GOLF®
MAGAZINE

PRIVATE
LESSONS™

REVISED & UPDATED EDITION

LESSONS ™

REVISED & UPDATED EDITION

THE BEST OF THE
BEST INSTRUCTION

DAVID DUSEK • ILLUSTRATIONS BY BARRY ROSS

ABRAMS, NEW YORK

CONTENTS

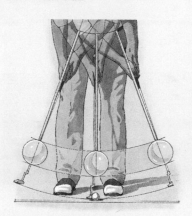

FOREWORD

Honestly, I can't remember too much about my first private lesson. I certainly can't remember the name of the pro who, after showing me how to hold the club, aim at a target and make a swing, suggested that I should probably take up another game.

But that was a long time ago and, happily, I chose not to heed his advice. As a writer, editor and publisher of golf publications in England and the United States for over 25 years, I have had the privilege of playing many of the world's greatest courses, such as The Old Course at St. Andrews, Pebble Beach Golf Links, Pinehurst No. 2 and the West Course at Winged Foot Golf Club. I have also had the good fortune to get more than my fair share of private lessons and swing pointers from some of the finest teachers in the game.

David Leadbetter, a GOLF MAGAZINE Top 100 Teacher, gave me a fantastic lesson once that focused almost exclusively on my grip. If you are anything like me, you probably think about your grip about as often as you think about your spare tire. But Leadbetter's advice helped me understand that my faulty grip was actually at the root of my problem. After he helped me adjust it, I started hitting the ball farther and straighter. And that helped me have more fun.

A few years later, Mike Malaska, another Top 100 Teacher, pointed out to me that my grip appeared to be a little off. He suggested that if I tweaked it, just a touch, I would get better results. *Presto!* I immediately started hitting the ball better. And once again, I started having more fun.

Great teachers like Leadbetter and Malaska have a knack for being able to cut through complicated ideas and deliver simple advice that can have a profound impact on your game. So does *Private Lessons*, which has been appearing on its trademark recycled paper in Golf Magazine for over 20 years.

Sure, most of the instruction focuses on how to hit the ball better, but many articles and tips offer insights into how to play *the game* better using the swing you've got. What you hold in your hands is a collection of the finest articles that have appeared in *Private Lessons* over the past several years. And, while it will make any coffee table you set it on look good, it's meant to be used, read, written-in and referred to often. This is a how-to book in the truest sense, and our goal in producing it is for you to learn how to play better golf and have more fun.

As you read *Private Lessons*, you may notice that some pieces of instruction seem to be repeated in different areas. You might initially wonder why we chose to do that, but the answer is simple: The game's best teachers have an uncanny ability to describe something in a number of different ways, ensuring that every student walks away knowing exactly what he meant. Since all of us learn in different ways, repeating some vital concepts using different words and images is an insurance policy that will allow more readers to have an epiphany and suddenly have everything "click."

I sincerely hope that you enjoy this book as much as we enjoyed creating it.

Editor
Golf Magazine

THE BASICS

When the most accomplished players in the world develop a problem with their game, they find its root—as well as its solution—by examining their swing and breaking it down into its simplest elements. They might start by examining the way they stand and address the ball, how they start the club back or where it is positioned at the top of the backswing. More often than not, this is all that's necessary to get them back on track.

But what you definitely will not see the pros do is seek the answer by making things more complicated. And you are not going to see any pro start looking for some *magic bullet* cure to help him suddenly start to play better. When things get tough, the pros try to make things very simple.

For proof of just how attuned to the fundamental's the pros are, spend some time around the driving range, short game area and putting green the next time you have a chance to attend a PGA or LPGA event. Pay close attention to how the players address each ball before they hit it, how they go through a well-orchestrated routine before every shot and how they examine such things as their alignment, posture and stance. Remember, this is just their practice and pre-round warm-up. If they pay such close attention to the basics here, imagine how meticulous they must be inside the ropes!

Now be honest: Do you even remember the last time you talked to your pro about your grip, your takeaway or the way you shift your weight forward as you swing down to the ball? Have your really thought about the reasons why your chip shots seem to lack consistency?

While the pros may swing faster and harder than you, focusing on the game's fundamentals can often fix your faults too. Unfortunately, if you are like most players, you take the basics of the game—like your grip, your stance and good balance—for granted. If you start to spray a few shots around during your round, you probably don't make a note of it or try to notice any patterns. Instead, if you have the time, you head to the range, buy a big bucket of balls and proceed to hit them rapid-fire into the empty field in front of you in hopes that one shot will feel just right and remind you of what you really want to do.

That kind of "practice" will do nothing but grind blisters into your hands. Seriously, it's a waste of time.

This chapter offers you a simple, no-frills look at the most common shots that you will encounter during a typical round of golf. It covers the grip, posture and swing mechanics, as well as offering situational tips on chipping, pitching, bunker play and putting. Think of this first chapter as a jumping-off point, and as a place you can immediately turn to the next time your swing starts to feel a little less than perfect. You will be surprised how concentrating on some simple, time-tested techniques can have a profound impact on your game.

Make sure your palms face each other when you're taking your grip.

GRIP: MAKE YOUR HANDS WORK TOGETHER

The hands are your only connection to the club and are ultimately responsible for squaring the clubface at impact. To be certain they function together, make sure your palms face each other when you take your grip. For example, if you prefer a strong left-hand position with three knuckles showing at address, your right hand should be turned slightly under so the palms mirror each other. Here's an easy way to check: When your palms face each other, your left thumb fits snugly into the channel formed by your right thumb and palm. If that relationship doesn't exist, your hands will work against each other, costing you distance and accuracy.

Even with a strong left-hand position, your hands must mirror each other.

Your left thumb fits snugly between the right thumb and palm.

DRILL: SPLIT HANDS To train your hands to work as a unit, make some swings with your hands three inches apart on the grip. This makes it easier to feel if your hands are fighting each other for control.

The more you focus on making your hands work together, the better your chances of delivering a square club-face. When you go back to your normal grip, your hands will work as one.

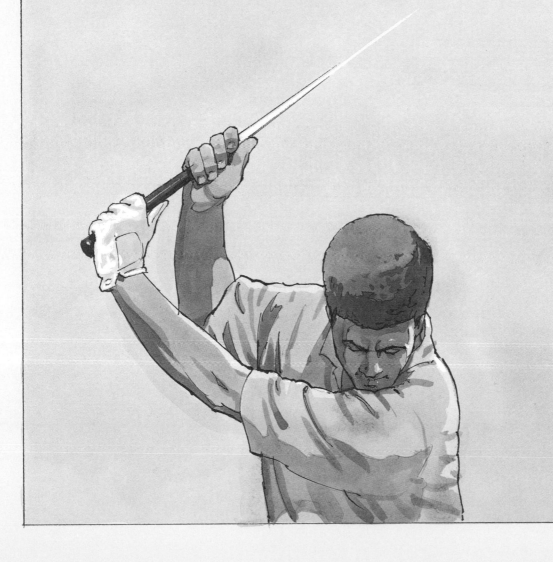

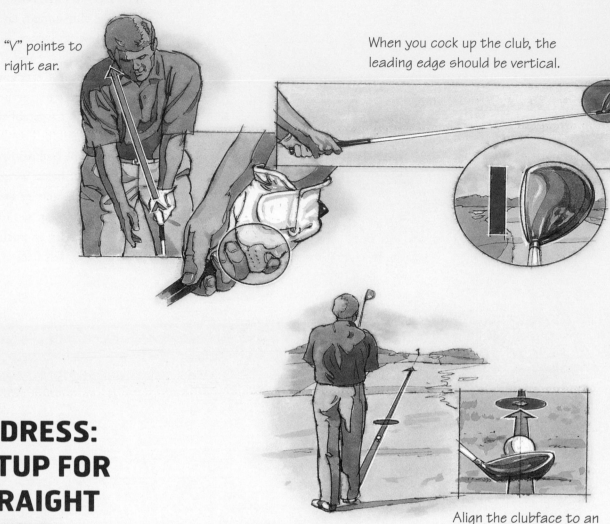

"V" points to right ear.

When you cock up the club, the leading edge should be vertical.

Align the clubface to an intermediate target.

ADDRESS: SETUP FOR STRAIGHT SHOTS

Many golfers never consider that their contact problems could stem from an inconsistent setup. But think about it: If you setup to the ball differently every time—adjusting your posture, shifting your aim or changing where you position the ball in your stance—how can you expect the club to be in the same impact position every time?

The following points will help you set up correctly for each swing.

STEP 1: CHECK YOUR GRIP

Place the club in the fingers of your left hand. The "V" formed by your left thumb and forefinger should point at your right ear. Add your right hand so your right ring finger is flush against your left forefinger, and your right pinkie rests between your left forefinger and middle finger. Then cock up the club so the shaft is parallel to the ground. If the club's leading edge is vertical, the clubface is square.

STEP 2: AIM THE CLUBFACE

Once you've completed your grip, stand behind the ball, facing the target. Pick an intermediate target—a spot on the ground a few feet in front of the ball and along the target line—then step in and sole the clubhead. Rather than trying to square the face to your ultimate target, aim it at the intermediate target. You'll find it much easier to set up to a nearby spot than to a distant one.

STEP 3: COMPLETE YOUR SETUP
With the club aimed, take a shoulder-width stance, flexing your knees slightly and tilting from your hips. Relax your shoulders and let your arms hang freely. Now establish your ball position: For short irons, play the ball midway between your heels; for mid-irons through fairway woods, move it an inch or two forward; for the driver, position it opposite your left heel.

Tilt forward from hips.

Flex knees slightly.

Heels shoulder-width apart.

DRIVING: UNDERSTAND WHAT SQUARE MEANS

Keeping the clubface "square" during the swing does not mean keeping it perpendicular to the target line. In fact, if you try to force the face to point at the ball as you swing back, you'll actually close it and set the stage for a hook.

Instead, keep the clubface perpendicular to your chest for the first several feet of your swing. Once it moves behind you, the face is tough to see. The good news is, face rotation happens naturally if you do two things. First, use a neutral grip with the "Vs" formed by the thumb and forefinger of each hand pointing at your right ear. Second, control your swing by turning back and through with no independent hand action.

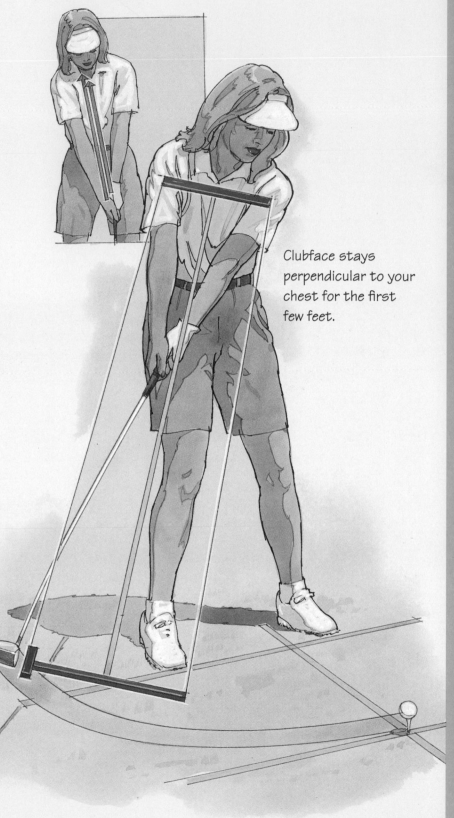

Clubface stays perpendicular to your chest for the first few feet.

IRONS: HIT DOWN TO GO UP

To make solid contact, the clubhead must hit the ball before the ground. Your swing should bottom out just ahead of the ball (on the target side). That's why you see the pros' divots in front of the ball, never behind.

If you're catching more turf than ball, you probably have the wrong idea about impact.

Rather than hitting down on the ball, you're trying to help it up. As a result, the clubhead reaches the bottom of its arc too early and gouges a large chunk of earth behind the ball. That's the definition of hitting it "fat."

To trim the fat, try the following: Stick two tees in the ground 12 inches apart and perpendicular to your target line. Place a ball between the tees and, with a 5-iron, swing away. Hit balls until your divots are consistently on the target side of both tees.

Remember: Down means up. Focus on shifting your weight to the front foot prior to impact. Your front leg should be nearly vertical (the knee still slightly flexed). This helps delay the clubhead's release until late in the downswing, creating the sharp, descending blow you want for a perfect divot.

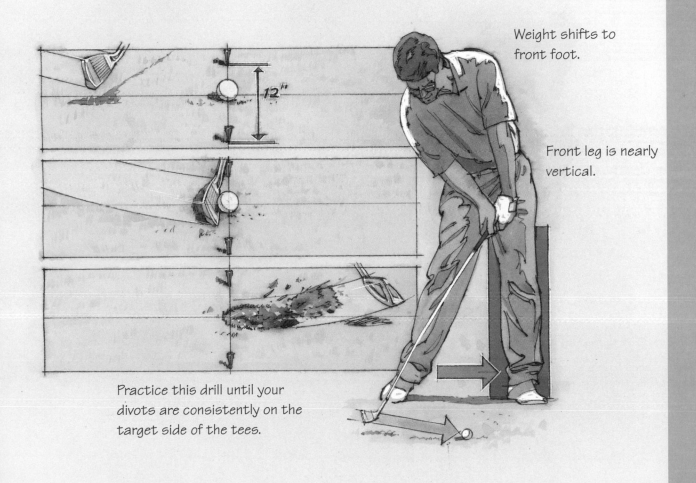

12"

Weight shifts to front foot.

Front leg is nearly vertical.

Practice this drill until your divots are consistently on the target side of the tees.

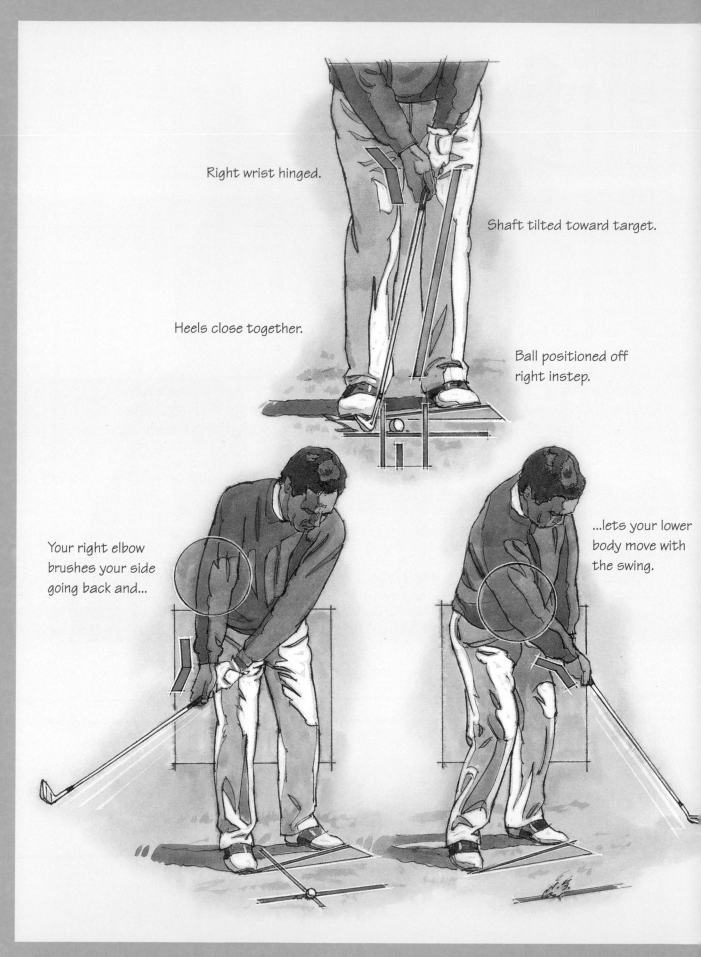

Right wrist hinged.

Shaft tilted toward target.

Heels close together.

Ball positioned off right instep.

Your right elbow brushes your side going back and...

...lets your lower body move with the swing.

CHIPPING: GET YOUR WRISTS, ARMS AND BODY IN SYNC

Smart golfers know they have to work on their short game. Specifically, if your chipping isn't up to snuff, you're throwing away strokes. Here's the basics.

MAINTAIN WRIST ANGLE

Crisp contact comes from a slightly descending blow. This only happens when the shaft is tilted toward the target at impact. Preset this forward lean at address: With your heels only a couple of inches apart, position the ball off your right instep and press your hands slightly ahead of it. Notice the angle formed at your right wrist. Ensure a descending strike by maintaining this angle.

SYNCHRONIZE YOUR ARMS AND BODY

Your hands should be close to your thighs so your right elbow can brush gently against your side as you swing back and through. In addition, your body should be free to move with your arms. Of course, your shoulders turn as your arms swing, but your lower body should also respond to the swinging motion, too.

DRILL: STICK TO YOUR RIBS Grip down to the metal on a 5-iron and let the handle rest lightly against your left side. Your right wrist is now at the proper angle for chipping. Make a series of chipping motions in the air, keeping the grip against your ribs. This drill teaches you to maintain the angle of the right wrist and to keep your body moving with the club.

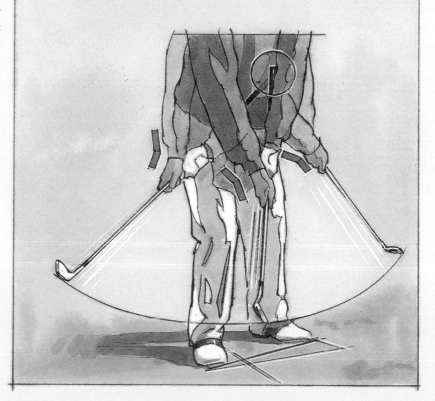

When pitching, set up with an open stance, the ball centered and your weight left.

Left wrist is flat.

Stay left as you swing back.

Control the down-swing by turning your torso left.

PITCHING: MAKE THE IDEAL STANCE, GRIP AND TURN

Since few golfers can overpower a course, good pitching is an essential scoring tool. The secret to crisp pitches is making a descending blow, with your hands leading the clubhead into the ball.

WEIGHT LEFT, TURN LEFT

For a basic pitch, open your stance, play the ball in the middle and favor your left side. Your hands should be an inch or two in front of the ball; the clubface should be square. Stay left as you start back and your wrists hinge the club upward.

Instead of flipping your wrists through impact, as many golfers do, control the downswing by turning your torso to the left. This keeps your left wrist flat and the clubface square as your body turns.

TAKE YOUR TIME

Good tempo is crucial for control, so maintain the same smooth, back-and-through feeling on every pitch shot. Never increase your swing speed to hit the ball farther. If you need more distance, simply use a longer swing.

DRILL: RIGHT FOOT PUSH One way to make sure your weight is on your left side at impact is to start the downswing with a push off your right foot. When practicing, exaggerate this move: Start your right knee toward the target before your arms finish swinging back.

FROM FIRM TO FLUFFY

To become a good bunker player, you need to understand not only the basics of the proper technique, but the differences between firm and soft sand. Here's what you need to know.

FEET FIRST

To gauge the quality of the sand, first step into the bunker and twist down into it with your feet. You'll know immediately whether the sand is firm, fluffy or somewhere in between.

WHEN IT'S FIRM

An explosion shot from wet or hard-packed sand requires a more descending angle of attack, so encourage this by moving the ball back in your stance. The clubface should be set just a little bit open to your target, which will make it easier for the leading edge to cut into the sand.

Cock your wrists as you begin the backswing, then bring the clubhead down and into the sand about an inch or so behind the ball. Avoid a classic mistake and remember to follow through: You should feel and hear the club *thump* the sand as the ball pops out.

Clubface slightly open.

Ball back.

Hinge your wrists early in the backswing.

Use a descending angle of attack.

WHEN IT'S FLUFFY

The ball tends to settle down in soft, fluffy sand, making it seem harder to impart backspin. But because the sand is lighter, the club cuts through it more easily, which actually helps to create backspin. The key to cutting through the sand and getting the maximum height and spin is to swing through on a shallow angle so the club does not dig down and get buried.

Start by moving the ball an inch forward in your stance and leaning the handle back to expose plenty of your sand wedge's bounce. This will keep the club from digging. Open your stance a little, but swing the club back and through along your target line. This will keep your angle of attack shallow. You'll move more sand than usual, but the ball will splash out with plenty of backspin to help you control the shot.

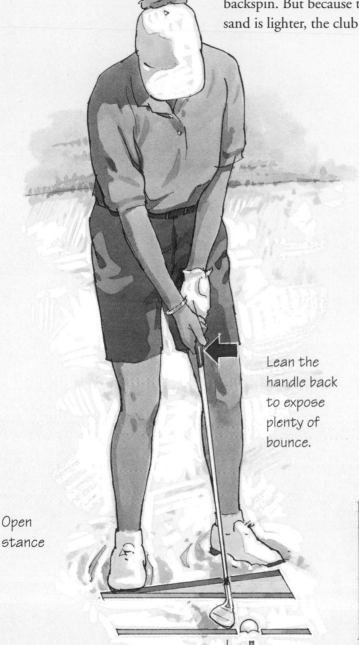

Lean the handle back to expose plenty of bounce.

Open stance

Ball forward

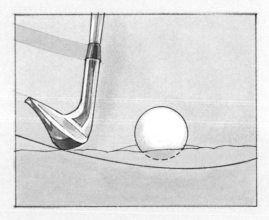

Shallow angle of attack

PUTTING: PREPARE FOR A PERFECT ROLL

Your eyes should be directly over the target line.

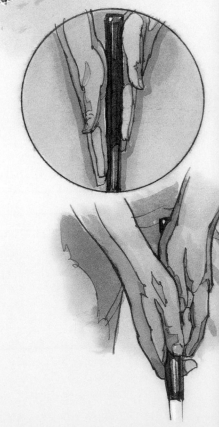

The grip sits in the palms of both hands.

You can't learn good touch overnight. But there is something you can accomplish right away: Make sure your setup allows a straight-back, straight-through stroke that puts a true end-over-end roll on the ball. If you can do that, you will master the more difficult aspects of putting, like distance control, faster. Here are some keys for an ideal putting setup.

MAKE YOUR EYELINE YOUR TARGET LINE

How you see the putt's line is directly related to the position of your eyes as you stand over the ball. To create an undistorted view, your eyeline must be directly over the target line.

Stand over a putt, then hold your putter horizontally in front of your chest and over the target line. When you look down, you should see the shaft run through the ball directly on top of the target line. If you don't, adjust until everything is on the same line, then return the putter to address.

HANDLE IN PALMS

In putting, there should be no movement in your wrists; let the bigger, more reliable shoulder muscles control your stroke. Instead of resting the handle in your fingers, as you do in a full swing shot, you should set it in the palms of both hands. With your palms facing each other, wrap your fingers around the handle, locking them in place for a wristless stroke.

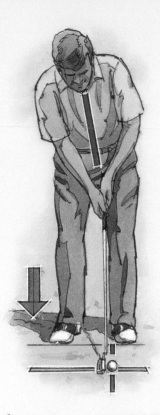

Encourage contact on the upswing by playing the ball forward and favoring your back foot.

FAVOR YOUR BACK FOOT

To impart the truest roll, and thereby sink the most putts, you must hit the ball as the putterface is moving horizontally or slightly on the upswing. To encourage this, position the ball inside your left heel and set more weight on your back foot. This tilts your spine slightly away from the target, moving the low point of the stroke behind the ball and eliminating any chance of striking it with a descending blow.

DRILL: GROOVE YOUR STROKE Find a flat section of the practice green about five feet from a hole. Lay two clubs parallel and pointing to the hole. The channel formed by the shafts should be an inch wider than the putterhead. Place a ball between the clubs and putt without bumping the shafts with the putterhead.

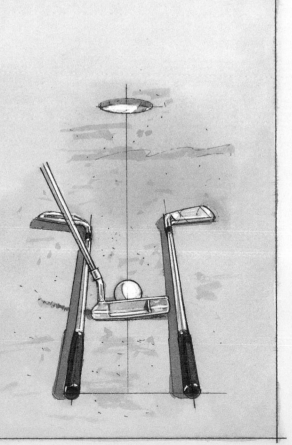

ADDRESS, SETUP AND PRE-SWING

Before you swing, how you hold the club, position yourself next to the ball and stand can determine whether you split the fairway or send your shot into the woods. Humble as they are, these basics are the foundation of a good swing, and too often, golfers overlook them.

On a positive note, when your grip, posture and setup are solid, hitting good shots is a lot easier because the need for in-swing compensations is eliminated. This chapter's goal is to arm you with the knowledge you need to put yourself in a position to hit good shots more often.

KEEP YOUR PRE-SHOT ROUTINE SHORT

While it's important to take your time on the course, taking too long to hit a shot paves the way for negative thoughts.

Try to keep your pre-shot routine under 20 seconds. Here's how to do it:

1. Stand behind the ball to choose your target and visualize your ball flight to that target.

2. Align your feet, hips and shoulders down your target line.

3. Don't waggle the club more than twice.

4. Fire away!

It's important to repeat this routine on every single shot. If you can develop consistency with your pre-shot routine, you will be relaxed and ready every time you address the ball. And keeping your routine short may even inspire your playing companions to pick up their pace too!

Align your body to the target line.

Choose your target and picture your ball flight.

Waggle, then fire away.

CRITICAL POSTURE ANGLES

Posture can be defined simply as the angles formed by your body. Two critical posture angles are those created by the upper body when tilting forward (toward the ball) and to the side (away from the target). The correct forward tilt sets up an on-plane swing, which helps keep the clubface square, while the proper side tilt determines the bottom of the swing arc, ensuring solid contact. Perfect these two tilts, and you'll become a better ball-striker.

FORWARD TILT: SET THE PLANE

To reach the ball, bend forward from the hips, not the waist, approximately 35 degrees. To see if you have enough forward bend, swing to the top without changing your spine tilt, take your left hand off the club and place it on your right knee without bending further. Your hand should cover the knee.

Maintaining this forward tilt will help the club remain on plane. Plane refers to the angle of the shaft relative to the ground, and you can stay on plane by swinging the left arm at 90 degrees to the swing's axis—your spine.

Bend forward from the hips about 35 degrees.

At the top, you sho[uld] be able to cover the side of your right kn[ee] with your left hand.

The left arm swings at a 90-degree angle to the spine.

At address, your spine should angle eight to 10 degrees away from the target.

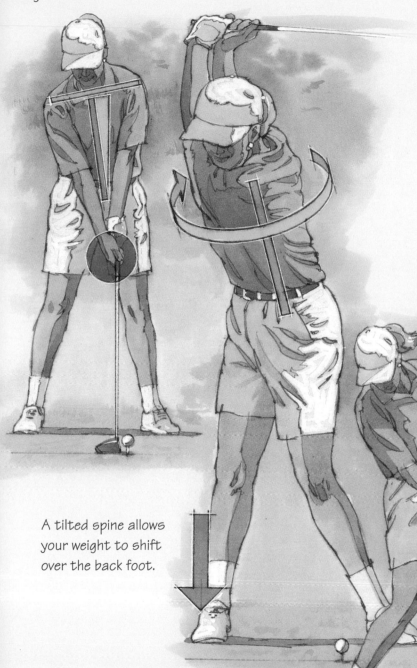

A tilted spine allows your weight to shift over the back foot.

SIDE TILT: ESTABLISH CONTACT

Your spine should be angled eight to 10 degrees away from the target. This is because your right hand holds the club below your left, dropping your right shoulder and tilting your spine away from the target. Nearly level shoulders result in a reverse weight shift at the top—your body leaning toward the target rather than loaded over your right side.

Tilting your spine allows your weight to shift onto your right leg on the backswing, setting up a powerful coil. With your power stored over your right side, your swing will naturally shift to the front foot during the downswing. This moves the bottom of the swing arc forward, which ensures solid contact.

The result is maximum power and solid contact.

Address

Impact

Fred Couples has a strong grip, which pre-sets the clubface in a released position.

WHY STRENGTH- ENING YOUR GRIP CAN BE GOOD

Strengthening the left-hand grip is usually prescribed to golfers seeking more distance. It encourages a faster closing of the clubface through impact, producing a powerful release and longer shots. However, a stronger grip can help those players who already hit the ball powerfully but lack accuracy, as well.

Long hitters already release the club effectively, but their wrist action can be hard to control, causing accuracy problems. A strong grip can eliminate the need to release by pre-setting the clubface in a released position, so you won't have to rely on your hands and wrists.

With your hands and wrists remaining relatively quiet, you must make a body-and-arm swing. This is a more consistent move, exemplified by Fred Couples, who has a strong left-hand grip and swings the club back to the target line with little wrist action. With fewer moving parts, the club won't rotate as much through impact. This swing adjustment can become an effective weapon when you're looking for control.

A subtle pre-swing motion can trigger a smooth takeaway.

USE A TRIGGER FOR A SMOOTHER TAKEAWAY

If you stand rigidly still at address, you're inviting muscular tension and a jerky takeaway. Instead, use a trigger—a subtle movement that puts your body in motion just before you start the club back. Try pushing your hands toward the target an inch or two—a forward press—or tapping your feet or pumping your knees. Any of these pre-swing motions will help you keep your body loose and set the tone for a smooth swing.

REHEARSE YOUR WAGGLE

If your club moves out of position during the takeaway—too far inside or outside the target line—the rest of your swing becomes a series of compensations. A rehearsal waggle can help; it's a preview of the positions you want to reach. Here's how a rhythmic rehearsal waggle—one of the keys to the success of Mike Weir and Chris DiMarco—can help you keep the club on track.

STRAIGHT AND SQUARE

First, be sure the clubhead is moving back along the target line for the first 12 inches before gradually swinging inside and up. Start by rotating your shoulders—your arms and hands will follow naturally.

Second, check that the clubface stays square—not to the target, but to your torso. As the clubhead reaches hip height, the toe should point to the sky.

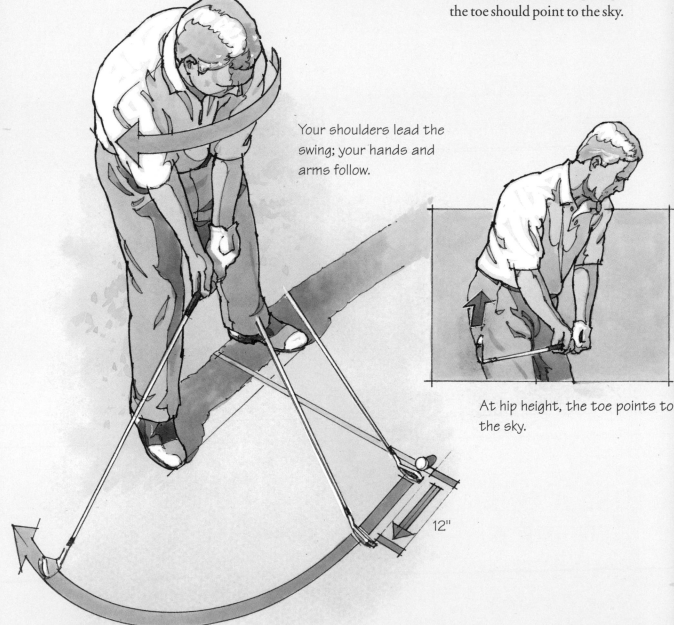

Your shoulders lead the swing; your hands and arms follow.

At hip height, the toe points to the sky.

12"

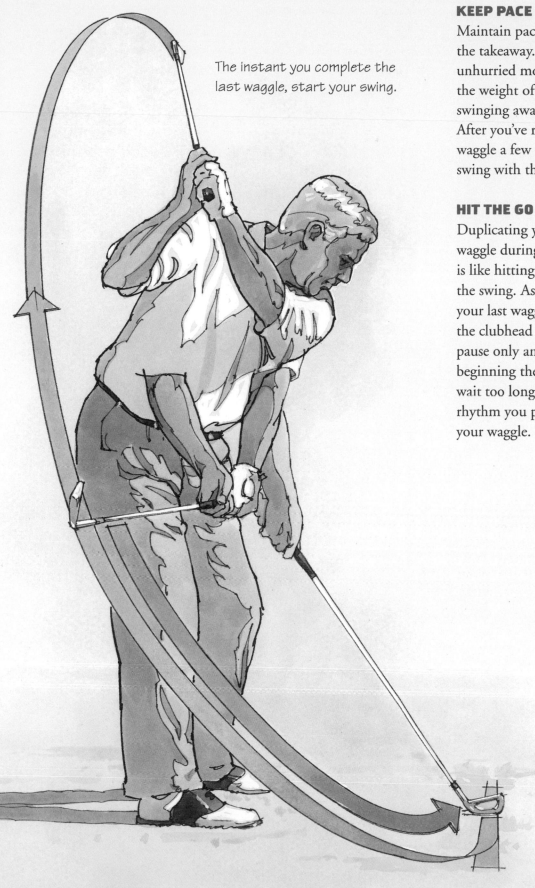

The instant you complete the last waggle, start your swing.

KEEP PACE

Maintain pace as you practice the takeaway. Make a smooth, unhurried motion, and feel the weight of the clubhead swinging away from the ball. After you've repeated the waggle a few times, begin your swing with the same pace.

HIT THE GO SWITCH

Duplicating your rehearsal waggle during the takeaway is like hitting a go switch for the swing. As you complete your last waggle and return the clubhead to the ball, pause only an instant before beginning the swing. If you wait too long, you will lose the rhythm you programmed with your waggle.

TEE BOX STRATEGY

For many golfers, the tee box is simply the place where the hole starts. What these golfers may not understand, however, is that the tee box and tee markers are strategically placed to increase or decrease the difficulty of a hole. A smart player knows that he can use the position of the tees to his advantage. Imagine, for example, a par 4 with a slight dogleg right, a bunker to the right of the green and the pin tucked in on the right. To avoid having to hit an approach shot over the bunker, you should ideally hit your drive to the left side of the fairway, and to make this as easy as possible, you should tee up your ball as close as you can to the right tee marker. This will give you the largest possible margin of error, and help you place your drive on the left side of the fairway. Teeing the ball in the middle or the left side would

Set up on the right side of the tee box to leave the most room to hit to the left side of the fairway.

only make this hole more difficult—the idea is to set up on the right side of the tee box to leave the most room to hit it left, and the left side for the most room right.

You can use the same strategy on a par 3. Make sure to consider not only where you want to hit the ball, but also where you definitely don't want the ball to go. You may notice that the pin is on the left and then immediately tee up on the right, but if there's also potential trouble to the left of the green, such as a bunker or water hazard, make sure to give yourself a larger margin of error—tee your ball a little closer to the middle for the easiest line to the fat part of the green. Even if it means giving up a few yards to the left or right, you'll still be putting for birdie—even if you hit a slightly errant shot—instead of scowling because of trouble around the green.

Tee up where you have the largest margin of error when hitting to a well-guarded pin.

SQUARE THE CLUBFACE AT ADDRESS

Your address position is perhaps the most important factor in hitting a great shot. If your swing is flawed at address, it'll usually just get worse by impact. To prevent problems with alignment, take an extra second at address to ensure that your clubface is square to your target line. When your feet and shoulders are aligned, it's easy to take it for granted that your clubface is, too, but that's not always the case.

You can check your clubface alignment on the practice tee by laying a ruler perpendicular to the target line on the grass behind the ball. This will make it obvious whether the clubface is open, closed, or square. Repeat this drill several times, and you'll break a bad alignment habit in no time.

Once your feet and shoulders are aligned, take a moment to ensure that your clubface is square to your target line.

Check your clubface alignment by laying a ruler perpendicular to the target line on the grass behind the ball.

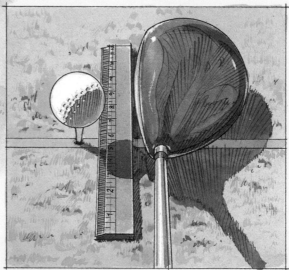

Compare the leading edge of the clubface with the edge of the ruler.

VISUALIZE A SPECIFIC SHOT

Visualization—picturing the shot you want to hit in your mind before you try to hit it—should be an important part of your pre-shot routine. If you can picture what type of shot you want to hit, the images become like a set of instructions sent from your mind to your body, telling your muscles what to do. So make those images as detailed as possible: Rather than simply picturing the ball landing in the fairway or on the green, picture how the swing looks, what the trajectory will be like and the precise spot where the ball will land. For approach shots, visualize the depth of the divot and how the ball is going to bounce after hitting your target. On the greens, see the ball fall into the hole. Does it drop on its last revolution or ram into the back of the cup? The more specific your mind is, the better your body understands what you want to do, and the more likely it is to deliver.

The more specific your pre-shot images are, the better the result.

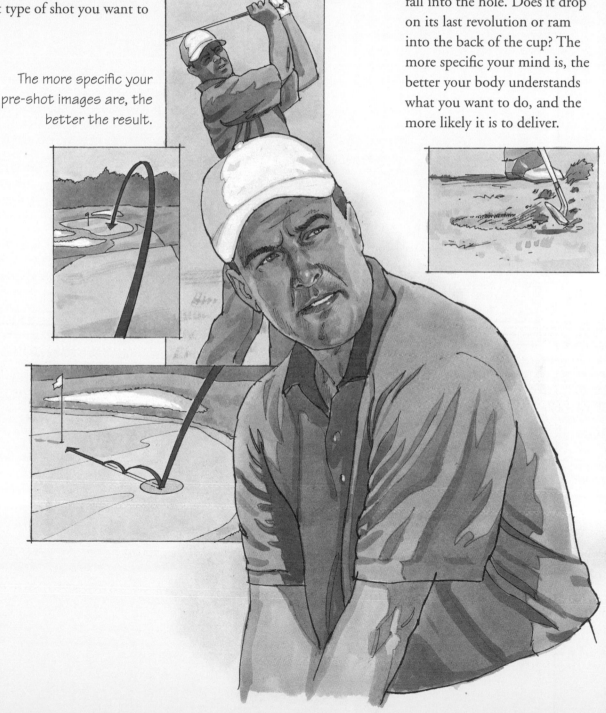

DRIVING

Skills you develop in one sport often make learning another easier. For instance, if you know how to throw a football or pitch a baseball, you can probably develop a good serve in tennis because the motions are similar. But the golf swing is unique, and few sports teach you skills that translate well. We tell you this not to be discouraging, but instead to make you realize that every great player, from Bobby Jones to Jack Nicklaus to Tiger Woods, started his golf career missing fairways. The game can be humbling and frustrating, but that's why hitting good shots is so gratifying.

Thanks to high-tech materials, innovative clubhead designs and lighter and stronger shafts, it's never been easier to hit the ball long and straight. Once you master a few simple moves, such as how to initiate your swing, make solid contact and properly rotate your body, you might be surprised at just how much progress you make.

A PEACHY TAKEAWAY DRILL

Snatching the club up and away from the ball like an axe is a common mistake made by players looking to increase distance off the tee. But this move encourages a choppy downswing and results in pop-ups, topped shots and weak slices. Sound familiar?

Here's an image from *GOLF MAGAZINE* Top 100 Teacher Mitchell Spearman that can help improve your first move away from the ball. Picture a ripe peach sitting just behind your clubhead at address.

If you snatch the club back quickly, you'll whack the peach and bruise it. But start back slowly and smoothly, and the clubhead pushes the peach away gently. This low, slow takeaway promotes a full body coil and results in solid contact and better shots.

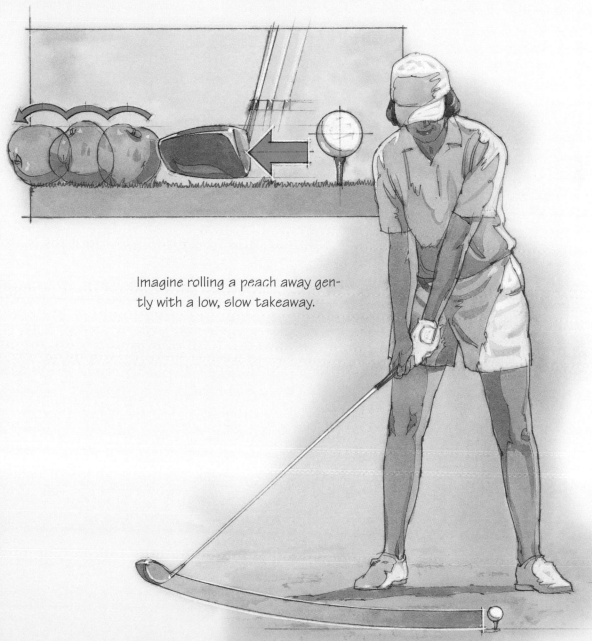

Imagine rolling a peach away gently with a low, slow takeaway.

LET YOUR HEAD MOVE

Your buddies mean well when they offer advice. But the problem is that a simple comment, like "keep your head still," really doesn't help. As World Golf Teachers' Hall of Fame instructor John Jacobs pointed out, "It's like strapping a straitjacket onto a golfer—it restricts the full, free turn that is so essential for both power and accuracy."

Video analysis of tour pros shows that instead of keeping their heads rock steady as they swing, almost all let their head move away from the target between address and impact.

Instead of trying to keep your head "down" or "still," think "keep your head behind the ball." This frees your body to coil fully over your right side during the backswing.

Keeping your head behind the ball also preserves the leverage created during the backswing, allowing your arms to pass your body and fully release the club, a critical element to longer, straighter shots.

Focus on contacting the inside-back quadrant of the ball with the clubhead at impact. If you concentrate on that quadrant, your head will likely stay behind the ball—where it belongs.

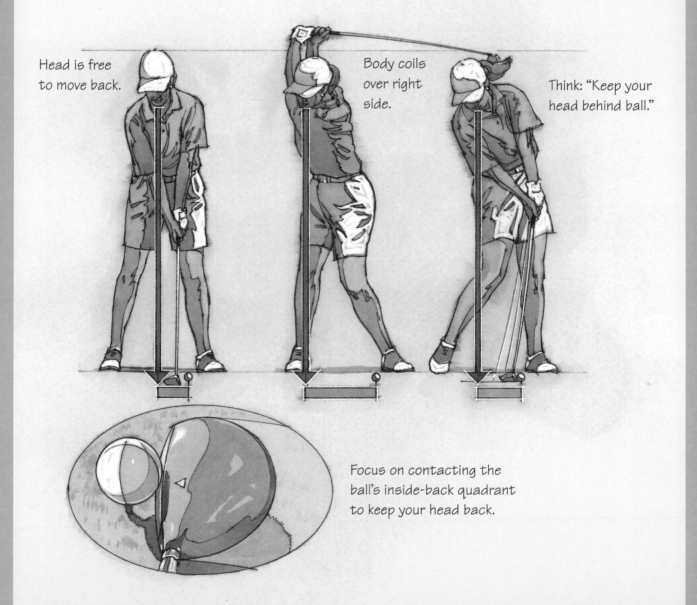

Head is free to move back.

Body coils over right side.

Think: "Keep your head behind ball."

Focus on contacting the ball's inside-back quadrant to keep your head back.

CHOKE DOWN FOR MORE CONTROL

As players try to hit the ball farther, they often make a larger swing arc to increase clubhead speed and power. That's great as long as you can maintain control. Unfortunately, the longer your swing, the more chances there are for mistakes to occur, and it can be especially difficult to control a wide swing arc when you are under pressure. While a smaller, more compact swing is easier to control, it would be both difficult and unwise to try to alter your natural swing length and rhythm. Instead, when accuracy is a priority over distance, choke down on your club by about an inch and a half. This effectively shortens both the club and your swing arc without altering your swing. You will lose about a half club's worth of distance, but what you'll gain in control will be well worth the trade-off.

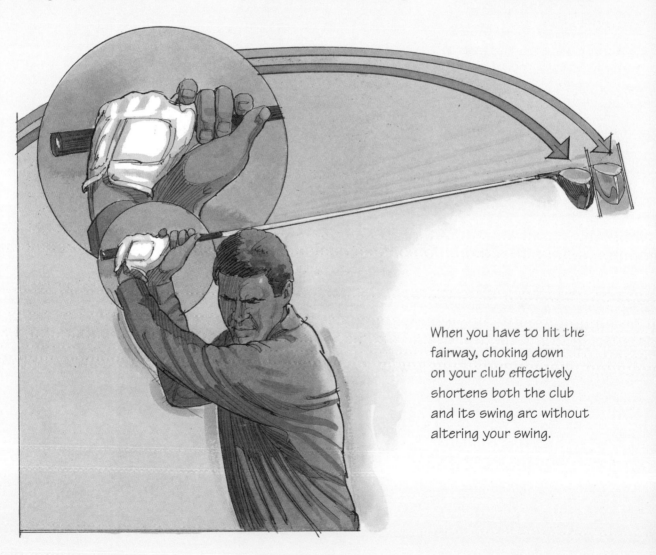

When you have to hit the fairway, choking down on your club effectively shortens both the club and its swing arc without altering your swing.

FIRM UP YOUR FRONT SIDE

Weight transfer is crucial to solid contact. But moving too aggressively to your front foot on the downswing will cause your body to slide instead of rotate through impact. That leads to misses on both the left and right sides of the fairway.

Firming up your left side through impact eliminates the hip slide and keeps your swing moving in the correct sequence. Picture a wall just outside your front foot and try to swing so that your torso—from your belt buckle to your chest—touches the wall at the finish. To make your upper body rotate that far, your left leg must stay firm as your hips turn through the strike.

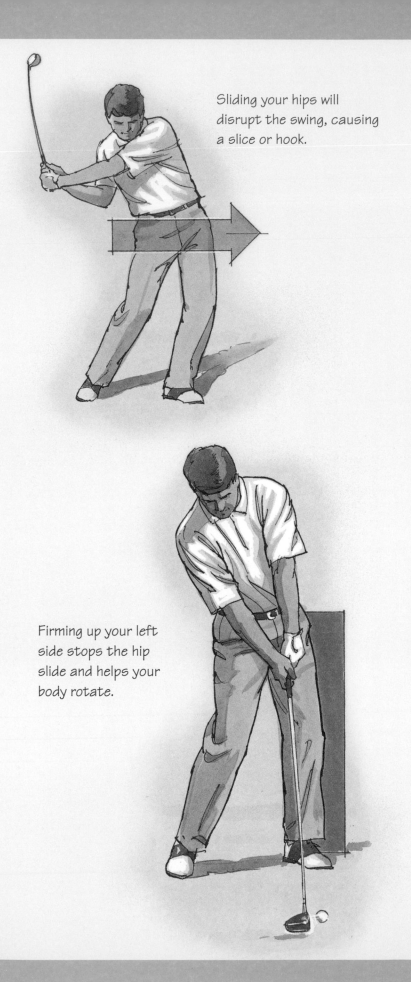

Sliding your hips will disrupt the swing, causing a slice or hook.

Firming up your left side stops the hip slide and helps your body rotate.

Imagine a wall beside your front foot and try to finish with your torso pressed against it.

Hand action dictates hook or push.

Overdriving your legs toward the target leaves your arms behind your body.

Body and arms swing together, keeping the club on plane.

Shift gently onto your left side while keeping your weight between your feet.

CREATE MORE ROOM TO SWING

FAULT: BODY WINS THE RACE

"Getting stuck" is caused by the overuse of a major power source: your legs driving toward the target in the downswing. When overdone, your body leaves your arms behind, causing the club to drop too far behind your body and your swing path to become too flat. From here, the clubhead approaches the ball on a severe in-to-out path, forcing your hands to flip the club through impact in an attempt to square the face.

This hand action determines shot direction. Too much hand rotation produces hooks; not enough leads to pushes. It all happens in a split second, and only perfect timing will result in straight shots. No one can do that every time.

FIX: HANDS IN FRONT

To get unstuck, keep your body in sync with your arms during the downswing by curbing lateral motion. Rather than making your first move down a powerful lower-body move toward the target, shift gently onto the left side while keeping your weight between your feet. This allows your body and arms to swing together, keeping the club on-plane and eliminating the need for compensations by your hands.

Done correctly, the club should feel as if it is swinging down in front of your body, rather than behind it.

DRILL: MISS THE SHAFT Stick a shaft or umbrella four inches outside your front foot at address. Hit balls while trying to avoid bumping the shaft with your left leg or hip during the downswing. This will stop the excessive lateral drive that causes the body to out-race the arms.

FLATTEN THE BOTTOM OF YOUR SWING

If you want to see more of the short grass, without easing off the throttle or laying up off every tee, you are not alone. One way is to increase the flat spot at the bottom of your swing. The following keys will help.

TEE IT HIGH

A high tee encourages a shallow angle of attack, which is the main element of a long flat spot. Get some extra-long tees, and tee the ball so its bottom is level with the top line of the clubface. This encourages a sweeping angle of attack so contact is made just as the clubhead starts to ascend. The result is less backspin and more accuracy.

GET BEHIND THE BALL

To create a long flat spot, your body must stay behind the ball. Focus on your head: At address, it should be completely behind an imaginary line drawn straight up from the ball. On the backswing, your head may slide a few inches farther back, so it is over your right knee. That's good: It's a sign

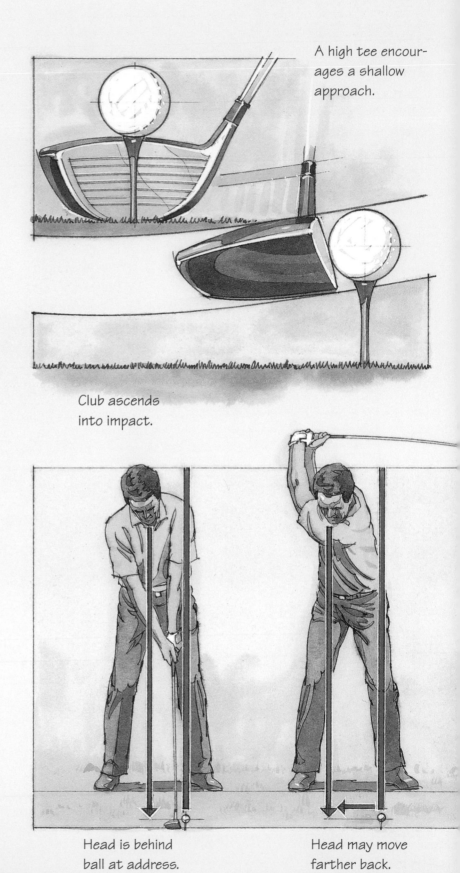

A high tee encourages a shallow approach.

Club ascends into impact.

Head is behind ball at address.

Head may move farther back.

of a proper pivot. At impact, although your weight has shifted forward and your torso is turning, your head should remain behind that imaginary vertical line. Practice posing the impact position to get a feel for it.

SWING DOWN WIDE

You probably know that extending your arms during the takeaway moves the club back along the target line. The same principle applies to maximizing the flat spot. To make sure the clubhead travels down the target line for as long as possible, focus on keeping your hands away from your body as the club swings down.

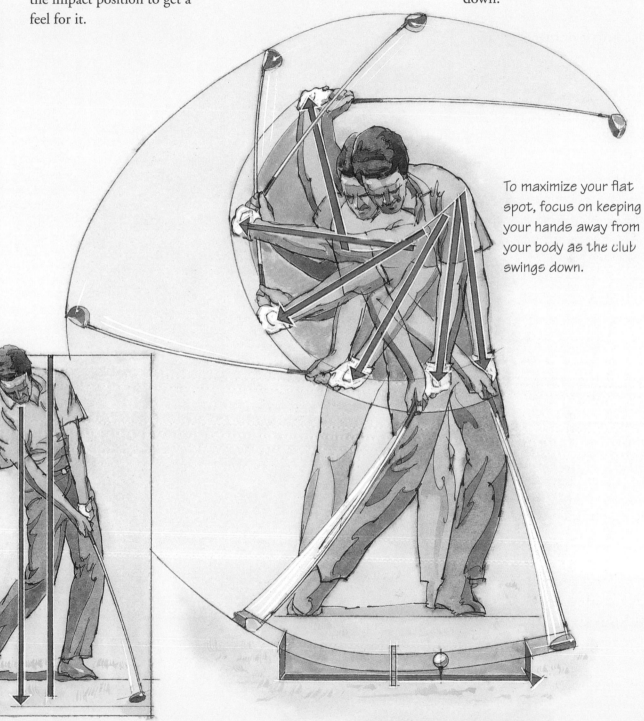

To maximize your flat spot, focus on keeping your hands away from your body as the club swings down.

Head remains behind ball at impact.

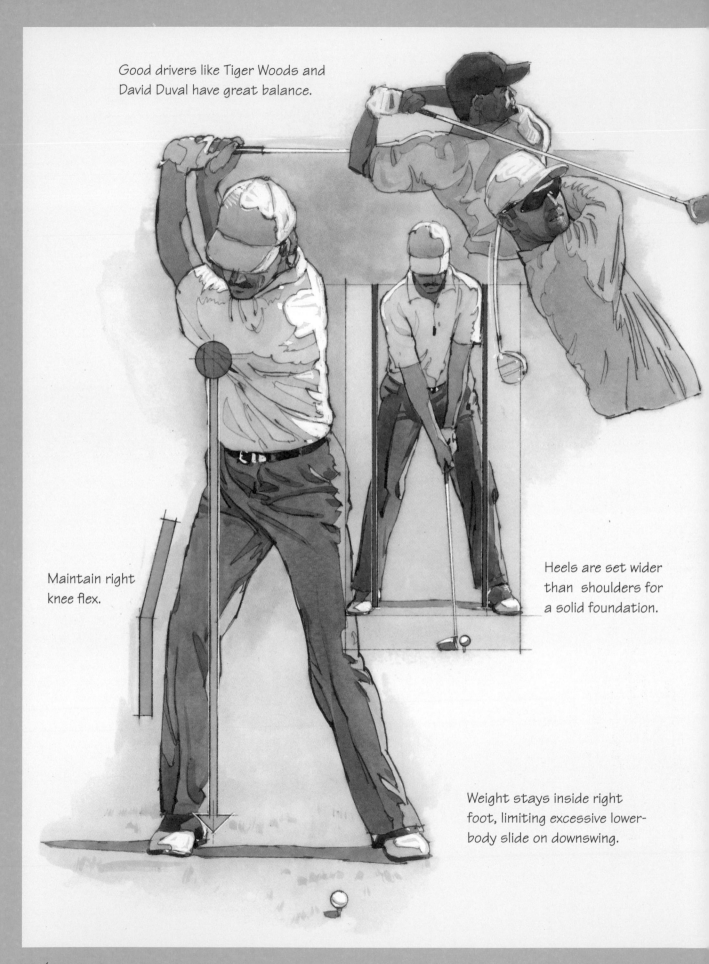

Good drivers like Tiger Woods and David Duval have great balance.

Maintain right knee flex.

Heels are set wider than shoulders for a solid foundation.

Weight stays inside right foot, limiting excessive lower-body slide on downswing.

HOW TO MAINTAIN GREAT BALANCE

Good drivers have great balance, enabling them to maintain control while generating tremendous clubhead speed. And the key to good balance is your feet and legs.

START WIDE

Good balance starts with width at address. Using a driver, your heels should be set wider than your shoulders. An overly narrow stance will result in a loss of balance and poor shots.

STAY INSIDE

During the backswing, maintain the flex in your right knee, which will keep your body weight centered over the inside of your right foot. Letting weight spill outside your right foot leads to an excessive lower-body slide toward the target during the downswing; as a result, the club gets left behind your body with its face open. Legs that stay stable and balanced will rotate properly and allow the clubface to return to impact squarely.

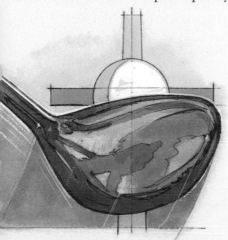

Clubface returns to impact squarely.

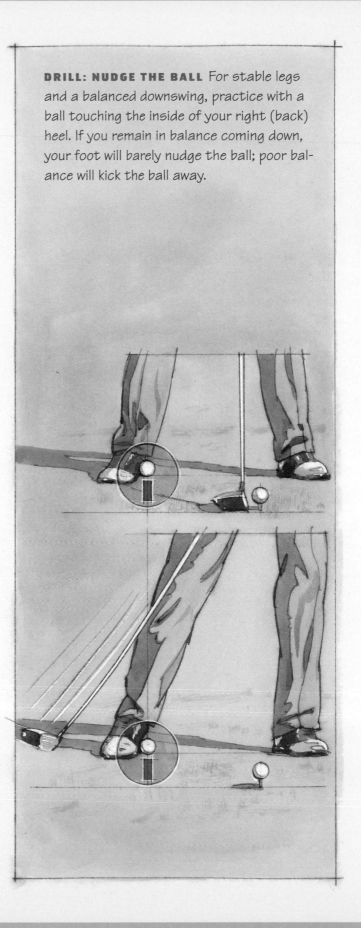

DRILL: NUDGE THE BALL For stable legs and a balanced downswing, practice with a ball touching the inside of your right (back) heel. If you remain in balance coming down, your foot will barely nudge the ball; poor balance will kick the ball away.

TIGHTEN YOUR SWING FOR GREATER ACCURACY

Crushing the ball is satisfying, but for more accuracy you may have to tighten your motion and make a more compact move. If you don't believe it, look at long hitters like Davis Love III, Sergio Garcia and Greg Norman. All three of these big hitters shortened their swings for better ball striking and control. Here's how you can do the same.

CHECK YOUR GRIP

A controlled swing starts with proper grip pressure. Focus on the last three fingers of your left hand and the point where your right palm makes contact with your left thumb. Slide a tee between the grip and the last three fingers of your left hand and a dime between your left thumb and right palm. If you can swing without either item falling out, your grip pressure is good.

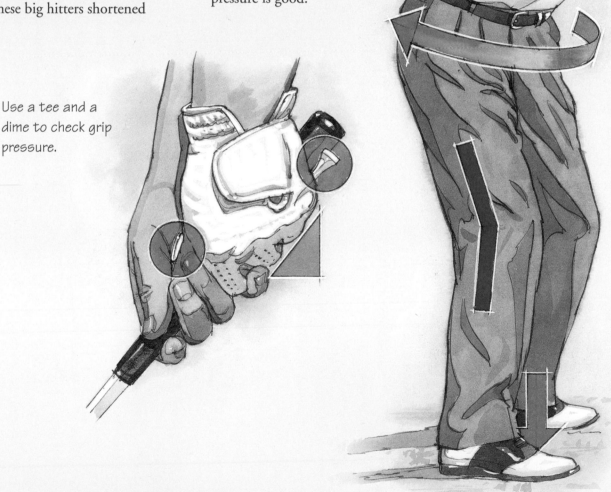

Your right knee must stay flexed going back.

Use a tee and a dime to check grip pressure.

RIGHT KNEE FLEX

Your right knee anchors your backswing; when it buckles or straightens, your hips slide or over-rotate and the swing becomes too long. To make a good hip turn, your right knee must remain slightly flexed going back with your weight over the inside of your right foot.

SHOULDERS SAY WHEN

Most overswings are caused when your arms keep swinging after your shoulders have reached their limit. When this happens, your torso tends to tilt toward the target, making solid contact difficult. Try to move your arms and shoulders in unison. When your shoulders stop, everything stops.

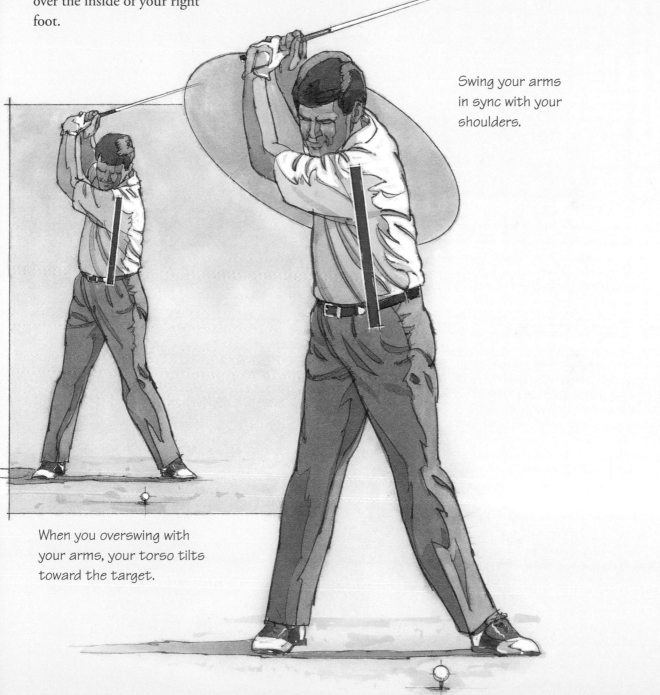

Swing your arms in sync with your shoulders.

When you overswing with your arms, your torso tilts toward the target.

Tee the ball high.

Ball moved forward one inch.

Keep the clubface pointing at the target.

INCREASE YOUR LAUNCH ANGLE

Whether you're cutting the corner on a dogleg, hitting to a wet fairway or trying to land the ball softly on a long par 3, the high-trajectory tee shot is a weapon you need in your arsenal. At address, move the ball an extra inch forward in your stance and tee it so the bottom of the ball is level with the top of the clubface. As you swing through impact, try to keep the clubface pointing at the target a split second longer than normal. These adjustments add loft at impact to produce the launch angle you are trying to achieve.

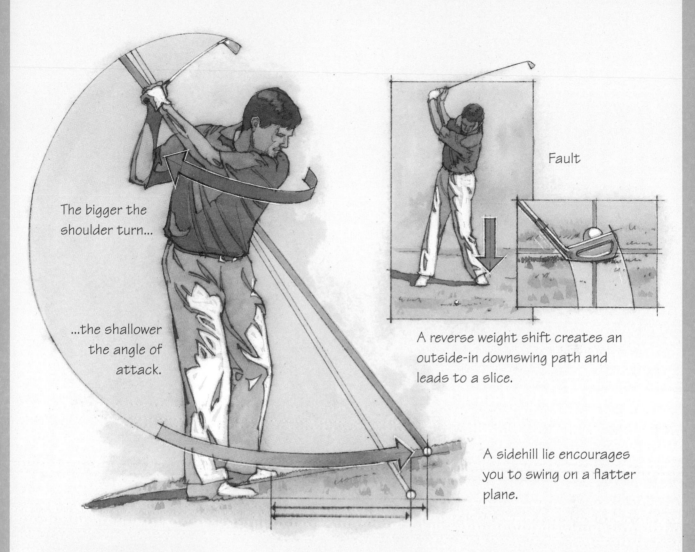

The bigger the shoulder turn...

...the shallower the angle of attack.

Fault

A reverse weight shift creates an outside-in downswing path and leads to a slice.

A sidehill lie encourages you to swing on a flatter plane.

SLICERS: HIT THE SLOPES

Hitting from a sidehill lie with the ball above your feet is no picnic. Yet this trouble shot offers the perfect solution to one of golf's most common faults: the slice.

Most slicers lift the club too steeply on the backswing, usually because of poor posture or a faulty takeaway.

A steep swing restricts lateral motion, leading to a reverse weight shift (leaning toward the target) at the top. From this position, the tendency is to bring the clubhead down on an outside to in path. Even if the clubface is square to the target line, the shot will curl to the right because of the spin imparted to it.

Hitting off a lie that puts the ball several inches above your feet forces you to stand farther from the ball and swing more around your body. This flatter swing plane promotes a bigger shoulder turn and a shallower angle of attack. The club approaches the ball from slightly inside the target line and launches a straighter, more powerful shot. So practice hitting shots from this sidehill lie to begin feeling, and remembering, a better swing.

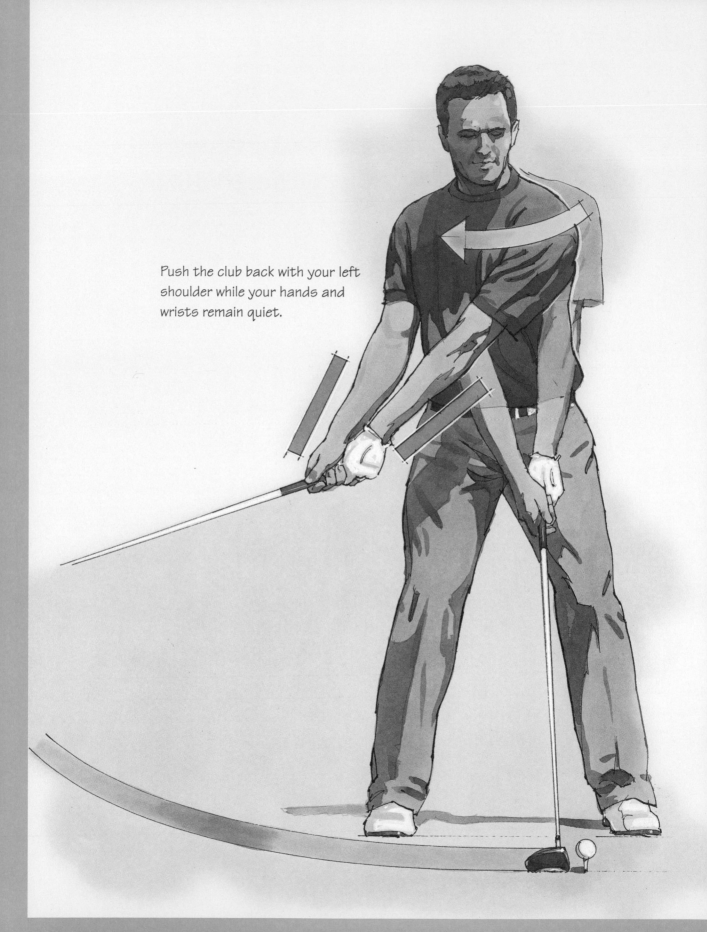

Push the club back with your left shoulder while your hands and wrists remain quiet.

ADD POWER IN YOUR TAKEAWAY

When you think of creating power, you probably think about making a big shift toward the target or whipping the club through impact. But a much simpler move has a huge bearing on your power potential: your takeaway. A wide, smooth takeaway sets up maximum clubhead speed, while a faulty one will cost you valuable yards.

KEEP IT TOGETHER

Your hands, arms and shoulders should move as a unit to start the club away from the ball. This keeps the club on plane and the clubface square, making the move back to the ball simple. Feel as if your left shoulder pushes the club back while your hands and wrists just react to the momentum.

WATCH YOUR TEMPO

The slower you start the club back, the easier it is to create a wide arc, which is a major key to maximizing clubhead speed. A smooth start also sets the tone for good rhythm and tempo during the swing. There's no need to rush: You're at your most powerful when the clubhead gradually builds to top speed without any sudden bursts of acceleration.

DRILL: GET A HEAD START To encourage a wide, smooth takeaway, grab your 5-iron and set up without a ball, then move the club about two feet toward the target. Both arms should be fully extended as they would be after impact. From here, swing back normally. Starting from a full extension will widen your takeaway arc, a feeling you should carry over into your regular swing.

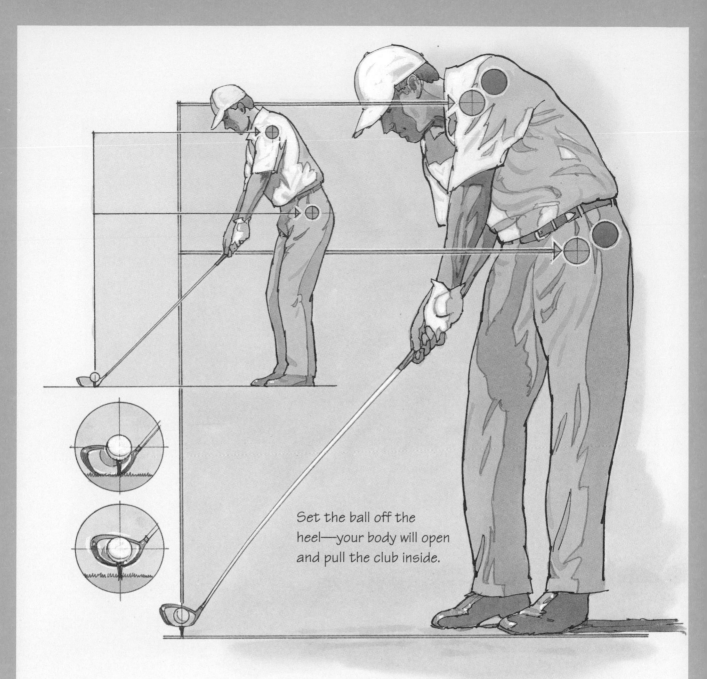

Set the ball off the heel—your body will open and pull the club inside.

ADDRESS ADJUSTMENT FOR TOE HITS

To hit the ball in the middle of the clubface, often referred to as the *sweetspot*, where should you position it at address? It seems obvious to put the sweetspot directly behind the ball, but some tour pros actually address the ball away from the sweetspot—closer to the clubhead's heel.

Here's the logic: At address, your hips and shoulders should be parallel to the target line, but the force of the downswing opens them as the club approaches impact. This can pull the clubhead to the inside. This explains why better players usually mis-hit shots toward the toe. If you struggle with toe hits, try addressing the ball opposite the heel.

LET YOUR LEFT HEEL COME UP

Only the most limber players can make a full turn with both feet flat on the ground. Don't worry if you can't. Instead, give your turn a boost by letting your left heel lift off the ground during the backswing, giving your hips and shoulders more room to turn.

Be warned: There's a right and wrong way to lift that heel. Don't move it straight up and down as if tapping your foot; let it roll. As your backswing progresses, your left foot rolls inward while the heel comes up, letting your left knee kick toward the right knee. This move ensures that your hips maximize their rotation.

Lifting your heel will create more turn.

Left foot and knee lean inward for greater rotation.

Don't play the ball too far forward.

THREE CAUSES FOR TOPPING

The topped shot is usually a beginner's mistake, but it can sneak up on good players, too. A slight miscue is all it takes to make contact above the ball's equator, particularly when hitting your driver or a fairway wood. Here's how to stop the top.

Coming down, turn your front hip to the left to prevent a lateral slide.

To maintain your posture, keep your knees flexed and your eyes level.

BALL TOO FAR UP

It's easy to top a shot if the clubhead has begun to move upward. To make contact while the clubhead is moving down—or level for tee shots—position the ball no farther forward than an inch inside your front heel (opposite page, top).

STANDING TOO SOON

If you pull your body up before impact, your swing arc rises with it. Keep your knees flexed and your eyes level until after the strike; you'll maintain your forward tilt from your hips and keep your upper body—and swing arc—set for solid contact.

TOO MUCH SLIDE

An aggressive move from the top can cause you to slide toward the target. That moves the swing's low point forward; the club comes down almost on top of the ball, producing a thin or topped shot. Coming down, focus on turning your left hip behind you.

DRILL: STRESS TEST To prevent a lateral slide, have a friend stand in front of you and hold the grip of a club against your left ear. Make slow practice swings, then work up to hitting shots at full speed. If the pressure against your head increases during the downswing, you're sliding toward the target. Work on rotating your left hip through the shot until the pressure stays constant.

FIGHT THE HOOK

Though most golfers would kill to move the ball from right to left, a draw that turns into a hook means trouble. Not only will you miss fairways and greens, but after visiting the left rough a few times, you may overcompensate, leading to a big block to the right. You need to rein in the hook without going too far in the other direction.

UNDERSTAND THE CAUSE

A big hook usually results from a simple sequence of events. It starts with your hips, which slide too aggressively toward the target to start the downswing. This move drops the club too far behind you, causing it to approach the ball on an extreme in-to-out path. To prevent the ball from going right, your hands flip the clubface closed. Timed perfectly, this produces a gentle draw, but when your hands close the clubface too soon, as is often the case, that draw becomes a hook.

When your hips slide too aggressively toward the target, the club swings down sharply from the inside.

To prevent a pushed shot, your hands flip the club-face closed, which leads to a hook.

A neutral grip helps square the clubface at impact.

START IN NEUTRAL

The solution is to eliminate flipping at impact, and that starts with your grip. Better players often take a strong grip, which encourages a closed clubface at impact. A neutral grip—two knuckles visible on the left hand and the "Vs" of both hands pointing between your chin and right shoulder—helps to square the clubface at impact.

DRILL: SLICE AWAY YOUR HOOK Next time you're at the range, try to hit big slices. Push your hands down and away from your body to start the downswing. It will feel as if you're cutting across the ball at impact and hitting a nasty slice, but you'll probably launch it straight; you're so used to the in-to-out hook that a swing on the proper path feels wrong.

Fault: Your weight shifts to your rear foot on the downswing.

Fix: Imagine a grip against your cheek to promote a more level shoulder rotation and a weight shift to your forward leg.

FINISH FOR POWER

If you are one of the lucky players who naturally finds a lot of fairways, you probably wish you could squeeze out just a few more yards from your swing. Fixing these two common power leaks could do just that.

FAULT 1: REVERSE PIVOT

It's frustrating to a see a shot fly directly at the flag but fall well short. When this happens, check where your weight finished after your swing. If it is over your back foot, you are finishing poorly because of a reverse pivot.

A reverse pivot occurs when you dip your left shoulder and tilt your upper body toward the target on your backswing. From there, you naturally fall back—away from your target—on your downswing, and have to scoop under the ball to make contact. Usually, the shot goes too high and lacks forward thrust, so it lands short.

Fix this problem by keeping your head at the same level throughout your backswing.

Imagine someone is holding the grip end of a club against your target-side cheek as you start the club back, and try to maintain contact with that grip throughout your swing. Your shoulders will rotate on a more level plane, which will help you shift your weight to your forward leg as you swing through the ball.

Fault: Your arms cannot swing freely when your lower body slides aggressively toward the target.

Fix: To straighten your shots, shorten your backswing and rotate your weight around your left leg on the downswing.

FAULT 2: THE REVERSE "C"

In your quest for more power, it's tempting to get your lower body too active at the start of your downswing. A sure sign is when you start missing fairways and your back suddenly aches. A reverse "C" finish is the likely culprit.

When your lower body slides too aggressively toward your target to start your downswing, your arms can't swing down freely. That free swing is what squares the clubface, so your shots will fly straight but land in the right rough (unlike a slice, which curves through the air). Also, your upper body will tilt away from your target and contort into a reverse C-shape, which is the reason for your back pain.

Add some power by shortening your backswing and rotating your weight around your left leg on the downswing. Shortening your backswing will help you keep your lower body and upper body in sync. Rotating over your front leg will clear more room for your arms to swing, so the clubface can square up naturally through the hitting zone. You should start to see longer shots that fly straight and hit the fairway.

ADDING POWER

There is no question that increasing power and gaining distance with not only your driver, but your fairway woods and irons as well, can be a big advantage. It's modern golf. But how you go about trying to add distance is important.

On the pages that follow are a variety of tips to add yards. You will see how subtle things like a grip adjustment can help you get the ball farther down the fairway. You will also see how tweaking your takeaway and improving the quality of your impact can lead to distance gains. So turn the page and get ready to add more horse-power to your game.

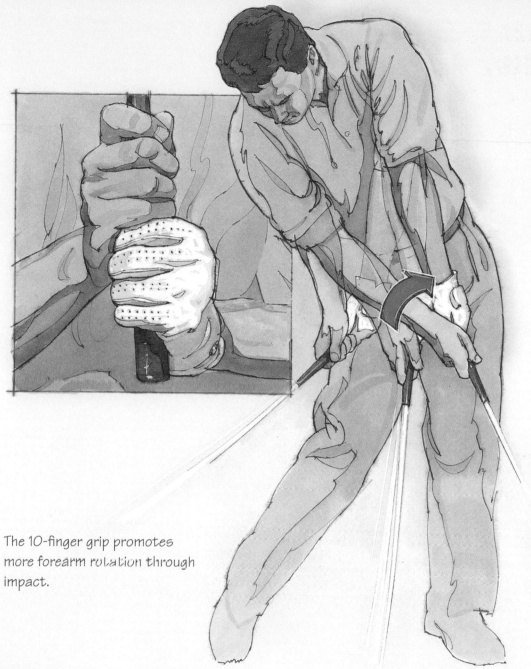

The 10-finger grip promotes more forearm rotation through impact.

CREATE A POWER GRIP

Increasing your forearm rotation is a good way to add extra snap through the hitting area. To encourage this, try the 10-finger grip. It's only a slight adjustment from more traditional grips—your right pinkie wraps around the grip instead of overlapping or interlocking with the fingers of your left hand.

During the swing, however, it will feel significantly different. With your entire right hand gripping the club, there is more mobility in your wrists, allowing for an aggressive rotation of your right forearm through impact. Make a few baseball swings with this grip before hitting balls; it will give you a good sense for how your right forearm is rotating. Key on this rotation through the bottom of the swing for more power and better contact.

"RELEASE" YOUR UNTAPPED POWER

One of the most important elements of maximizing your power is timing the release of your wrists at impact. Ideally, your hands and forearms should be rotating toward the target as the clubhead nears impact. But some players tense their hands, wrists and forearms in an effort to swing hard at the ball, which results in a blockage of the natural rotation that takes place at the bottom of your downswing. To make your release the best it can be, keep your left-hand grip pressure relaxed throughout your swing. It may feel as though you're closing the clubface on the downswing, but you're actually squaring it. This will generate more clubhead speed and encourage a right-to-left ball flight, which can also help to add distance.

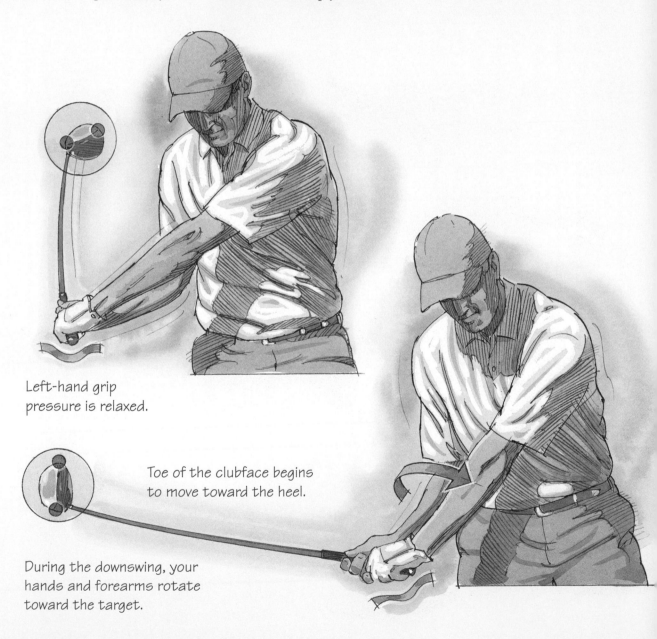

Left-hand grip pressure is relaxed.

Toe of the clubface begins to move toward the heel.

During the downswing, your hands and forearms rotate toward the target.

Wrists and
forearms
continue
to rotate
toward the
target
through
impact.

Clubface square to target at impact.

Toe of clubface passes heel after impact.

WATCH YOUR WIDTH

A wide stance might feel powerful, but it can cost you distance by inhibiting body rotation and weight transfer. Your goal should be to balance stability with freedom of movement.

When hitting woods and long irons, spread your feet shoulder-width apart. The insides of your heels should be in line with the outsides of your shoulders. If you're like many golfers, you flare out one or both feet, so use your heels as a guide.

Stability is less of an issue with shorter clubs, so narrow your stance when hitting them. But don't go overboard. A stance that's too narrow makes it hard to stay balanced during the swing; it can cost you solid contact and distance control when you need them most.

For woods and long irons, spread your feet shoulder-width apart.

The shorter the club, the narrower your stance.

Mid-irons

Short irons

START BACK LOW LIKE DALY

Many golf purists have criticized John Daly's unorthodox swing; it's unusually long and includes movements sure to keep chiropractors busy. However, if you are not satisfied with how far you hit the ball off the tee, there is one crucial element of Big John's swing that is worth copying: the extremely low takeaway.

You can increase your driving distance by copying John Daly's extremely low takeaway.

A low takeaway creates a wide swing arc that promotes more clubhead speed and longer shots. However, most golfers break their wrists too early in the swing, setting the club on a much narrower arc. The result is a lack of power.

Daly nearly drags the clubhead along the ground for the first 18 inches of the backswing. If you do the same in your takeaway, you are likely to add some precious yards to your drives.

A low takeaway creates a wide clubhead arc that promotes longer shots.

18"

DELAY THE RELEASE

A late release is a fundamental power producer. But keeping your wrists fully cocked until the instant before impact is a difficult concept. Here's a tip that can help.

Imagine that your club is an ax and you're using it to chop down a tree. The task calls for maximum force, so you'll forget about your wrists and use the big muscles in your back and legs. Those muscles are the basic keys to power—if you rely on them to drive your swing, that late release of the wrists will take care of itself.

Imagine your club is an ax: Drive the swing with your big muscles and let the release happen naturally.

POWER PRIMERS

If you are one of the many players who have lost flexibility in your muscles and joints as you've gotten older, don't assume that means you're doomed to be short off the tee. Solid fundamentals can help you send the ball deep down the fairway.

DEVELOP A POWERFUL TURN

The more you can coil your body as you take the club back, the more power you will generate on the downswing. Just make sure it's the right type of coil—that is, don't let your weight sway outside your right foot. When you do that, your balance is sacrificed and it will be very tough to shift back into the correct position on your downswing and make solid contact.

The ideal backswing turn should position your weight over the inside edge of your back foot. Feel this by placing an old head cover under the outside half of your right foot. As you swing, the head cover will brace your leg so you can't slide your weight too far right. Make a few practice swings, and as you take the club back, feel your weight over the inside edge of your right shoe. Finally, take the head cover away and re-create that sensation while hitting your driver. You'll have a better coil going back and deliver extra power to the ball.

Practicing with an old head cover under the outside of your back foot will keep you from swaying and promote a powerful turn.

SWEEP YOUR FOREARMS

The more clubhead speed you create, the farther you can hit the ball. And to really make the clubhead accelerate, you must rotate your forearms on your downswing. You can practice this move by swinging a broom like a golf club.

Hold a broom as you would a driver, with the bristles facing your target. Take your address position and slowly swing the broom back to the top. When it is parallel to the ground on your backswing, your left forearm should be rotating over your right. As you swing down and the broom reaches parallel on your follow-through, your right forearm should be rotated over your left. If someone were facing you, he would see one side of the bristles on your backswing and the other side of the bristles on your follow-through.

Swinging the broom faster and faster while going through those positions will build strength in your hands, arms and shoulders, and will teach you how to rotate your forearms effectively to generate more clubhead speed.

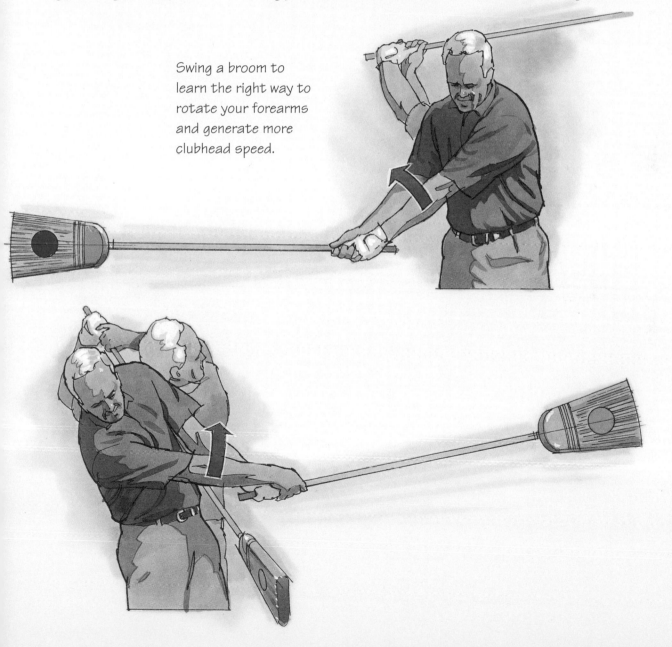

Swing a broom to learn the right way to rotate your forearms and generate more clubhead speed.

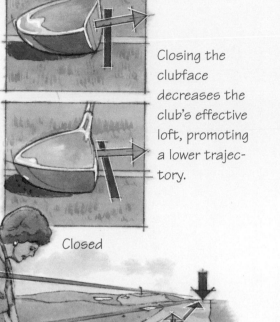

Square

Aim your stance to the right of the target, with your clubface directly at it.

Closing the clubface decreases the club's effective loft, promoting a lower trajectory.

Closed

HOW TO ADD 17 YARDS

Many short hitters can pick up distance by drawing the ball, that is, curving it from right to left. A draw goes farther because closing the clubface to the target line decreases the club's effective loft and the ball's launch angle. The shot has less backspin and a more penetrating flight, causing it to roll more after landing.

Robots swinging a driver at 90 miles per hour—the typical clubhead speed of most amateurs—proved that a draw travels, on average, 17 yards farther than a fade (233 yards vs. 216 yards). Here's how you can get your 17 yards, and maybe more.

SETTING UP FOR A DRAW

Aim your stance and body to the right of your target, while aiming the clubface directly at it. Swing along your stance line both back and through. The clubhead will reach impact closed to your stance line, producing right-to-left spin.

If this isn't enough, strengthen your grip—rotating your hands clockwise on the club—to promote faster clubface rotation through impact.

By swinging along your stance line, the clubface will reach impact closed to the stance line.

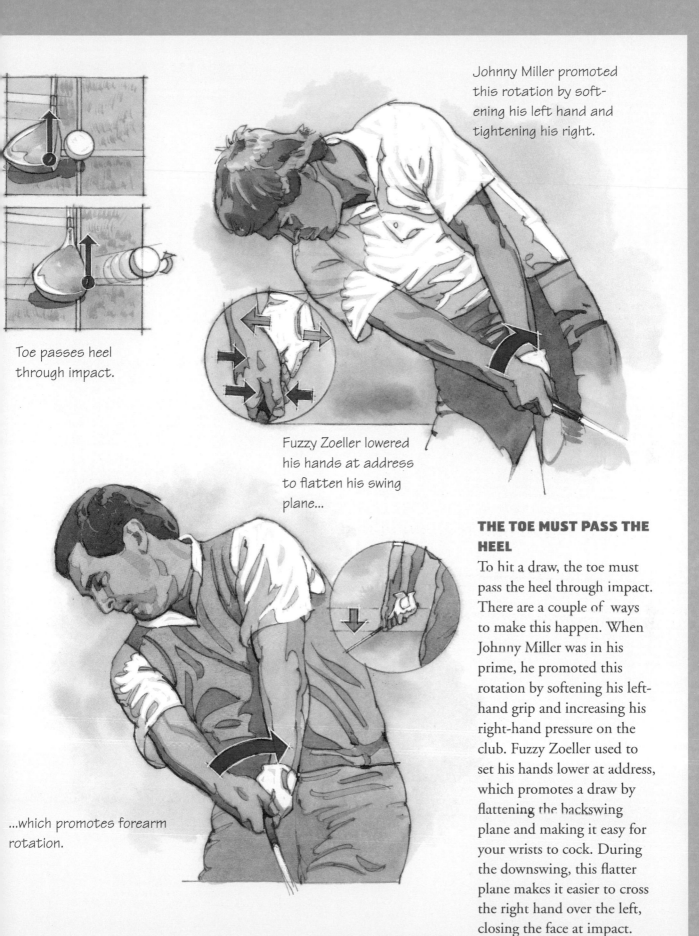

Toe passes heel
through impact.

Johnny Miller promoted
this rotation by soft-
ening his left hand and
tightening his right.

Fuzzy Zoeller lowered
his hands at address
to flatten his swing
plane...

...which promotes forearm
rotation.

THE TOE MUST PASS THE HEEL

To hit a draw, the toe must pass the heel through impact. There are a couple of ways to make this happen. When Johnny Miller was in his prime, he promoted this rotation by softening his left-hand grip and increasing his right-hand pressure on the club. Fuzzy Zoeller used to set his hands lower at address, which promotes a draw by flattening the backswing plane and making it easy for your wrists to cock. During the downswing, this flatter plane makes it easier to cross the right hand over the left, closing the face at impact.

Mimic Snead's footwork and leg action to develop "the squat."

SQUAT LIKE SAM SNEAD

If you want more distance, but don't want to hit the weight room, forget about hitting a left-to-right fade and start hitting right-to-left draws instead.

A draw's inside-to-square downswing path demands good leg action, and nobody was better at that than the late

Right hip and leg hold steady at the top.

Left foot rolls inside.

The downswing is initiated by rolling the left foot and knee toward the target, while the right foot remains planted.

Sam Snead. His downswing was characterized by a squat: He started down by letting his left leg shift toward the target while holding his right leg and hip steady. This created the squat.

By restricting the right side as he swung down, Snead maintained his posture and created plenty of room for the club to swing into the ball from inside the target line. Most golfers start the downswing by releasing the right hip, which blocks the inside path to the ball. As a result, the club approaches the ball from outside the target line, which usually produces a weak slice.

FANCY FOOTWORK

Copy Snead's footwork to develop the squat. Without a ball, swing to the top and feel your weight over your right side. You should feel the right hip supporting your body's weight and the left foot rolled inward. Start down by rolling the left foot toward the target while keeping the right foot planted. This will put you in the squat position. Only as your weight shifts to your left side and the club passes impact should the right foot come up onto its toes.

DRILL: DROP THE BALL Groove the squat that will help you hit a draw by making practice swings holding a beach ball or soccer ball between your knees. At the top of the swing, your knees should hold the ball in place. As you start the downswing, your left knee should shift toward the target, causing the ball to drop before the clubhead reaches impact.

APPLY YOUR POWER

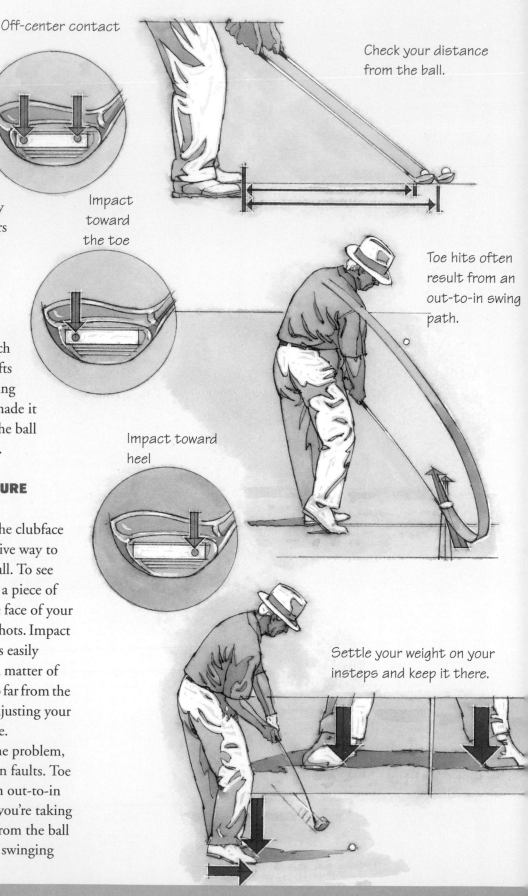

Off-center contact

Check your distance from the ball.

Impact toward the toe

Toe hits often result from an out-to-in swing path.

Impact toward heel

Settle your weight on your insteps and keep it there.

Believe it or not, some golfers have power to spare. But chances are, you're probably fighting for every yard. You can stay competitive with players who can really boom it if you can make solid contact and maximize clubhead speed. That's easier than you think with today's clubs, which have longer, lighter shafts and larger, more forgiving faces. Technology has made it easier than ever to hit the ball solidly and swing faster.

NOTHING BEATS A PURE STRIKE

Hitting the middle of the clubface remains the most effective way to transfer power to the ball. To see how you're doing, stick a piece of masking tape across the face of your driver and hit some tee shots. Impact toward the toe or heel is easily corrected if it's simply a matter of standing too close or too far from the ball at address. See if adjusting your setup makes a difference.

If a poor setup isn't the problem, check for other common faults. Toe hits often result from an out-to-in swing path. Make sure you're taking the club straight away from the ball on the backswing, then swinging

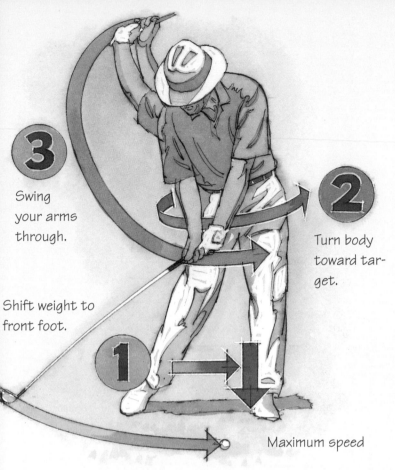

3
Swing
your arms
through.

Shift weight to
front foot.

2
Turn body
toward tar-
get.

1

Maximum speed

out to the target through impact. Heel impact follows from leaning forward, onto your toes, during the swing. Start with your weight on your insteps and feel it stay there through impact.

POSITION YOUR FAST POINT

Many golfers jerk the club down from the top, which wastes speed too soon in the downswing. Control your speed by working on the sequence of your downswing. Starting from the top, you should: 1) Shift weight to your front foot, 2) Turn your body to the target, and 3) Swing your arms through. Follow this sequence and clubhead speed will max out at impact.

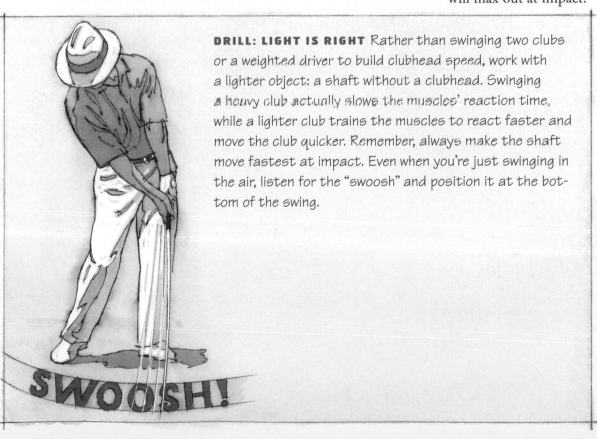

DRILL: LIGHT IS RIGHT Rather than swinging two clubs or a weighted driver to build clubhead speed, work with a lighter object: a shaft without a clubhead. Swinging a heavy club actually slows the muscles' reaction time, while a lighter club trains the muscles to react faster and move the club quicker. Remember, always make the shaft move fastest at impact. Even when you're just swinging in the air, listen for the "swoosh" and position it at the bottom of the swing.

SWOOSH!

Flare your left foot only a few degrees to optimize your hip turn.

To activate your hands, practice half-swings and feel the shaft's rotation through the hitting area.

LESS FLARE AND BETTER HANDS

You can usually squeeze out a few more yards if you pay extra attention to the power producers in your swing—and enhance them as much as possible.

LESS FLARE, MORE TURN

Torso rotation is a huge power generator. But flaring your left foot out at address, which many golfers do, can hold it back. So why not toe it in? Unfortunately, that restricts your hips on the through-swing. Try the happy medium instead, flaring your left foot open a few degrees. That position allows you to make a full hip turn on the backswing while giving your hips the freedom to drive through impact.

ACTIVATE YOUR HANDS

When your hands are functioning properly, the toe of the club points up when the club is halfway down, and again when it is halfway through. To get a feel for this, make half-swings back and through and create the toe-up positions. The faster you rotate the shaft, the more effective your hands will be in increasing clubhead speed.

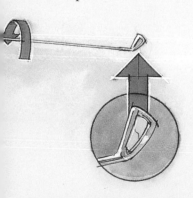

DRILL: CHECK YOUR POCKETS To ensure your hips are doing their part, use your two front hip pockets as checkpoints. Going back, rotate the hips so your left hip pocket is behind the ball at the top. Swinging through, rotate the right hip aggressively through the impact zone until it faces the target at the finish. If you can hit these two marks, your hips and torso have made a full turn back and through.

FIRM UP YOUR LEFT SIDE

You don't have to be big and strong to create a lot of clubhead speed. More distance will come if you use the right technique.

TWO PARTS TO A RELEASE

At impact, the body and club should release, creating a burst of clubhead speed. The power comes mainly from your arms, specifically their rotation and unhinging of your wrists. These motions happen naturally—if you let them.

As your arms pass in front of your body on the downswing, your right forearm naturally wants to roll over your left. This rotation adds some speed and, more important, squares the clubface at impact. Also, the weight of the clubhead causes your wrists to hinge during the backswing and unhinge as the club approaches impact. This unhinging is a major source of clubhead speed.

Power comes from the rotation of your right forearm over your left, and the unhinging of your wrists.

Rotation squares the clubface at impact.

SWING IN CEMENT

To make the most of arm rotation and wrist unhinging, your body must provide leverage. This occurs when the front side stays firm, forming a brace that your arms and clubhead swing past. Many short hitters slide toward the target as the club approaches the ball, throwing away a lot of leverage.

As you swing down, pretend your front foot is mired in cement and your front leg is solid. You'll have more hitting power.

To increase leverage, your arms must swing past a firm left side.

Imagine your front foot is in cement.

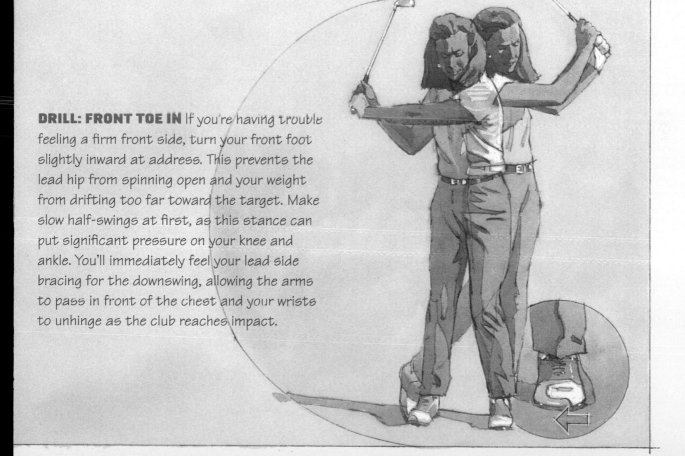

DRILL: FRONT TOE IN If you're having trouble feeling a firm front side, turn your front foot slightly inward at address. This prevents the lead hip from spinning open and your weight from drifting too far toward the target. Make slow half-swings at first, as this stance can put significant pressure on your knee and ankle. You'll immediately feel your lead side bracing for the downswing, allowing the arms to pass in front of the chest and your wrists to unhinge as the club reaches impact.

TEE IT HIGH TO STRETCH YOUR DRIVES

Maximizing your distance off the tee without flexing your muscles or straining your back may seem like a tall order, but believe it or not, you can get all the length you need with your driver by simply teeing your ball at the proper height.

The simple truth—proven countless times in tests—is that a ball teed higher tends to fly farther than a ball teed lower. Years ago, the standard advice was to tee the ball up so that half of it was visible over the top of the driver. Nowadays, with most drivers measuring 460 cubic centimeters, you should tee the ball so that three-quarters of it is visible over the top of the clubhead. The added height will allow you to catch the ball with an upward blow, which will cause the ball to fly farther and give you the extra yards you're looking for.

Tee the ball up so that you can see three-quarters of the ball over the top of the clubhead.

The added height will allow you to catch the ball with an upward blow.

The ball will fly farther.

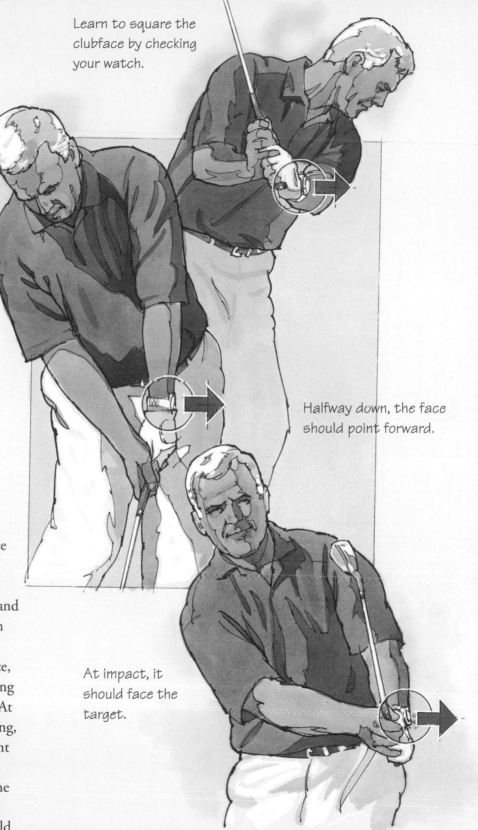

Learn to square the clubface by checking your watch.

Halfway down, the face should point forward.

At impact, it should face the target.

At halfway through, it should point behind you.

SQUARE THE FACE

A quick way to add distance is to square the clubface at impact. Leaving it open, as many golfers do, adds loft and creates left-to-right sidespin that costs you yards.

To learn to square the face, make practice swings wearing a watch on your left wrist. At hip height on the downswing, the watch's face should point directly in front of you; at impact it should point at the target; and at hip height in the follow-through, it should point behind you. If you hit these marks, you'll square the face and boost your power.

Keep your wrists fully cocked until the club is near impact.

At hip high, the club's leading edge should match your spine angle.

CASTING ROBS YOU OF POWER

In fishing, good casting is essential if you want to catch the big one. In golf, casting—flicking the wrists at the start of the downswing—causes high, weak drives and fat iron shots.

A good swing is characterized by the wrists remaining fully cocked well into the downswing, storing energy until the last possible moment before impact. If your drives lack power and your irons seem to fall from the sky, one of the following cures should eliminate your cast.

THE INSIDE STORY
Many casters immediately pull the club to the inside going back. This leads to over-rotating the left forearm and swinging the club so far behind the body that casting is the only way to get the clubhead back to the ball.

To check your backswing, lay a club on the ground, extending it straight back from the toes of your back foot. Holding another club, swing back until its shaft is parallel to the one on the ground: Your hands should be directly above the grip of the club at your foot. The club's leading edge should match your spine angle.

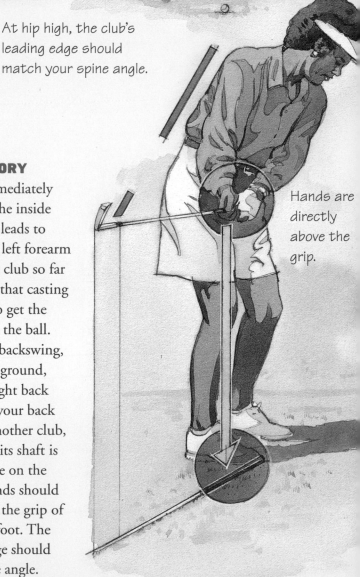

Hands are directly above the grip.

"Cupping" at the top commonly leads to casting.

DON'T BREAK THIS RULE(R)

Swing a club to the top, stop and look at your hands. Is there a noticeable angle between your left wrist and forearm? Bending or "cupping" your wrist at the top of the swing often leads to casting.

To get the feel of a straight wrist, slip one end of a plastic ruler or Popsicle stick under your watchband, the other end under a rubber band around your hand. Now swing: The ruler should lie flat across the wrist and back of the hand. If it bends, you're still cupping.

Use a ruler and a rubber band to feel a straight wrist.

Holding a tee under the left pinky also can reduce casting.

CONSTANT PRESSURE

Yes, it is possible to grip the club too lightly. If your left hand doesn't have a firm hold, it will let go of the club at the top, then regrip too tightly. The ensuing tension often leads to casting.

At address, be sure to take a firm grip with the last three fingers of the left hand. Slide a tee under your left pinky and make practice swings with the tee staying in place. Holding on with the pinky also keeps pressure on the ring and middle fingers, and will cure your casting.

SWING THOUGHT: SHIFT LIKE A PITCHER

Many similarities to the golf swing can be found in the motion of a Major League pitcher.

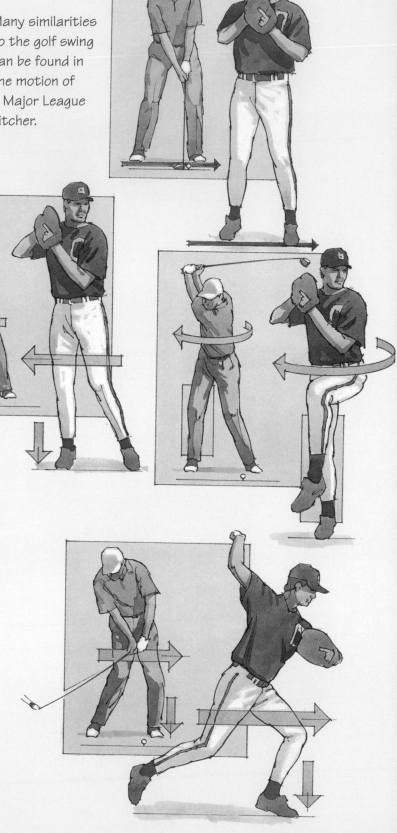

To understand how much power a good coil and weight transfer can produce, study the motion of a baseball pitcher and notice the similarities to the golf swing.

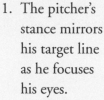

1. The pitcher's stance mirrors his target line as he focuses his eyes.
2. He shifts his weight onto his back foot to start his motion.
3. He coils his body around his back leg to store power.
4. He transfers his weight to his front foot as the body unwinds and his arm whips forward.

Pitchers talk about having strong arms, but without the support of their legs, hips and torso they'd lose serious velocity. The same applies to the golf swing; your swing will only produce extra yards if you have a good weight shift to support your arm motion.

Practice a one-piece take-away to help you square the clubhead at impact.

TRACK YOUR TAKEAWAY

Hitting long drives is great, but in your quest for power, if too many of your shots are "long and wrong," you might have too much of a good thing. Length comes from developing lots of clubhead speed, but if your arms, wrists and hands are too loose, it can lead to a poor backswing path, which makes it difficult to hit the ball straight.

Here's a drill to straighten your takeaway so you can maximize your power without sacrificing accuracy. Setup with the butt end of a club against the center of your chest and hold the club with your hands well down the shaft. Make a few swings, feeling your hands, arms and wrists moving in unison with your body. Practicing this one-piece takeaway will help you keep your arms, hands and wrists in check during the first few feet of the swing. Then you'll be able to use them when it really counts—at impact.

FAIRWAY WOODS

Whether it's the tee shot on a long par 3 or the second shot on a long par 4 or par 5, a fairway wood can be your best friend. And with their wide soles, fairway woods work through rough much more easily than long-irons, making them a smart choice from some ugly spots off the fairway.

But even with all this versatility, many players still hit these clubs poorly. Should you swing a fairway wood like your driver and sweep the ball off the ground, or swing it like an iron and try to trap the ball against the turf? This chapter's goal is to answer those questions, and many others, to help you get the most out of these important clubs.

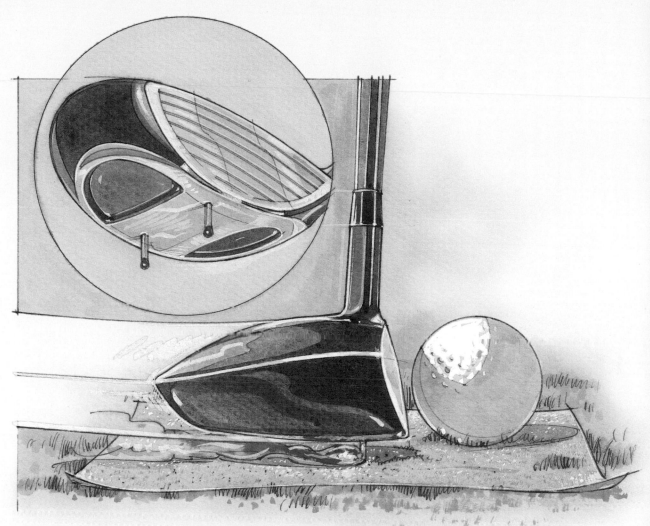

Think about striking matchsticks and sweeping straight through the ball.

MAX OUT YOUR FAIRWAY WOODS

To hit solid fairway wood shots, focus on sweeping the grass at impact. *GOLF MAGAZINE* Contributing Teacher Martin Hall suggests that you imagine that the ball is sitting on a strip of sandpaper and the club has the tips of two matchsticks stuck to the sole. As you swing, imagine you're lighting the matches by dragging them along the sandpaper at impact. This image encourages a shallow, sweeping blow, which allows you to hit the sweetspot more often. The dragging image also promotes acceleration through impact. With a faster, more level strike, you're sure to get maximum distance from these crucial clubs.

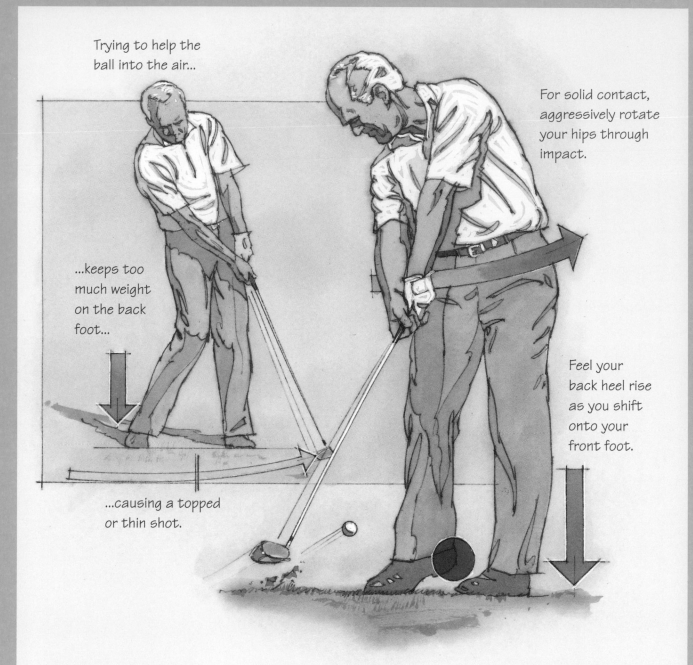

Trying to help the ball into the air...

...keeps too much weight on the back foot...

...causing a topped or thin shot.

For solid contact, aggressively rotate your hips through impact.

Feel your back heel rise as you shift onto your front foot.

KEEP YOUR 3-WOOD RELIABLE

Most golfers hit their 3-wood eight to 10 times a round—more than most non-driver full-swing clubs. So if you're not hitting it on the well, your scores will suffer.

The mistake many golfers make is trying to help the ball into the air. They know they're working with relatively little loft, so they feel the need to swing up on the ball, their weight staying on the back foot. That usually results either in a topped shot or a weak line drive.

For solid contact, you must transfer weight to your front foot on the downswing, which will force your back heel to come off the ground as you swing through the hitting area. Aggressively rotating your hips through impact is the trigger that pulls your heel up, but it also signals a proper weight shift, as your heel won't come up until your weight has shifted forward. Focus on this move the next time your 3-wood starts acting up.

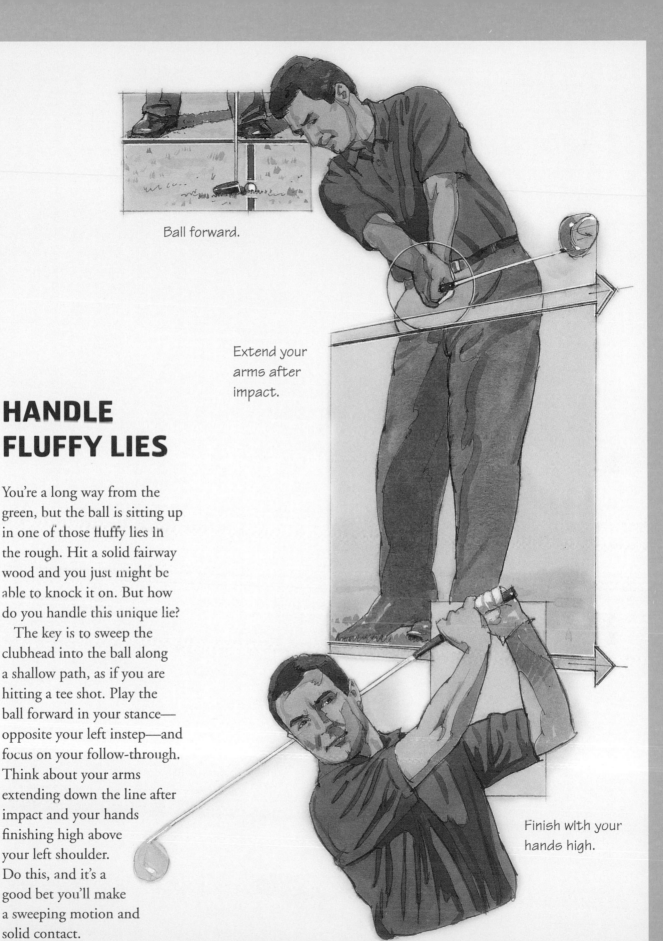

Ball forward.

Extend your
arms after
impact.

Finish with your
hands high.

HANDLE FLUFFY LIES

You're a long way from the
green, but the ball is sitting up
in one of those fluffy lies in
the rough. Hit a solid fairway
wood and you just might be
able to knock it on. But how
do you handle this unique lie?

The key is to sweep the
clubhead into the ball along
a shallow path, as if you are
hitting a tee shot. Play the
ball forward in your stance—
opposite your left instep—and
focus on your follow-through.
Think about your arms
extending down the line after
impact and your hands
finishing high above
your left shoulder.
Do this, and it's a
good bet you'll make
a sweeping motion and
solid contact.

MASTER YOUR 3-WOOD

Hitting a crisp 3-wood from a tight lie will be extremely challenging, but avoiding the club will only hurt your game. The 3-wood is the longest club in your bag after the driver, so you're sacrificing distance and the chance to hit shorter irons into the green when you leave it home.

Unlike irons—which are most effective when the ball is struck with a downward blow—fairway woods require a sweeping motion that strikes the ball as the clubhead moves parallel to the ground. To practice this technique, take a wide stance similar to the one you use with your driver.

Position the ball opposite your left heel with your weight balanced comfortably on the balls of your feet. Start the swing on a low path that almost skims the grass, and try to replicate that shallow path on your downswing. Remember to keep your right shoulder level and to pull through firmly with your left hand. Keep your head and upper body behind the

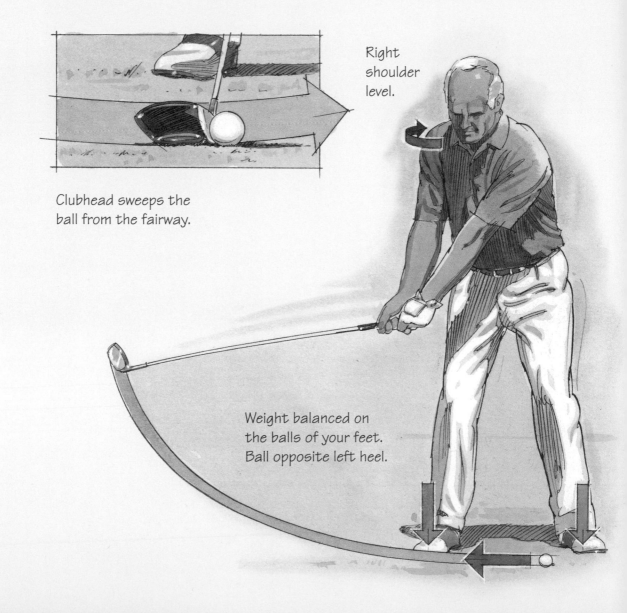

Clubhead sweeps the ball from the fairway.

Right shoulder level.

Weight balanced on the balls of your feet. Ball opposite left heel.

ball through impact. Brush through the ball and make sure to extend your arms toward the target on your follow-through.

A 3-wood isn't meant to go sky high, so don't feel as though you need to help it get airborne—just try to keep the clubhead on a level path through impact. The loft on a 3-wood is more than enough to send your ball on its way.

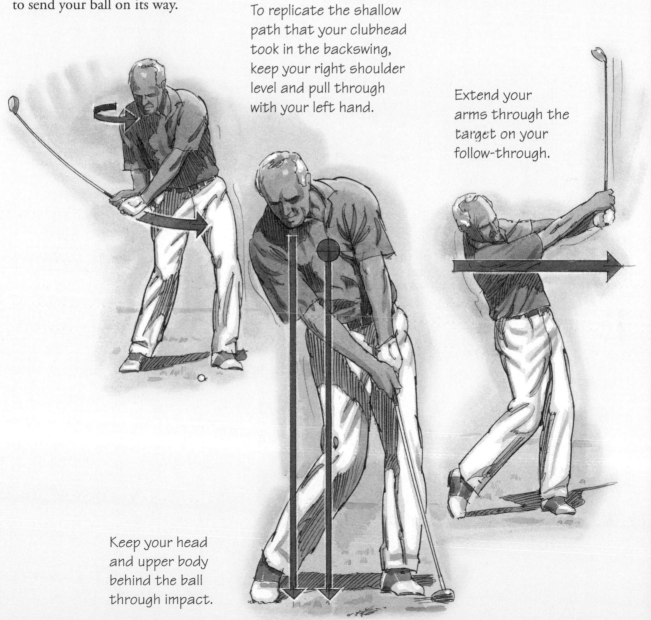

To replicate the shallow path that your clubhead took in the backswing, keep your right shoulder level and pull through with your left hand.

Extend your arms through the target on your follow-through.

Keep your head and upper body behind the ball through impact.

TWO VERSATILE HYBRID CLUB SHOTS

As playable as fairway woods but with a shorter shaft for more control, hybrid or *rescue clubs* are a great alternative to long irons. But their real advantage is versatility, as they can also provide options for two finesse shots close to the green.

THE BUMP-AND-RUN

You're short of the green with 20 to 30 yards of fairway between the ball and the putting surface. The bump-and-run is a good call, but using a 7- or 8-iron requires near-perfect contact. Because a hybrid clubhead is heavier and has a wider sole, you can focus almost exclusively on gauging the shot's length.

Hybrid club

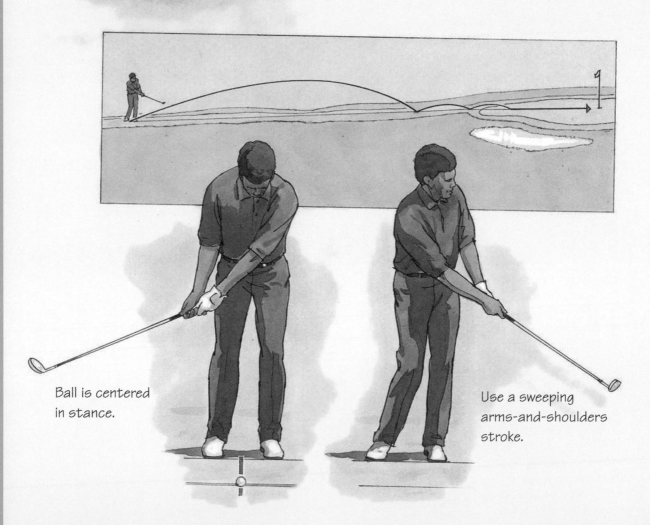

Ball is centered in stance.

Use a sweeping arms-and-shoulders stroke.

Play the ball in the middle of your stance and keep your wrists quiet during the swing. Use a sweeping arms-and-shoulders stroke and follow through. The ball will bounce onto the green, then roll to the hole.

THE KNOCKDOWN

You're 75 yards out, there's a strong headwind, and the last thing you want to do is throw a high wedge shot up into the gale. You could try to punch the ball low with a 9-iron, but with a lofted hybrid—say, 23-degrees or so—you can hit the same low shot with far less manipulation.

Take your normal address and ball position, then narrow your stance slightly. Grip down an inch or so and make a half-swing, similar to a long pitch shot. The hybrid's loft will get the ball airborne, but not high enough to balloon in the wind. This shot uses a simple, reliable motion that's easier to control than a punch.

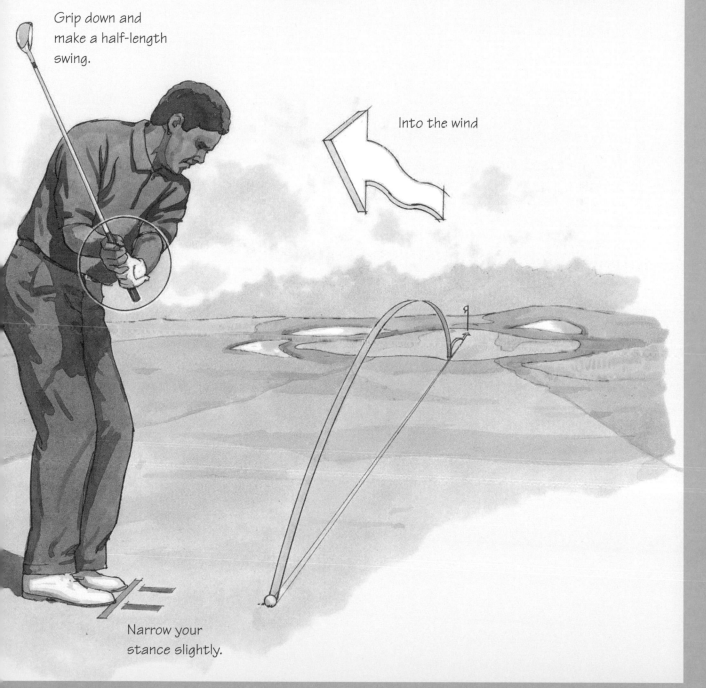

Grip down and make a half-length swing.

Into the wind

Narrow your stance slightly.

IRON PLAY

Developing a precise, accurate iron game is one of the most important keys to scoring well. You can hit every fairway on the course,
but if your irons are erratic, you won't be lining up many birdie putts.

But like drivers, irons have become more forgiving and easier to
hit thanks to improved technology and modern designs. At the same
time, the fundamentals of good iron play remain the same as they
were for Ben Hogan, Gene Sarazen and Byron Nelson. This chapter sheds some light on those swing keys, shows you how to adjust
the trajectory of your shots and ways to increase your accuracy. In
short, we will help you become a marksman.

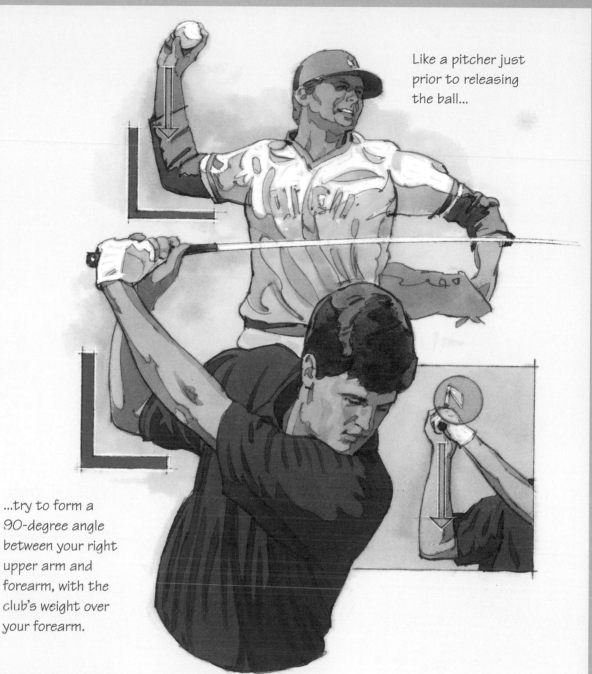

Like a pitcher just prior to releasing the ball...

...try to form a 90-degree angle between your right upper arm and forearm, with the club's weight over your forearm.

BACKSWING: THROW A STRIKE

To hit the ball with power and accuracy, you must be able to control the club at the top of the swing. Lose control, and there's no telling where the ball will end up. To set the club

at the top, picture a baseball pitcher just before he releases the ball: His right arm is bent at the elbow, forming a 90-degree angle. His right forearm is directly beneath the ball, allowing the pitcher to hold the baseball with minimal effort.

Try to set this 90-degree angle in your golf swing. Supporting the club's weight

over your right forearm keeps the club in the correct position at the top. From here, you can swing the club down freely.

Copying this pitching windup also allows your right wrist to bend back naturally. This prevents your wrist from bending too much at the top of the backswing, which encourages a square clubface.

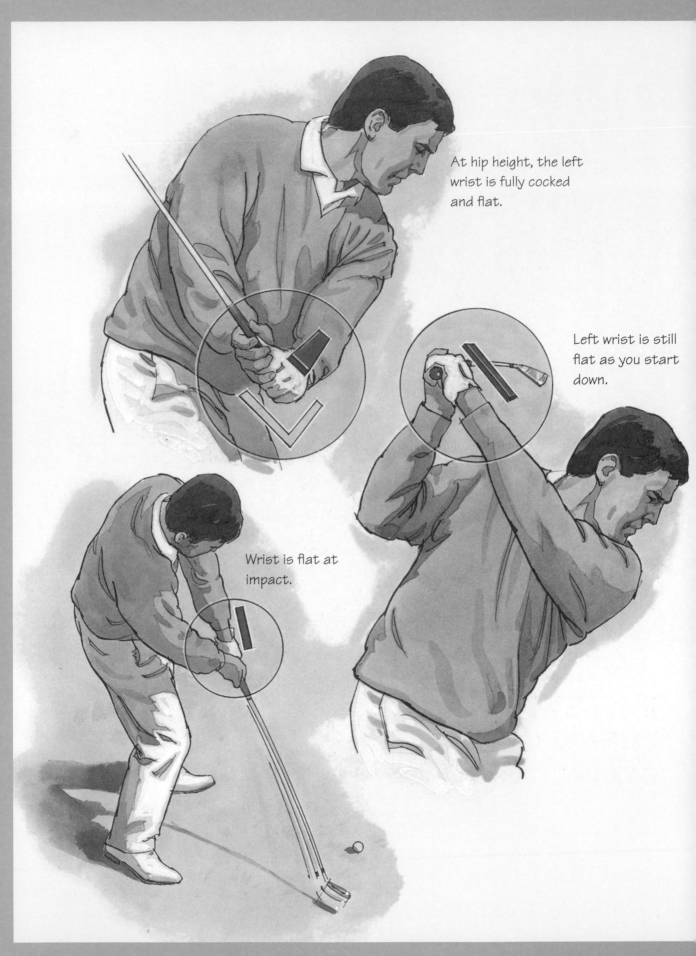

At hip height, the left wrist is fully cocked and flat.

Left wrist is still flat as you start down.

Wrist is flat at impact.

FLATTEN YOUR WRIST AT IMPACT

You won't find much consensus on whether or not the left wrist should be flat at the top of the swing. Nicklaus and Woods do it, but Hogan's left wrist was always cupped, and it's the same with Fred Couples. One thing is certain: For low, penetrating iron shots, your left wrist must be flat at the most important point—impact. The best way to achieve that is to have it flat when beginning the downswing.

HINGE AND FLATTEN

As your hands reach hip height in your backswing, the left wrist hinges and flattens. By the time your left arm reaches parallel to the ground, the left wrist is fully cocked but flat. From that point, your arms swing the club up, with the back of the left wrist forming a plane with the shaft. When you form this plane correctly, the shaft will point at the target. When you hold this left wrist angle in place as you start the downswing, you'll be able to hit the shot with a strong, piercing ball flight.

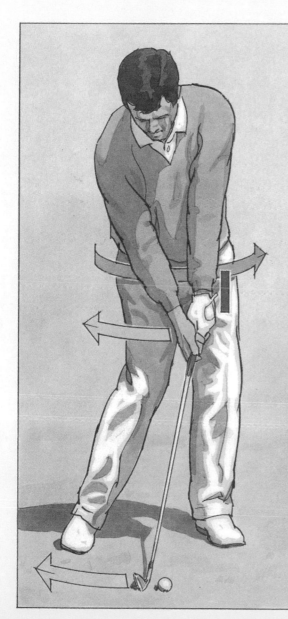

DRILL: POSE IMPACT To connect the dots between the top of the swing and impact, start from a posed impact position. Address the ball, then rotate your hips left and push your hands toward the target so your left wrist is flat and the clubface is hooded. Hold this position for a couple of seconds, then make your swing. During the downswing, focus on returning to the pre-set impact position. When you've hit several shots squarely, go back to a normal address and try to make the same contact.

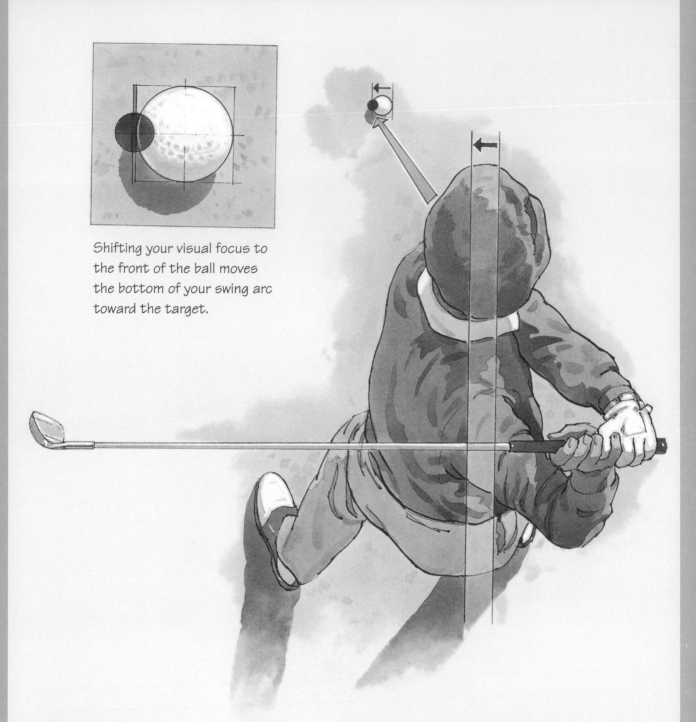

Shifting your visual focus to the front of the ball moves the bottom of your swing arc toward the target.

MAKE BALL–FIRST CONTACT

Sometimes a change in perspective is all it takes to fix a fault. Take inconsistent contact with your irons, for example. If you continually hit the ground on some shots, then make thin contact on others, start focusing your eyes on the front edge of the ball (target side) before and during your swing. It may not seem like much (the diameter of the golf ball is just 1.68 inches), but shifting your sight line forward even this small amount nudges your center of gravity toward the target. This forward shift will help the club reach its low point at the ball instead of behind it. *Presto*, better ball striking.

FIND YOUR REAL YARD-AGES

If you're like most players, your approach shots often finish short of the target. The reality is that you probably hit your maximum distance only once in every 10 tries. Your *average* distance with each club may be 10 yards shorter than you think.

To check your yardages, hit a dozen shots with each of your irons, then pace off the distances. Use the averages the next time you've got an iron shot to the green. Choosing an approach club based on your true average distance will give you more birdie putts—and fewer recovery shots from in front of the green.

Check your yardages by pacing off the distances you hit different clubs.

Grip down.

Make a three-quarter-length swing and pull the club down with both hands.

Center the ball with your hands forward and weight favoring your front foot.

Abbreviate the follow-through.

Keep the weight on your left side.

BETWEEN CLUBS? HIT A PUNCH SHOT

You're in-between clubs. Swinging easy with the longer iron can feel awkward to some players, and crushing the shorter stick doesn't guarantee accuracy. The trick is to make an aggressive yet controlled swing. Enter the punch shot.

Take the longer of the two irons, grip down about two or three inches and position the ball midway between your heels. Set your hands slightly ahead of the ball and lean toward your front foot. Instead of making a full weight transfer, stay set over your front foot to restrict your backswing to three-quarters length.

From the top, pull the club down with both hands. You can expect a deeper-than-usual divot, an abbreviated follow-through and a low, penetrating ball flight. Because of the limited lower-body shift, the punch shot allows you to make an aggressive arm swing. You'll maintain control and shave a few yards from the distance this club would normally fly, bringing your target into perfect range.

DRILL: THE WALK-THROUGH A successful punch shot demands you hit down through impact. Do this by setting your weight forward and keeping it there throughout the swing. Practice hitting shots with a walk-through swing—made famous by Gary Player—to avoid the tendency to fall back. Set up to play the punch, and as you follow through, let your right foot come off the ground and step past your left foot. The downswing and step-through should feel like one motion, and that leaves no doubt that your weight is over your front foot at impact.

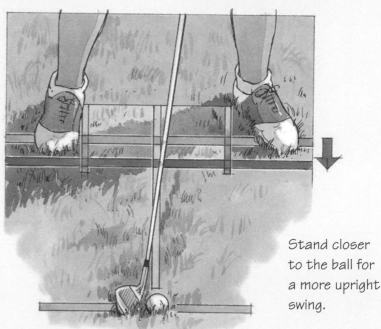

Choose the club that gives you the best chance at solid contact.

ESCAPE THE LONG GRASS

Full swings from the rough are always a gamble: The ball can jump, knuckle or squirt left or right—you never know until you hit the shot. You can, however, avoid "the big mistake," which is leaving the ball in the long grass. Keep the following keys in mind.

PLAY FOR GOOD CONTACT

Long irons are not designed to be played from the rough, so don't even consider using them. Choose the club that gives you the best chance at solid contact—preferably a short iron like an 8, but no more than a mid-iron, such as a 5. If it isn't enough club to reach the green, that's fine. You can handle a short pitch from in front, but you don't want another slash from the rough.

SETUP, HIT DOWN

Position the ball midway between your heels, moving it back another inch or so if the rough is extra thick. Playing the ball back will help you strike down on it. This keeps the rough from grabbing the clubhead and twisting the face off-line before impact.

It also helps to stand an inch closer to the ball than usual. You'll make a steeper, more upright swing while minimizing the amount of grass the clubhead must cut through before reaching the ball.

Stand closer to the ball for a more upright swing.

Play the ball midway between your heels from moderate rough.

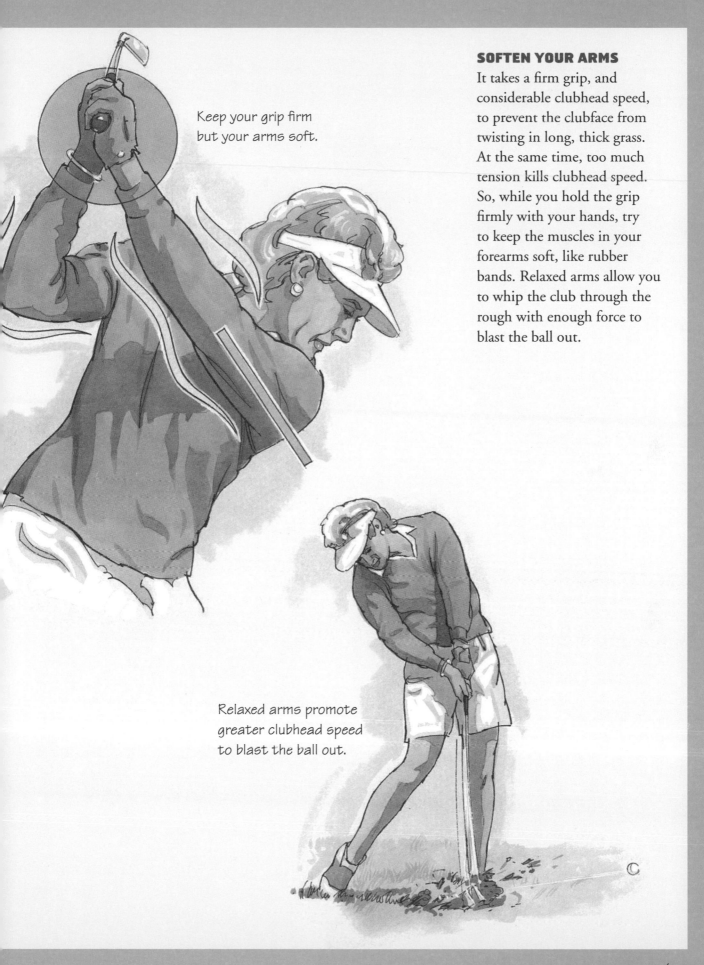

Keep your grip firm but your arms soft.

SOFTEN YOUR ARMS

It takes a firm grip, and considerable clubhead speed, to prevent the clubface from twisting in long, thick grass. At the same time, too much tension kills clubhead speed. So, while you hold the grip firmly with your hands, try to keep the muscles in your forearms soft, like rubber bands. Relaxed arms allow you to whip the club through the rough with enough force to blast the ball out.

Relaxed arms promote greater clubhead speed to blast the ball out.

TAKE ADVANTAGE OF TRICKY LIES

There is no greater confidence boost after a wild drive than a recovery shot that goes over, under or around trouble.

But many players don't check the lie and put themselves in an even worse spot after trying an ill-conceived shot. Here's how to tell if a lie will allow you to try a bold recovery—or make you take a more conservative route.

HIGH SHOT

Look for a flyer lie, where the ball is sitting on top of the rough. This will allow the club to slide under the ball and use its full loft. For extra height, let the clubhead pass your hands at impact and swing into a high finish while keeping your body back. The faster you swing, the higher the ball will fly.

LOW SHOTS

Almost any lie will do, but it helps if the ball is sitting down a little or on a bare patch of ground, such as hardpan. In either case, play the ball back in your stance, keeping your hands ahead of the ball to de-loft the club, and make sure you hit the ball before the ground.

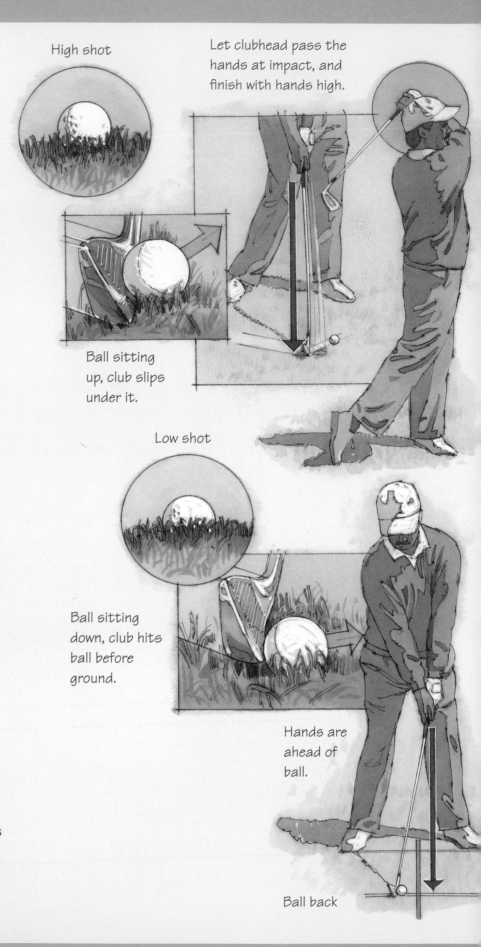

High shot

Let clubhead pass the hands at impact, and finish with hands high.

Ball sitting up, club slips under it.

Low shot

Ball sitting down, club hits ball before ground.

Hands are ahead of ball.

Ball back

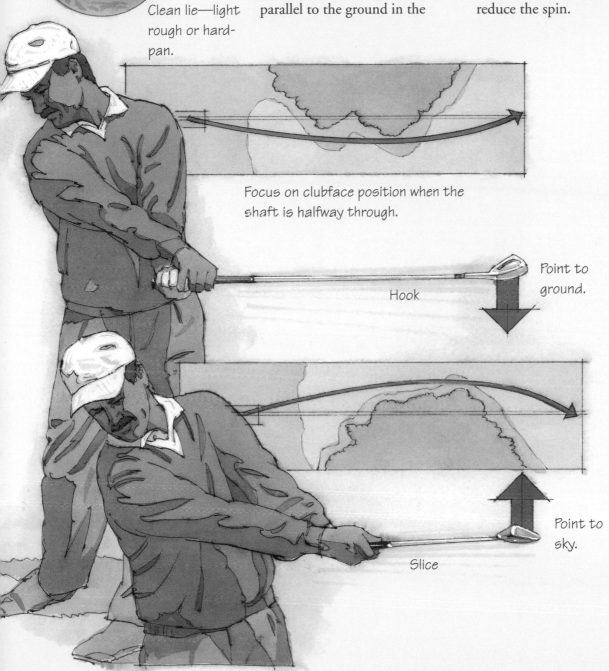

Curve shot

Clean lie—light rough or hardpan.

CURVED SHOTS

To apply sidespin, you want as little grass as possible between the club and ball. So look for clean lies—light rough or hardpan—where most of the ball is visible. To curve the ball, focus on the position of the clubface when the shaft is parallel to the ground in the follow-through: To hit a hook, the face should point to the ground; to hit a slice, the face should point to the sky.

Don't try to curve the ball from high rough or very wet grass, as any grass and water that gets trapped between the ball and the clubface will reduce the spin.

Focus on clubface position when the shaft is halfway through.

Hook

Point to ground.

Slice

Point to sky.

HITTING A DRAW

Want an extra 10 yards and a great scrambling tool all in one shot? Add an intentional draw to your iron game. With less backspin than a fade, the right-to-left draw flies lower, runs hotter and can help when you need to hit a recovery shot. Best of all, it isn't hard to learn: With a few setup adjustments, you can draw the ball with your normal swing.

BODY TO THE RIGHT

Body alignment determines the ball's initial direction, so pick a spot right of the target (say, the right edge of the fairway) and align your feet, knees, hips and shoulders to that point. This allows for the shot's curve.

CLUBFACE STRAIGHT

With your body aligned right, aim the clubface directly at your target. By setting the clubface closed to your body line, you'll create the right-to-left sidespin that curves the ball back to the target. Remember: Align your body where you want the ball to start; aim the clubface where you want it to finish.

Align your body right and aim the clubface straight.

Setting the clubface closed to your body line will promote a draw.

SWING ALONG YOUR BODY LINE

Use your normal swing. The closed clubface will take care of curving the shot back toward the target.

To move the ball right-to-left, the clubface must turn over through impact—try to muscle it and there's a good chance the face will stay open and the shot will stay right. Keep your forearms soft to promote clubface rotation through impact. The ball should start down the right side and run back to the target.

When you swing along your body line, the closed clubface will produce right-to-left sidespin.

MASTERING THE SHORT IRON DRAW

If you suffer from pulls or hooks, the short-iron draw (from an 8-iron down) is a technique that can save you from a lot of trouble spots. The key is that you've got to be able to generate enough clubhead speed to work the ball from a short distance.

To execute the short-iron draw successfully, aim well away from the trees impeding your sightline to the green, set up squarely to your line of flight, then close your stance by moving your right foot about an inch back from the target line.

Take the club back on a slightly inside swing plane and pull the clubhead through with your hands. Keep your head down until you've completed the swing—this will encourage your hands to over-release a bit, creating the draw spin you need. The shot will fly lower and farther and have a bit more roll than usual, so make sure that you take that into account when making your club selection.

Aim well away from the trees and set up square to the target line.

After you've aligned, pull your right foot back from the target line.

Take the club back on a slightly inside swing plane.

Keep your head down until you've completed your swing to foster an over-release.

Pull the club through with your hands.

The clubhead should touch down at the ball, not behind it.

FAT FIGHTERS

When it comes to mis-hits, the old saying is, "Thin to Win." Indeed, hitting the ball fat is guaranteed to rob your shot of distance—and it's a common mistake that developing players make. Here are two common causes of fat shots and tips for overcoming them.

THE FALLING CIRCLE

The clubhead essentially moves in a circle and the lowest point of that circle should be at the ball or just ahead of it. Fat shots occur when the low point drops behind the ball. This is often caused by sagging posture during your downswing.

Train yourself to maintain your posture by making practice swings without a club while your head is pressed against a wall. The wall will keep your head from dipping and your body from sagging as you swing down.

If your posture sags on the downswing, you'll probably hit the ball fat.

Learn to stay in posture by practicing without a club and with your head against a wall.

A reverse pivot can cause fat shots.

If you can lift your back foot at the finish, your weight transfer is correct.

THE REVERSE PIVOT

This fat-producing fault occurs when your weight moves toward your target on the backswing, then falls away on the downswing. For solid contact, the opposite must happen.

As you turn away from the ball, most of your weight should move to the inside of your back foot. On the downswing, shift to your front foot so nearly all of your weight ends up on the outside of the foot. Here's a test: If you can lift your back foot off the ground at the finish, your weight transfer was correct.

PLAY LONG IRONS AND WOODS FROM FAIRWAY SANDS

Playing a shot from a fairway bunker can be tough—especially on a long hole. One way to keep yourself in the hole from a fairway bunker is to develop confidence using your fairway woods or long-iron hybrids from the sand.

It's important to make sure that the lip of the bunker is low enough to clear with a longer club, and if it is, a successful shot is possible using the following technique:

Dig your feet into the sand just enough to create stability over the ball—you don't need to go as deep as you would in a greenside bunker. To avoid a sway, tilt the sole of your right shoe inward slightly to act as a brace.

Choke down slightly on the club and play the ball about an inch behind your left heel. Stand slightly straighter at the knees and waist to pick the ball cleanly from the sand.

Keep your takeaway low and limit your backswing to three-quarter length. Sweep the clubhead through the ball with your head still and spine angle consistent until well into your follow-through.

Stand slightly straighter at the knees and waist.

Choke down on the club.

Make sure you have a good lie and a very low front lip.

Tilt your right foot inward as a brace.

Play the ball just inside your left heel.

Three-quarter-length swing.

Keep your head still.

Maintain a consistent spine angle into the follow-through.

CHIPPING AND PITCHING

You may never hit your driver 300 yards because of your level of fitness, a lack of flexibility or an inability to generate the necessary clubhead speed. But everyone is capable of chipping and pitching the ball just as well as the pros. Power is not the issue here, but rather distance control, touch and a little practice.

What is the difference between a chip and a pitch? A chip stays low and rolls most of the way to the hole, while a pitch flies most of the way. When should you go with one technique instead of the other? This chapter will teach you, along with the smartest ways to hit these par-saving shots.

HOVER FOR SOLID CHIPS

Crisp chips require a descending blow. That means the clubhead must reach its lowest point after impact. At address, you may be tempted to press the club into the grass, but that presets the swing's low point at a spot behind the ball. The likely result: fat contact.

Instead, address the ball with the clubhead's leading edge at the ball's equator. With the ball in the middle of your stance and the shaft angled slightly toward the target, you can make a descending strike for solid chips.

Hover the clubhead's leading edge at the ball's equator.

The clubhead should reach its lowest point after impact.

Hands ahead of the ball.

Narrow your stance with your weight favoring the left side.

Ball back

Arms and shoulders swing while wrists remain quiet.

Weight remains over front foot.

Slight knee motion toward target.

CHIPPING: ONE SWING, MANY CLUBS

You're more capable of creating shots around the green than you think. Using one basic chipping technique, you can hit a variety of shots simply by varying club selection.

Start with a narrow stance and play the ball off your back foot. Push your hands ahead of the ball and keep your weight left to encourage a descending blow. Similar to when you make a putting stroke, there is minimal contribution from your wrists as your arms and shoulders swing the club back and through.

Next, try chipping with different clubs to see how the ball responds. Go as high as a 5-iron, which will produce a low roller with just enough airtime to hop over the fringe. The same technique with an 8-iron gives you a little more carry, a hint of check when the ball hits the green and a little less roll. When you chip with the sand or lob wedge, you'll produce a lofted pitch with enough backspin to stop quickly once it lands on the putting surface.

Once you have the basics of chipping down, expand your shot selection by making slight variations in ball position. For instance, move the ball an inch forward in your stance for a higher shot or an inch farther back to bring the trajectory down. Experiment with these shots and have some fun while also expanding your short-game arsenal.

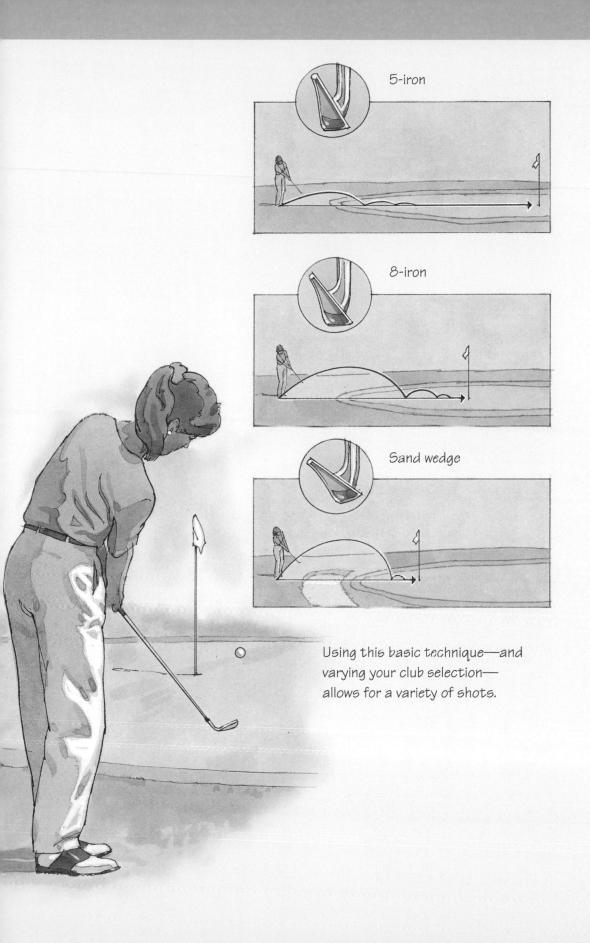

5-iron

8-iron

Sand wedge

Using this basic technique—and
varying your club selection—
allows for a variety of shots.

MORE PIVOT, LESS WRIST ACTION

During the full swing, unhinging your wrists through impact is a major contributor to power. In the short game, where control is more important than power, inconsistent wrist action produces inconsistent results. Too much or too little wrist hinge changes the club's loft at impact, affecting distance control. That's why some pitch shots "explode" and fly well past the hole, while others fall short of your target.

Maintain consistent loft by controlling your swing with your body pivot. Your hands and wrists should go along for the ride, not lead the motion. Focus on turning your body back and through, while keeping your hands in front of your chest throughout. You'll hit more pitches close to the hole.

Control your swing with your body pivot, letting your hands follow your body's lead.

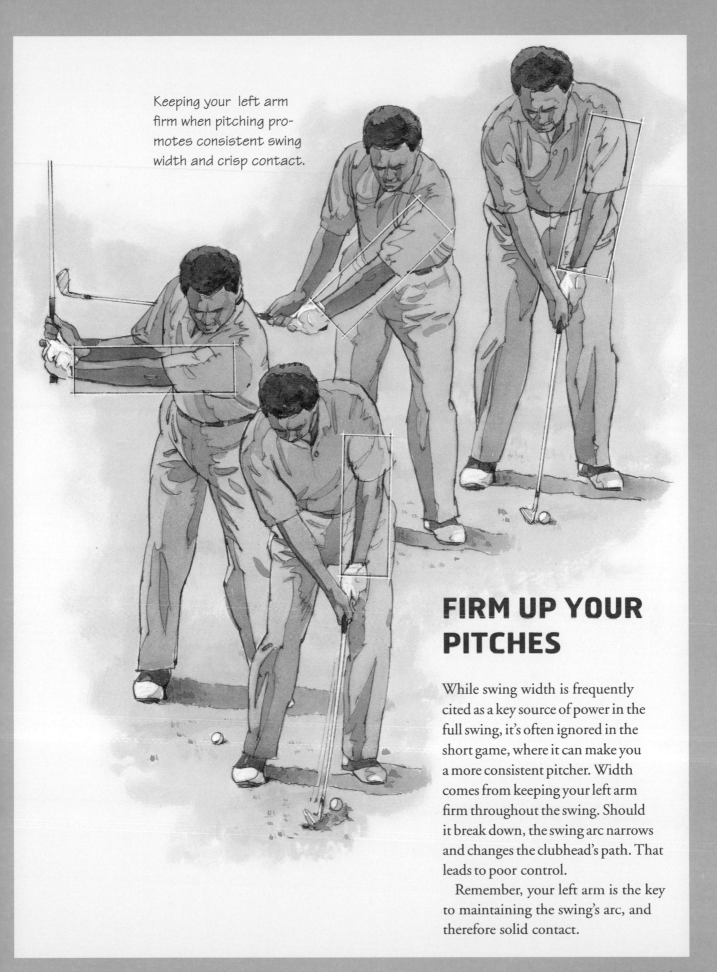

Keeping your left arm firm when pitching promotes consistent swing width and crisp contact.

FIRM UP YOUR PITCHES

While swing width is frequently cited as a key source of power in the full swing, it's often ignored in the short game, where it can make you a more consistent pitcher. Width comes from keeping your left arm firm throughout the swing. Should it break down, the swing arc narrows and changes the clubhead's path. That leads to poor control.

Remember, your left arm is the key to maintaining the swing's arc, and therefore solid contact.

Land the ball at least three feet onto the green.

Three feet

Avoid bouncing the ball on a crowned part of the green.

SPOT CHIPPING

To improve your chipping, focus on the landing spot. Picture a shot that carries only as far as necessary to get the ball rolling like a putt. Give yourself a healthy margin for error—at least three feet of green around the spot. That way, you'll have room for the ball to clear the rough even if you miss your target.

Check the green's contours. The flatter the area around your landing spot, the better.

Don't try to land the ball on a crowned part of the green—your ball might check up too soon or race past the hole. If there's a crown in your way, change clubs and aim for a flatter area.

DRILL: SHOOTING BASKETS Use a range basket as a target. Don't worry about roll; your goal is to learn which club will land the ball in the basket on the fly. Try various clubs and distances. Once you gain skill and confidence, picking a landing spot will seem like second nature.

Hands relaxed and quiet.

FINE-TUNE YOUR WEDGE GAME

From 30 to 60 yards off the green, all golfers want to be able to hit the ball close to the hole.

Stance open.

Imagine pitching a ball underhanded.

Arms swing freely.

Swing your right arm back and through like a pendulum.

However, from that distance you will usually be forced to hit a tricky "half wedge" shot that requires touch. Here are a few tips on how to play from this awkward yardage.

One way to think of a half wedge shot is to imagine pitching a ball underhanded.

When you pitch a ball, you swing your right arm back and through like a pendulum—the longer the throw, the longer the pendulum. The half wedge works the same way, except that instead of facing the target as you do when pitching a ball, this shot requires your stance and body to be well open to enable your arms to swing freely. Your hands stay relaxed and quiet, and the longer the shot is, the longer your arms swing.

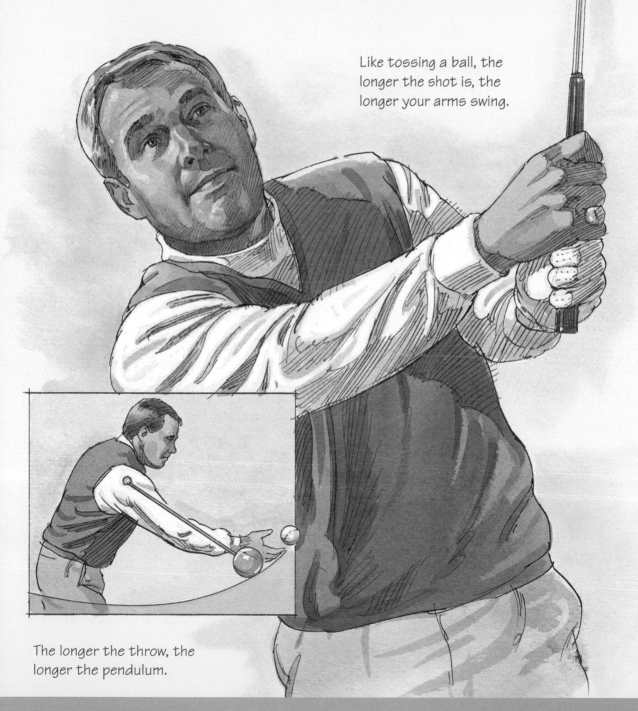

Like tossing a ball, the longer the shot is, the longer your arms swing.

The longer the throw, the longer the pendulum.

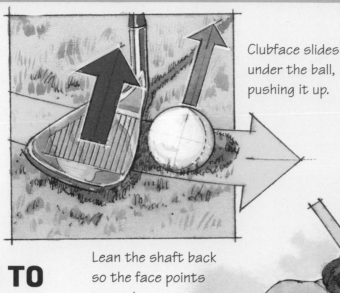

Clubface slides
under the ball,
pushing it up.

Lean the shaft back
so the face points
upward.

LEARN TO LOVE THE LOB

Anytime you play a course that requires lots of long approach shots, you are likely to run into your share of tricky up-and-downs. You need a lob shot in your arsenal: a soft pitch that flies almost straight up and lands very softly with almost no roll. Here's how to hit it.

THE BASICS

First, make sure your lie is fluffy: there needs to be room for the clubhead to slide under the ball. Then, take your sand or lob wedge and lean the handle back so the face points almost directly upward. Align your body about 30 degrees left and play the ball opposite your front instep. With light grip pressure and soft arms, make a long, lazy swing along your body line. The open clubface will send the ball almost straight upward.

Ball opposite front instep.

Open stance

Make a long, smooth swing along your body line.

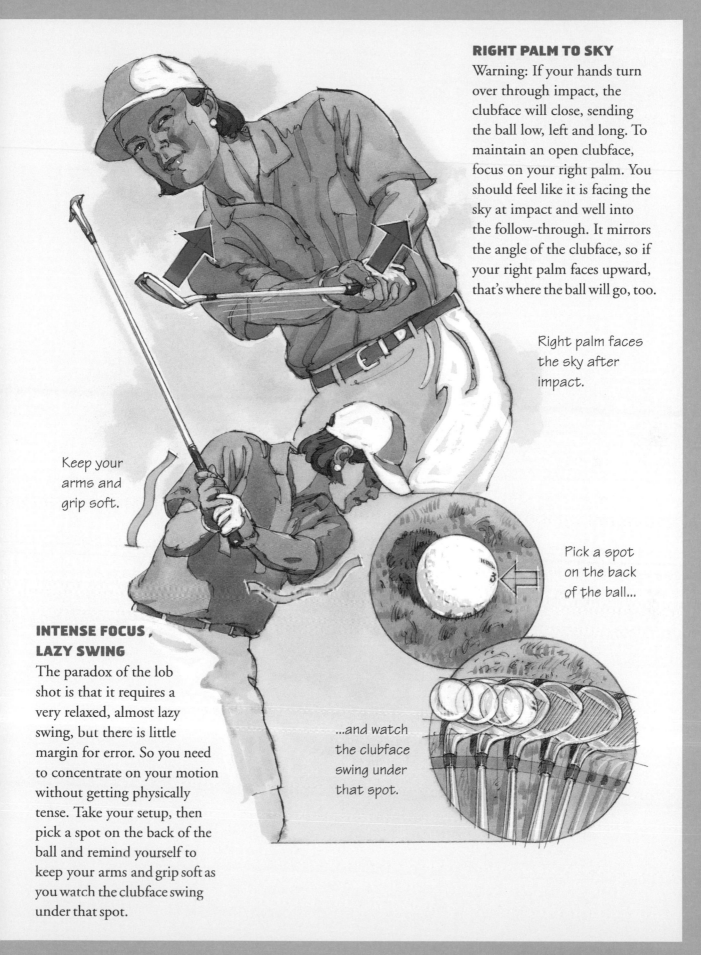

RIGHT PALM TO SKY

Warning: If your hands turn over through impact, the clubface will close, sending the ball low, left and long. To maintain an open clubface, focus on your right palm. You should feel like it is facing the sky at impact and well into the follow-through. It mirrors the angle of the clubface, so if your right palm faces upward, that's where the ball will go, too.

Right palm faces the sky after impact.

Keep your arms and grip soft.

Pick a spot on the back of the ball...

...and watch the clubface swing under that spot.

INTENSE FOCUS, LAZY SWING

The paradox of the lob shot is that it requires a very relaxed, almost lazy swing, but there is little margin for error. So you need to concentrate on your motion without getting physically tense. Take your setup, then pick a spot on the back of the ball and remind yourself to keep your arms and grip soft as you watch the clubface swing under that spot.

LEG ACTION AND PITCHING

Since pitching is about accuracy, not power, lower body action often gets overlooked. But your legs dictate your swing's rhythm and help control backspin. Here's how to use your legs to knock it stiff.

MAKE A MINI-SHIFT

Just like a full swing, your legs support your arm motion when you're pitching. So rather than trying to minimize their role, allow your weight to shift to your back foot on the backswing, then to your front foot as the club swings through impact. In fact, this weight transfer should trigger the transition from backswing to downswing, shifting your swing's low point ahead of the ball and preventing the clubhead from hitting the ground first.

Let your weight shift to your back foot on the backswing, then to your front foot.

USE YOUR KNEES

To help control backspin, tailor your knee action to the type of pitch shot you want to hit. In general, your front knee should slide away from the target going back, and your back knee should slide toward the target starting down.

For a low, spinning shot, kick your right knee aggressively toward the target as you start down. This will create a downward blow, with your hands ahead of the ball at impact. You'll trap the ball against the turf and create extra backspin.

For a higher, softer pitch with less spin, make a gentler forward move with your right knee. That will trigger a longer, lazier swing and let the clubhead pass your hands at impact for added loft on the shot.

For a pitch that runs after landing, minimize your knee action. Be careful with this one: You may lose some natural rhythm, but this produces a shallow path into impact and a shot with almost no spin.

Low, spinning shot: Aggressive right knee action.

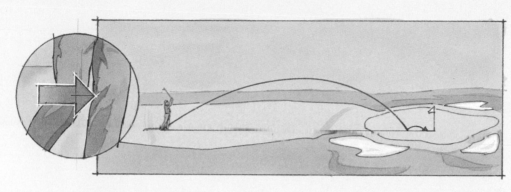

Higher, softer pitch with less spin: Moderate right knee action.

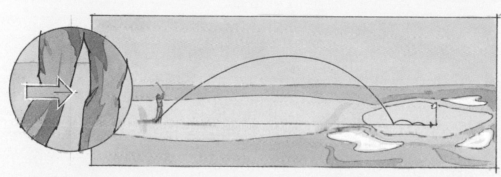

Pitch that runs after landing: Minimal right knee action.

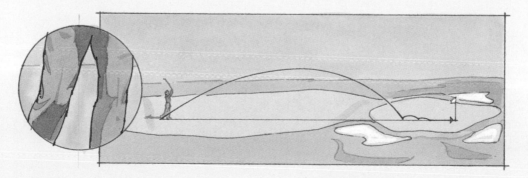

Take a moment to walk from your ball to the green and note any elevation changes.

READ YOUR PITCHES

It's great to have a variety of greenside shots in your bag, but to use them effectively, you have to know when to hit them. That starts with reading the terrain on and around the green to understand how the ball will react when it lands.

When time permits, walk along your target line to the green's edge before settling on a shot. Assess any elevation changes or uneven ground. If the green has a sloping false front, for example, choose a shot that will land on the flat part of the putting surface and still stop near the hole.

Take note of the grass fronting the green as well. Heavy rough dictates that you hit a more lofted shot that lands on the putting surface, while fairway grass generally allows you to consider a bump-and-run. But pay attention to the ground conditions. A soft, wet fairway will grab the ball, so be careful about hitting low, running chips when the ground is saturated. Along those same lines, avoid shots designed to stop quickly when the ground is dry and hard.

Rough fronting the green would call for a more lofted shot...

...while a fairway lie would allow for a bump-and-run.

MAKE THE WEDGE YOUR WEAPON

From 60 yards and in, the pros are usually automatic. What that means is that anytime they get a wedge in their hands and the ball rests in a decent lie, they know they're going to get it close to the hole. To play with that kind of confidence, you need good touch and an arsenal of different shots. Here are three you shouldn't be without.

LOW SPINNER

This is a great shot when there's a slight headwind or if the green slopes from back to front. Play the ball toward your back foot with your hands slightly ahead. Using a sand or lob wedge, make a three-quarter backswing, then think about pinching the ball off the turf as you swing down and through. This will make your hands a little more active through impact, which helps create backspin. The ball will skip once or twice toward the hole, then stop on a dime.

Setup with the ball back and your hands ahead.

Make a three-quarter backswing.

Focus on pinching the ball off the turf.

Ball will skip once or twice, then stop cold.

DEAD HANDS

When the pin is cut in the back of the green, the right call is a shot that lands and then rolls softly toward the cup. Quiet hands are the key. Take your normal setup with a sand or lob wedge, with the ball an inch forward of center in your stance. Make a three-quarter swing, but keep it virtually all arms, using minimal lag in your hands or wrists.

Make a three-quarter swing led by your arms.

Not un-cocking your wrists through impact slows the club-head just enough to take some of the spin off the ball, producing those few yards of roll you're looking for.

Ball is slightly forward.

Play the ball inside your left heel and grip down a little.

Focus on relaxing your hands through impact.

EASY DOES IT

When you're in between clubs, remember that wedges were made for control, not distance. So club down. For example, to hit a soft pitching wedge that flies high and stops quickly like a sand wedge, play the ball an inch inside your left heel and grip down a little. Make a three-quarter backswing, then focus on relaxing your hands through impact. Soft hands help the club release quickly, producing extra spin and a slightly higher trajectory.

SPECIALTY SHORT GAME SHOTS

Creativity is a skill that all great short game players possess. They not only see the obvious way to get the ball close to the hole, but they see every possible option, from every conceivable lie and stance.

In many cases, the closer you get to the hole, the more decisions you have to make. Take the ball in high or keep it close to the ground, land the ball on the hump or in the hollow. Be aggressive or play it safe. But you can only be creative and take advantage of the options you notice if you possess the skills necessary to hit the shots. The more shots you are comfortable playing around the greens, the more confidence you bring to your entire game.

If your ball is on bumpy fringe, grip down on a sand wedge.

FRINGE POP-UP

Your ball is only 15 feet from the hole, but it's sitting on scraggly fringe that could make the ball bounce off line. So grip down on a sand wedge and use your normal chipping stroke. By effectively shortening the club, you reduce clubhead speed at impact and deaden the shot. You'll get a soft pop shot that lands a foot or two past the fringe and rolls slowly to the hole.

TAKE THE LOW ROAD

Elegant, high-lofted pitches that stop close to the hole can be tough to control. So, in most greenside spots, remember that the less time a ball spends in the air, the easier it is to control. When confronting a chip or pitch, you should think, "How can I get this ball on the ground and rolling as soon as possible?" These three tactics should help you accomplish that goal.

CONSIDER THE FLAT STICK

The putter is the easiest club in the bag to hit, so take a good look to see if the conditions allow you to putt the ball even when you're off the green.

Putt the ball if the grass is cut short or the ground is extra firm.

Be smart: If there's any rough or thick fairway grass between you and the green, take a lofted club and chip the ball over it. But if the grass is cut short or the ground is extra firm, it won't slow down the ball's roll much, so give the putter a shot. Make a longer putting stroke, giving it just a little extra pop.

FAIRWAY: PLAY THE BUMP-AND-RUN

There's no rule that says your chip or pitch shot has to land on the green; you only want it to finish there. So if the path between your ball and the green is clear of obstacles, consider a bump-and-run: a shot that bounces a few times through the short grass before rolling to the hole. Play the ball back in your stance with a wedge or short iron, and make a smooth, chiplike stroke with little or no wrist action. The idea is to keep the ball bouncing until it's safely on the putting surface.

Play the bump-and-run if the path between the ball and the green is clear of obstacles.

Quiet wrists

Ball back

When you must fly the ball onto the green, a lower-lofted club allows you to make a more controllable pitch.

ROUGH: SQUEEZE IT ONTO THE GREEN

When you must fly the ball onto the green, challenge yourself to use the lowest-lofted club you can to get the ball over the rough, fairway or fringe (whatever is between you and the green) and still prevent it from rolling past the hole. Using a club with less loft, you can make a simpler, more compact pitching stroke. And that means the shot will be easier to control.

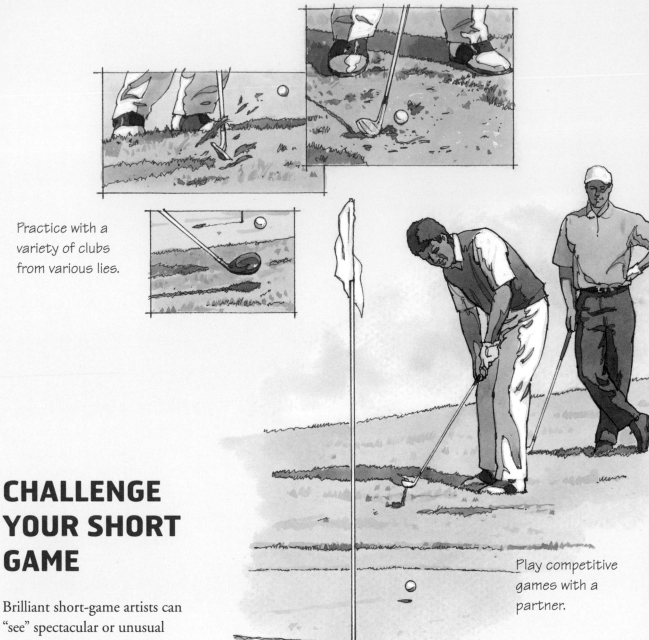

Practice with a variety of clubs from various lies.

Play competitive games with a partner.

CHALLENGE YOUR SHORT GAME

Brilliant short-game artists can "see" spectacular or unusual shots before hitting them. You can learn to do the same.

DARE YOURSELF

Instead of taking your sand wedge to the practice green and hitting 20 pitch shots from perfect lies, shake things up. Hit some pitches from hardpan. Chip from the collar with a fairway wood. Practice your lob shot from deep rough.

Invent as many situations as you can, and don't be afraid to use various clubs. For example, practice flop shots with your 7-iron. You may find untapped versatility in your bag. At the very least, you'll improve your touch and develop your imagination.

DUEL IN THE SUN

Two minds are more imaginative than one, so practice with a partner. Competitions like a short-game version of H-O-R-S-E for a few dollars can keep things interesting and sharpen your focus. Or try another, crueler game: Hit from various lies using clubs selected by your opponent.

DRILL: SIX OF ONE, HALF A DOZEN OF ANOTHER To vary your practice, choose a basic shot like a 30-yard pitch from the rough. Hit a few shots with the club you'd usually play (probably a sand wedge), then try it with five other clubs. The more awkward the club, the more imagination it will take to pull off the shot.

Now take the opposite approach. Use one club, such as an 8-iron, and practice six different greenside shots, from a standard chip to a high lob. You'll learn how changing clubface angle, swing speed and swing path can affect various shots.

USE A STRONG GRIP FOR CRISP CHIPS

Improving your short game is essential to lowering your handicap, and getting up and down more often is a surefire way to shave strokes off your game. Putting and chipping go hand in hand—good chipping will give you some easier saves on the green, and a bad chipping day can be salvaged if you can sink some long putts.

If you're suffering from high scores because of your play around the greens, it may be because your chipping game is not performing to its full potential. If your stroke is lackadaisical and your shots misdirected, you could benefit from strengthening your grip. Turn both hands

Turn both hands slightly to the right and hold on firmly with your left hand.

Keep your wrists firm and keep the back of your left hand moving down the target line.

slightly to the right and hold on firmly with your left hand. Concentrate on keeping your wrists firm when you make the stroke, and keep the back of your left hand moving down the line, facing the target. Hit down slightly on the ball without allowing your right hand to roll over your left, and keep the clubhead moving down the line after impact. With this method, you will feel increased control over the clubhead, and the ball should jump solidly off the clubface along your intended line.

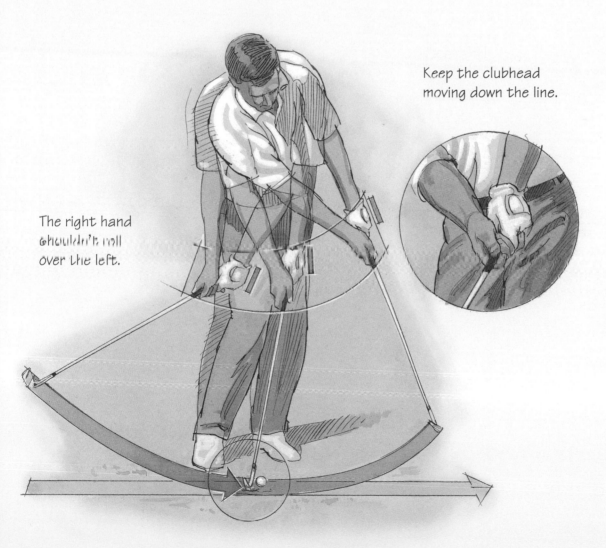

Keep the clubhead moving down the line.

The right hand shouldn't roll over the left.

Hit slightly down on the ball.

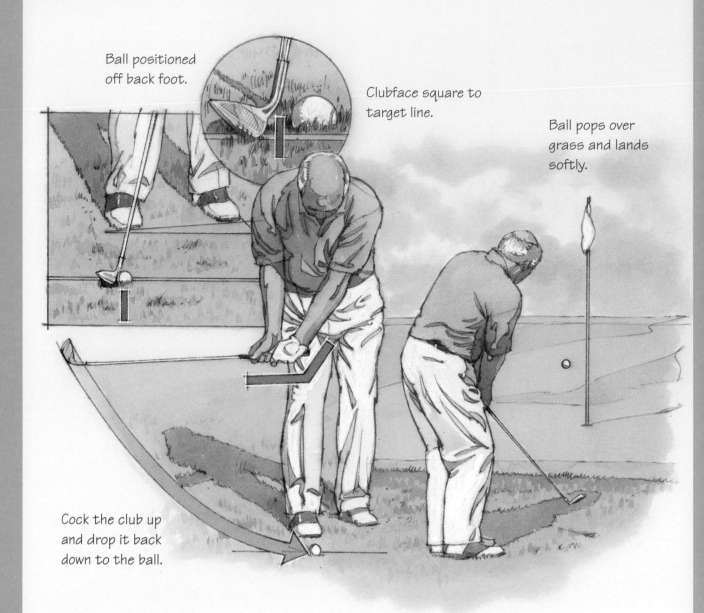

Ball positioned off back foot.

Clubface square to target line.

Ball pops over grass and lands softly.

Cock the club up and drop it back down to the ball.

LOB WEDGE CHIP

The lob wedge is your go-to club for high floaters, but it also can be valuable for chipping. In particular, it is useful when you need to pop the ball over some rough and stop it quickly. Why the lob wedge? Because you need all that loft to produce a shot that comes out soft and doesn't run away.

To execute the "lob chip," play the ball even with your back foot. This position will promote clean contact in the thick grass. Set the clubface square to the target line and simply cock the club up with your wrists and drop it back down to the ball with minimal follow-through. The ball will pop out, land on the green and dribble to the hole. It's the best way to get to a tight pin from thick stuff around the green.

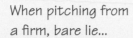

When pitching from
a firm, bare lie...

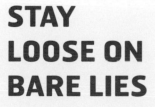

...maintain light grip
pressure as the club
swings through.

STAY LOOSE ON BARE LIES

Pitching the ball from a firm, bare lie cranks up your tension level; anything less than perfect contact can mean a skulled or chunked shot. To stay relaxed, focus on maintaining light grip pressure as you swing through impact. Softening your hands helps keep your arms and shoulders loose, giving your swing's natural momentum a chance to take over.

A FLOP SHOT FOR FLUFFY LIES

Unless you hit every green in regulation, you need a solid short game to salvage pars after errant tee shots or approaches. A flop shot is an extremely valuable tool to add to your repertoire, especially when you're faced with a shot over water or a bunker, or if you simply need to keep the ball from running too far on the green.

It's best to use your most lofted wedge to play a flop, but you'll still want to weaken your grip a bit and open the clubface slightly to achieve maximum loft. Play the ball off your left heel, cock your wrists sharply to take the club back, and keep your right elbow close to your side. Swing the clubface down with a wristy motion but a firm left arm. Focus on not letting the clubhead pass your hands through impact; you don't want to allow your wrists to

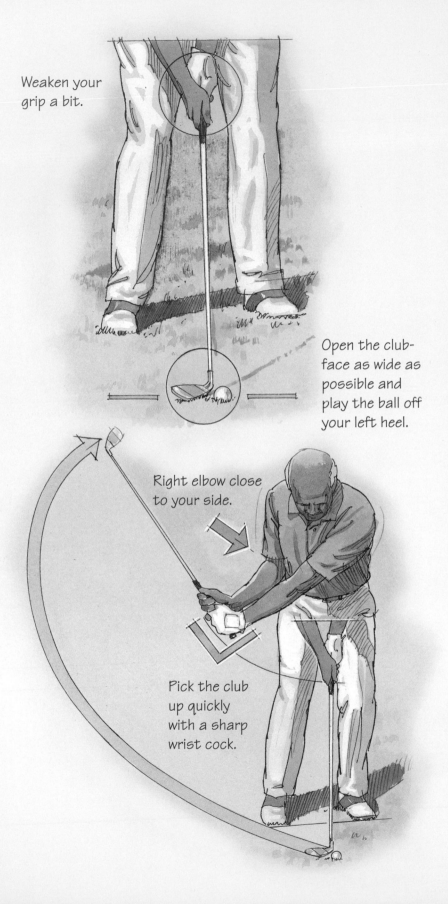

Weaken your grip a bit.

Open the club-face as wide as possible and play the ball off your left heel.

Right elbow close to your side.

Pick the club up quickly with a sharp wrist cock.

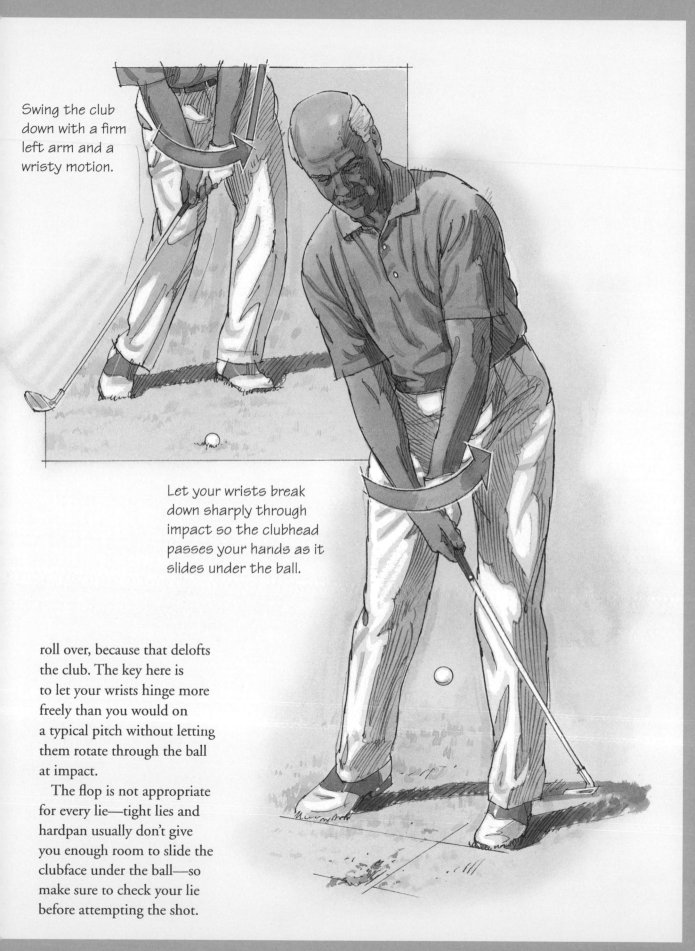

Swing the club down with a firm left arm and a wristy motion.

Let your wrists break down sharply through impact so the clubhead passes your hands as it slides under the ball.

roll over, because that delofts the club. The key here is to let your wrists hinge more freely than you would on a typical pitch without letting them rotate through the ball at impact.

The flop is not appropriate for every lie—tight lies and hardpan usually don't give you enough room to slide the clubface under the ball—so make sure to check your lie before attempting the shot.

KNOCKDOWN PITCH

The hole is all the way back on the green and you are 60 yards away. You could try flying the ball to the hole, but why not take advantage of all that green? A shot that flies lower and runs more is easier to execute than a high ball. Call it the "knockdown pitch."

ARMS CONTROL

The key to a good knockdown is minimizing backspin. Take a narrow, slightly open stance with the ball just back of center and your weight favoring your left side. Press your hands toward the target slightly to de-loft the clubface.

Now make an abbreviated swing controlled almost entirely by your arms. Don't consciously hinge your wrists going back. Coming down, pull the club through impact with your left arm. The club should thud against the ground, resulting in a low finish. The ball will bounce hard a couple of times and then roll like a putt.

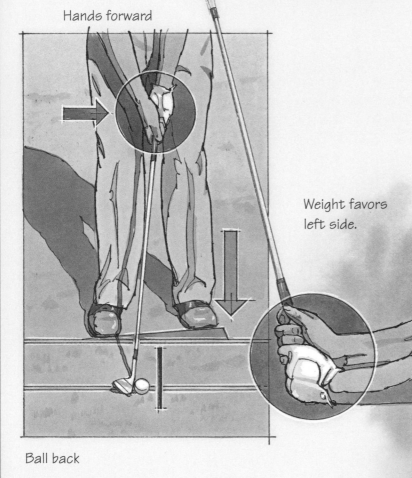

Hands forward

Weight favors left side.

Ball back

Make an abbreviated swing controlled by the arms.

PICK YOUR SPOTS

While the knockdown is easy to control for overall distance, it's difficult to be precise on the carry distance. If there is deep rough or a hazard near your landing spot, consider a normal, high-trajectory pitch that takes the obstacles out of play. Unless you know when to use it, the knockdown can be risky.

Make sure you have plenty of green to work with and no obstacles to carry.

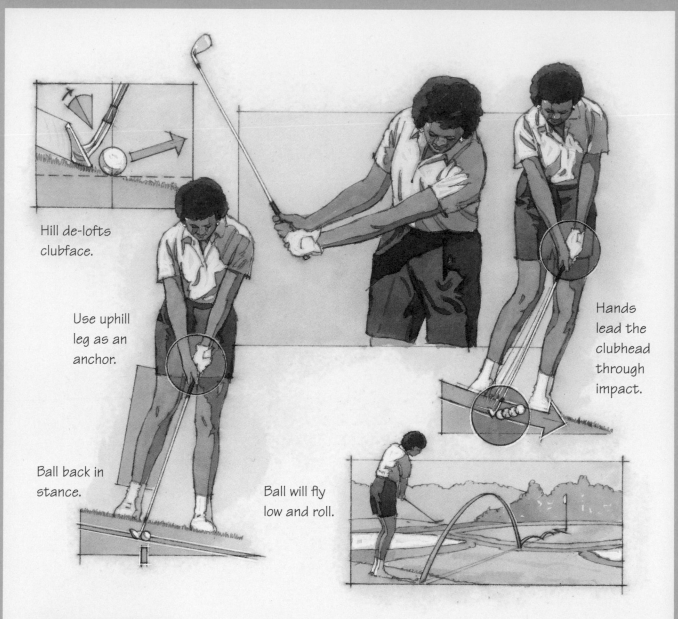

Hill de-lofts clubface.

Use uphill leg as an anchor.

Ball back in stance.

Hands lead the clubhead through impact.

Ball will fly low and roll.

LOSE YOUR FEAR OF DOWNHILL PITCHES

Your least favorite pitch is from a downhill lie. At least that's what 47 percent of readers said in a *GOLF MAGAZINE* poll. The down slope not only makes solid contact difficult, the shot is harder to control because the hill effectively de-lofts the clubface.

There are two keys to handling the downhill pitch. First, understand its limitations: Because the lie decreases loft, a soft, high shot—like a flop—is impossible. Accept the fact that a low, running shot is your best option, then determine where it has to land and how far it will run.

Second, make a few physical adjustments. Using your uphill leg as an anchor, play the ball well back in your stance (opposite your uphill foot) and angle your hands slightly ahead of the ball. Make a short backswing—remember, the ball is going to fly low and roll—and swing down and through, making sure that your hands lead the clubhead through the hitting area.

Stance and club are slightly open.

Wrists hinge the club up on the backswing.

Hands lead the club into impact.

MANAGING BERMUDA GRASS

Bermuda rough is normally kept short, but it's clumpy, so the ball tends to sit down. It's also tough and wiry and often snags the club's hosel on pitch or chip shots. A slight adjustment to your standard short-game technique is necessary to ensure crisp contact.

Because your club will not glide through the grass, you must make a steeper, firmer swing. Stick with your sand or pitching wedge and set up with your stance and clubface slightly open and the ball centered between your heels. From here, take the club back along your stance line, and allow your wrists to hinge. The wrist hinge will set up a descending blow. On the downswing, let your hands lead the clubhead through the ball. The grass may grab the clubface, so hold on tightly with your left hand at impact.

THE UPS AND DOWNS OF PITCHING

Once you know the proper adjustments in stance and setup for uphill and downhill pitch shots, pulling them off will be easier. Follow these rules.

UPHILL LIES

Step one when facing any hilly lie is aligning your body with the slope. For uphill lies, put most of your weight on your back foot. Position the ball even with the middle of your chest. Use one extra club, make a simple arms-and-shoulders swing and expect the ball to fly higher than normal.

Align your body with the slope.

Play the ball opposite the center of your chest.

Weight favors back foot.

The ball will fly higher than normal.

DOWNHILL LIES

Put most of your weight on your front foot. Again, play the ball even with the middle of your chest. This is a more awkward shot than the uphill pitch, as you'll instinctively feel like you have to help the ball up. Instead, focus on smooth tempo and balance. Plan for a low trajectory and plenty of roll.

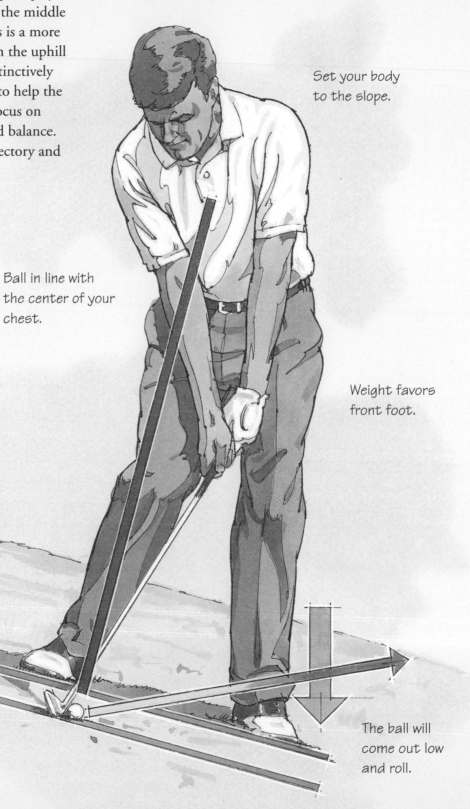

Set your body to the slope.

Ball in line with the center of your chest.

Weight favors front foot.

The ball will come out low and roll.

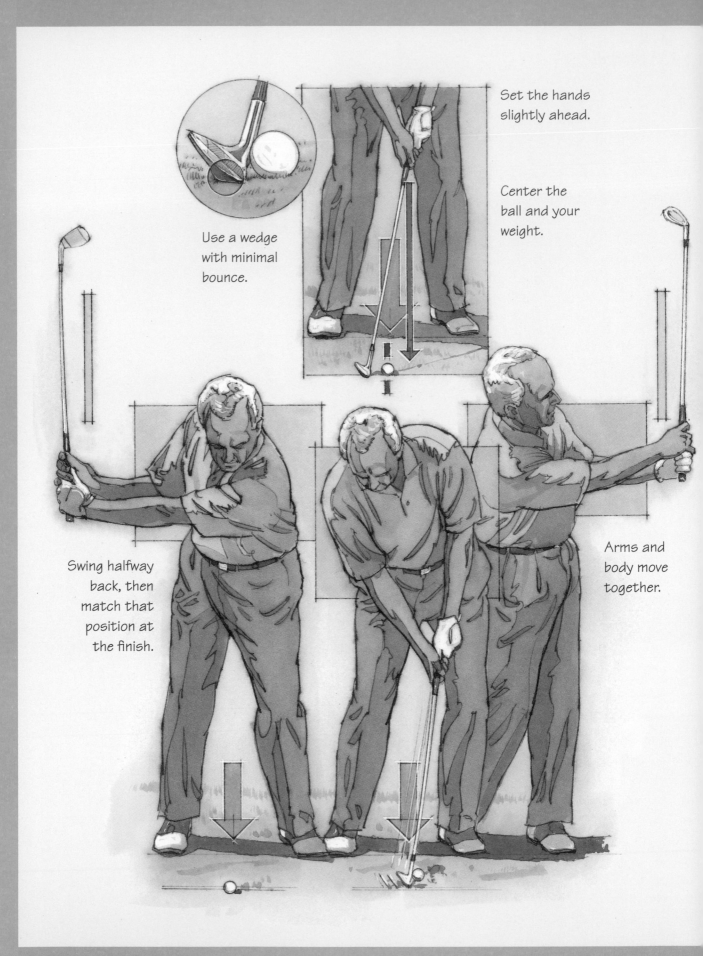

Use a wedge with minimal bounce.

Set the hands slightly ahead.

Center the ball and your weight.

Swing halfway back, then match that position at the finish.

Arms and body move together.

IMPROVE YOUR HALF-WEDGE SHOTS

Perhaps no shot in golf has a worse success rate than the half-wedge. It turns amateurs into basket cases. They feel caught between the full swing and the short game.

Don't fool yourself: This shot will always be a difficult one to judge. For that reason, you want to avoid situations that require a half-wedge; for instance, lay back and leave a full wedge into the green. Still, there will be times when only a half-wedge will do. Here's how to be fully prepared.

GET CENTERED, STAY CENTERED

Use a pitching or gap wedge without much bounce; the clubhead should cut a divot. Take a shoulder-width stance with the ball centered between your heels, and your hands set slightly ahead. Distribute your weight evenly between the feet, and keep it centered through the swing.

MIRROR-IMAGE SWING

The common mistake is to make a full-length backswing and then decelerate into the ball, trying to "hit it easy." Instead, focus on swinging no farther than halfway back, until the shaft reaches vertical, then match that position in the finish. As you swing, feel that your arms and body are linked, moving back and through together.

DRILL: STABLE BASE To ingrain the feeling of staying centered during the swing, take your normal stance and wedge a golf ball under the outside of each foot. With your feet pitched inward, your lower body will stay in place as your upper body rotates back and through without much lateral movement. Staying centered while swinging is the crucial key for good contact and consistency.

BUNKER PLAY

Professional golfers would rather face a greenside bunker shot than see their ball land in deep rough any day. But talk to most golfers who do not play for a living about greenside bunkers and you will hear one horror story after another. Why the difference of opinion?

The pros know how to use their sand wedge properly, make a few minor adjustments to their stance and work the club through the sand. It's really not too difficult if you give it some practice. And once you are comfortable and confident that you can escape from greenside bunkers, it gives you the green light to attack more flags on your approach shots. And that can lead to lower scores.

Practicing with only your left hand on the club will prevent skulling.

THE ANTI-SKULL GRIP

The short bunker blast drives you crazy. It's a fairly easy shot, but the impulse to scoop the ball out rather than slide the clubface under it can lead to a skulled shot that soars over the green.

Eliminate this error by practicing explosion shots with a simple grip adjustment: Take your normal left-hand grip, then wrap your right hand around the fingers of your left. With this hand-over-hand grip, you can't flip the club upward. Hit several shots this way, then return to your normal grip, keeping your left arm in check as you did during practice. And watch your bunker shots start to take flight.

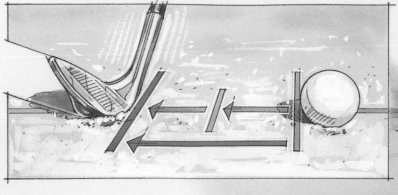

Extra-fat shot: Take twice as much
sand and make an aggressive swing.

SHORT-SIDED SAND SHOTS

Your ball is in a bunker, with the hole only a few tantalizing feet away. From this spot, too many golfers make tentative swings that leave the ball in the sand.

There are two ways to hit a short bunker shot. The first is to take twice as much sand as usual: Instead of entering the sand two inches behind the ball, as you would on a typical sand shot, make it four inches. But be sure to make an aggressive swing.

The second, more difficult method is the "pop shot." Lift the club abruptly with your hands and wrists, then imagine you're throwing a knife with your right hand. Bury the clubhead into the sand behind the ball. As long as the club cuts into the sand a couple of inches behind the ball, the ball will pop out. But beware: The pop shot takes practice.

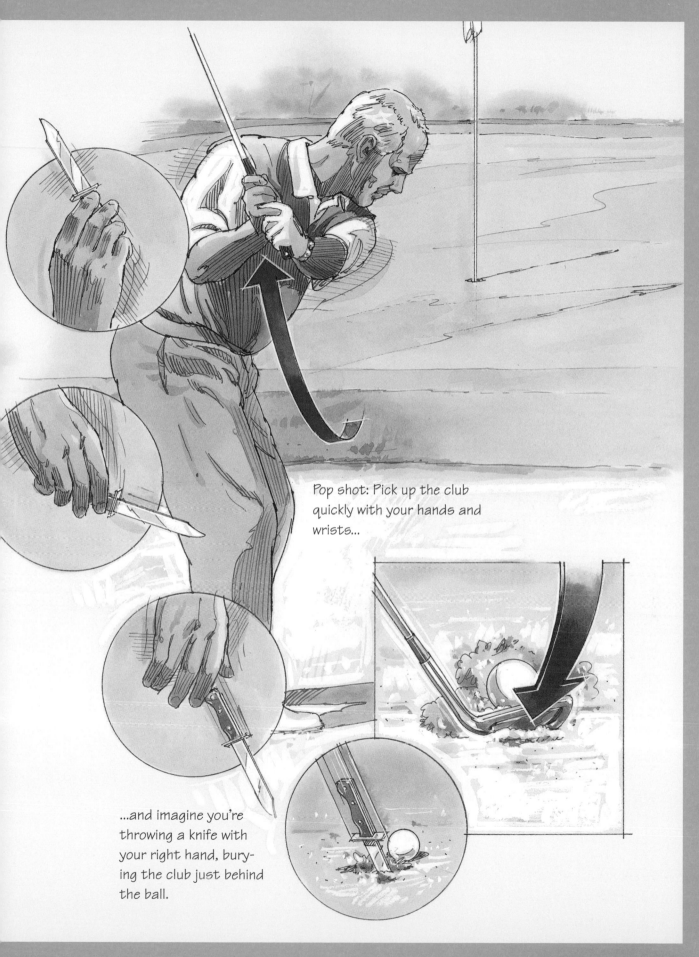

Pop shot: Pick up the club quickly with your hands and wrists...

...and imagine you're throwing a knife with your right hand, burying the club just behind the ball.

Make a larger swing.

Open the clubface 20 degrees right of the hole.

15 degrees

Play the ball off your left heel.

Open your stance slightly.

HIT IT LONG, SHORT, AND HIGH FROM THE SAND

Shots from the sand can be intimidating. What many inexperienced golfers don't realize is that playing from the sand is actually easier than it looks, and executing the right shot at the right time can save you lots of strokes. Here are some quick tips to hit it long, short and high from the sand:

LONG SHOTS

The tried-and-true explosion shot often doesn't cut it when you're over 25 yards from the hole. From this distance and longer, take a stance that is slightly open (about 15 degrees) and play the ball off your left heel. Keep the clubface square to slightly open and make a longer swing.

Make a shorter backswing.

Open stance 45 degrees.

Ball ahead of left foot.

SHORT SHOTS

When the pin is cut close to the bunker, open your stance to 45 degrees left of the hole and play the ball slightly ahead of your left foot. Open your clubface to 20 degrees right of the hole and make a shorter backswing. Be sure to accelerate through the ball to a full finish.

Open the clubface 20 degrees right of the hole.

Open the clubface 30 degrees right of the hole.

HIGH SHOTS

When you face a high lip in the sand, a high shot is in order. Set up as you would for a "normal" bunker shot, with your feet 30 degrees open and the ball set off your left foot. Lay the face of the club open to about 30 degrees. When you use your normal bunker swing, the open face will pop the ball high into the air so it clears the lip and still lands softly.

Use your normal bunker swing.

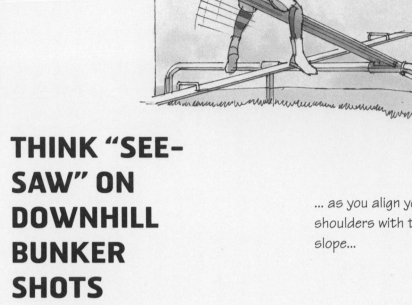

Think of a seesaw...

THINK "SEE-SAW" ON DOWNHILL BUNKER SHOTS

A downhill lie in a bunker makes it tough to get the ball airborne and nearly impossible to stop it on the green. But what if you tilted everything back, as if you were on a seesaw, making that downhill lie effectively flat? You'd just be facing a regular bunker shot over a high lip. That's a great image to have as you prepare to hit this shot.

With the seesaw in mind, set up with the clubface and your stance more open than usual. Dig your uphill foot into the sand.

Hinge the club almost straight up and chop into the sand about an inch behind the ball. To avoid closing the face, keep your right palm facing the target at impact.

... as you align your shoulders with the slope...

... dig your uphill foot into the sand...

... and open your clubface and stance.

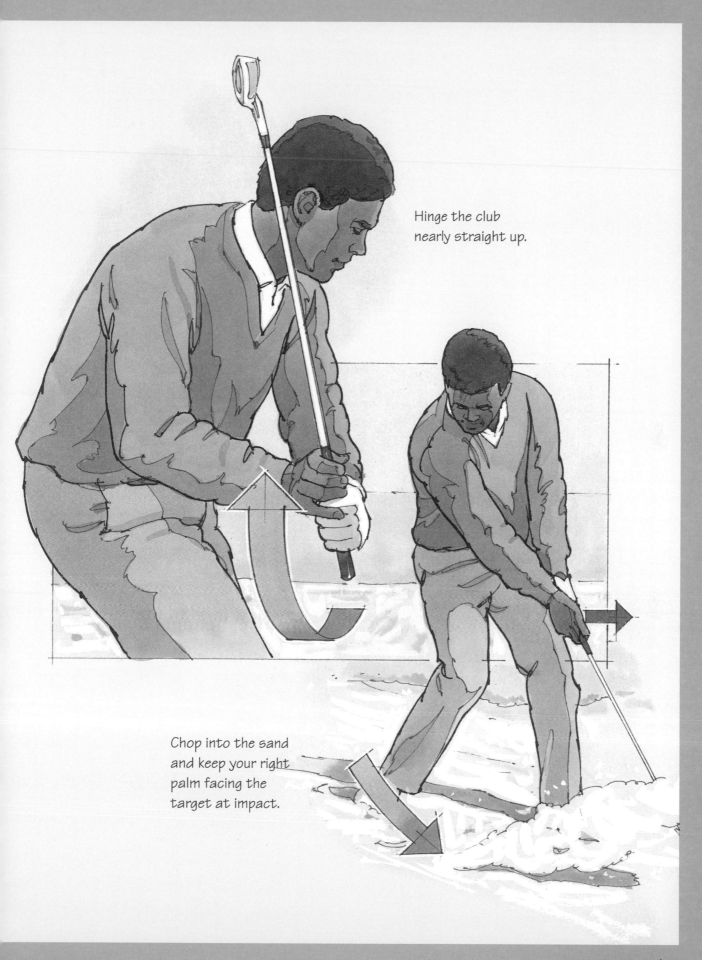

Hinge the club
nearly straight up.

Chop into the sand
and keep your right
palm facing the
target at impact.

As you dig your feet a few inches into the sand for stability, get a feel for its depth and texture.

In wet sand, open your clubface and stance slightly and aim for a spot an inch behind the ball.

LET THE SAND DICTATE YOUR SHOT

Not only are every course's bunkers different, but sand conditions can vary from day to day depending on the weather. It's important to take these factors into account when you find yourself in a bunker. In addition to calculating the distance of the shot you face, allow the texture of the sand to dictate your shot strategy. It is helpful to dig your feet a few inches into the sand to test its texture.

FIRM, WET SAND

You need a shallower angle of attack for this lie, because you'll want to take less sand. Open your clubface and stance slightly, and aim for a spot about an inch behind the ball.

DEEP, FLUFFY SAND

A full explosion shot is the ticket here. Your clubface and stance should be wide open. Take a full, steep swing to allow the club to move plenty of sand.

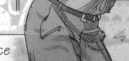

Take a full, steep swing.

Clubface and stance are wide open.

Square clubface and slightly open stance.

Make a three-quarter swing.

LOOSE, SHALLOW SAND

Shallow bunkers can be deceiving, because though the loose sand looks fluffy, the club will bounce off the surface, resulting in a long, bladed shot. Play this shot like a normal pitch shot instead, with a square clubface and a slightly open stance. Make a three-quarter swing and hit a half-inch behind the ball. Stay firm through impact and into the follow-through, and the ball will fly out like a pitch shot hit slightly fat.

PUTTING

According to *Golf Magazine*'s Top 100 Teachers, the fastest way to lower your scores is to improve your putting. Even more than distance off the tee, this is the area of the game that really separates the pros from the rest of us. Their mastery of distance control, keen ability to read greens and consistent strokes help them roll the rock with an artist's touch.

But for nearly all amateurs, putting can be one of the most frustrating parts of the game. Is there anything worse than facing yet another five-foot knee knocker?

On the bright side, putting has nothing to do with power or physical strength, so if you can learn a repeatable stroke, develop some speed control and better recognize the factors that make the ball bend and curve along the putting surface, you can definitely hole more putts.

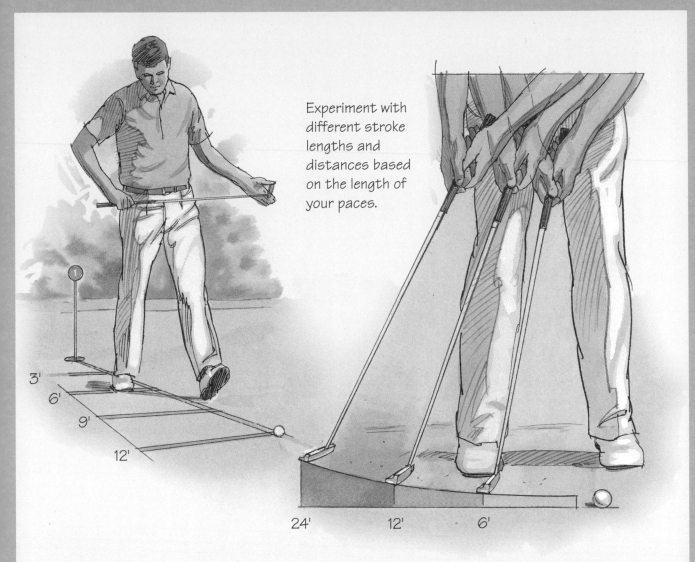

Experiment with different stroke lengths and distances based on the length of your paces.

3'
6'
9'
12'

24'   12'   6'

PUTT CONSISTENTLY FROM ANY DISTANCE

Often, three-putting is the result of coming up too long or too short on your first putt. Unlike the rest of the golf course, there are no distance markers on the green, so gauging the distance of your putt is up to you. One way to develop a feel for distance on the green is to pace off your putts. The length of most players' natural stride is about three feet; therefore, a putt that is five paces long is about 15 feet, 10 paces is 30 feet, and so on. When you have some time on the practice green, experiment with different stroke lengths and distances based on the length of your paces. You'll soon have a good idea of how long your stroke should be for various distances, and your three-putt percentage should diminish substantially as you gain confidence from every distance.

LET THE PUTTER SWING

In a good putting stroke, the putterhead is accelerating when it makes contact with the ball. But that doesn't mean you should make a short, jabby backstroke and then power through the ball. For consistent rhythm and reliable touch, a fluid back-and-through motion is ideal. Picture the stroke as a pendulum: Once you pull the putter back, imagine that gravity takes over and accelerates it into the ball. In this smoother version of the stroke, sense that the putter is swinging itself while letting your arms and fingers stay relaxed—this gives you better feel and distance control.

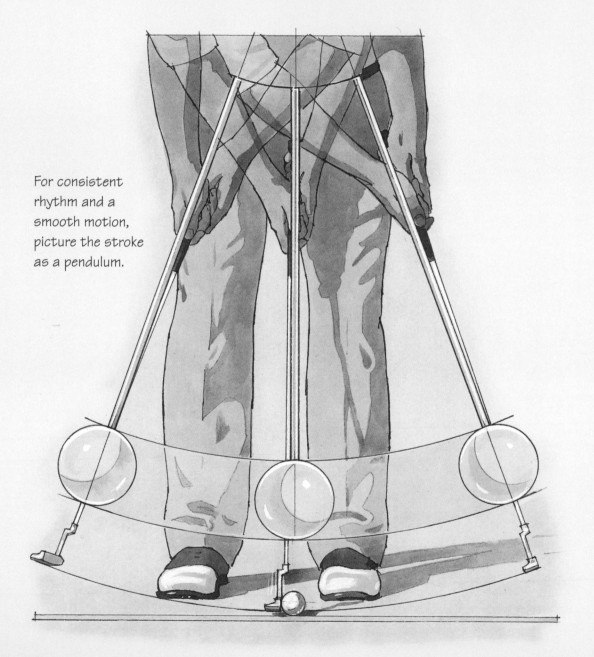

For consistent rhythm and a smooth motion, picture the stroke as a pendulum.

MARK WITH A LINE TO STAY ON LINE

If your ball continually burns the edge of the cup without dropping in, it may not be a green-reading issue—you could very well have a flaw in your putting stroke.

One way to find out is to draw a straight line around your practice balls and head out to the putting green for a practice session. Tour players often use lines on their balls not only for putting practice but also in tournament play, to study the roll of the ball. To check all your form, take 10 of the balls you marked with a line and hit a series of eight- to 10-foot putts. Keep an eye on the line on the ball. If it wobbles when you putt, you aren't taking the putter back and through squarely. Focus on squaring up your putting stroke until the line becomes a blur and the putts begin to drop!

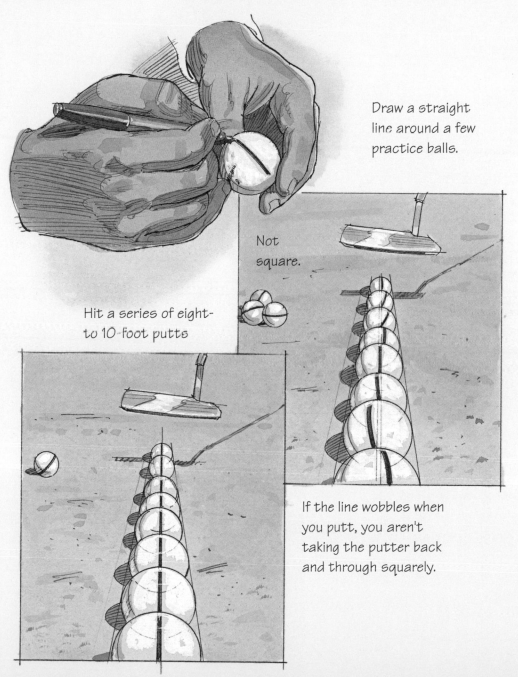

Draw a straight line around a few practice balls.

Not square.

Hit a series of eight- to 10-foot putts

If the line wobbles when you putt, you aren't taking the putter back and through squarely.

PUT YOUR GRIP IN REVERSE

The most common putting grip is the reverse-overlap, the left forefinger overlapping the last few fingers of the right hand. Make this grip work for you, concentrating on these positions.

PALM PILOT

Rest the club in the palm of your left hand—between the thumb pad and the heel—not in the fingers. This immobilizes your left wrist so it won't break down through impact.

Grip the putter so both palms run parallel to the putterface. This allows your hands to operate as a unit—a direct extension of your arms and shoulders—making it easier to swing the putter along the target line.

THUMBS ON

Both thumbs should extend down the top of the shaft on the flat portion of the grip. Besides providing stability, this keeps your palms parallel to the putterface.

When placing your right hand on the grip, make sure your right thumb pad covers your left thumb. Your remaining fingers wrap around the club, with your left forefinger resting on top of the right-hand fingers.

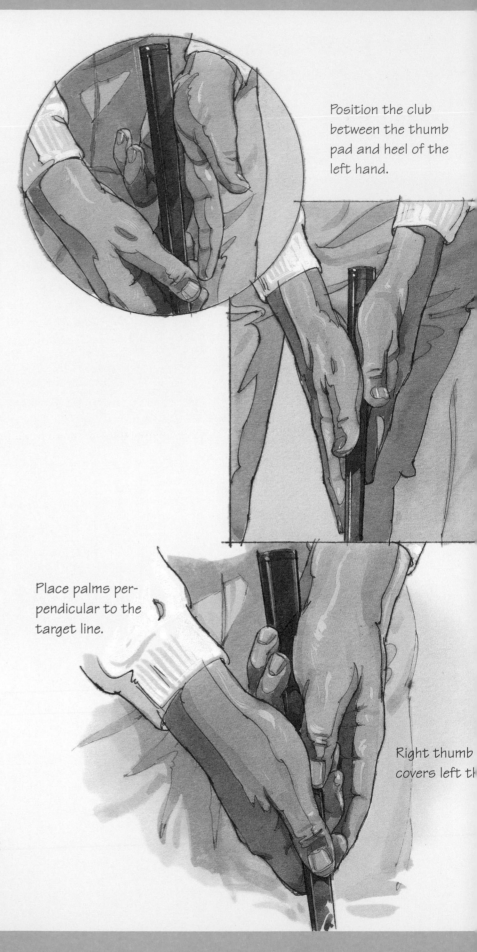

Position the club between the thumb pad and heel of the left hand.

Place palms perpendicular to the target line.

Right thumb covers left th[...]

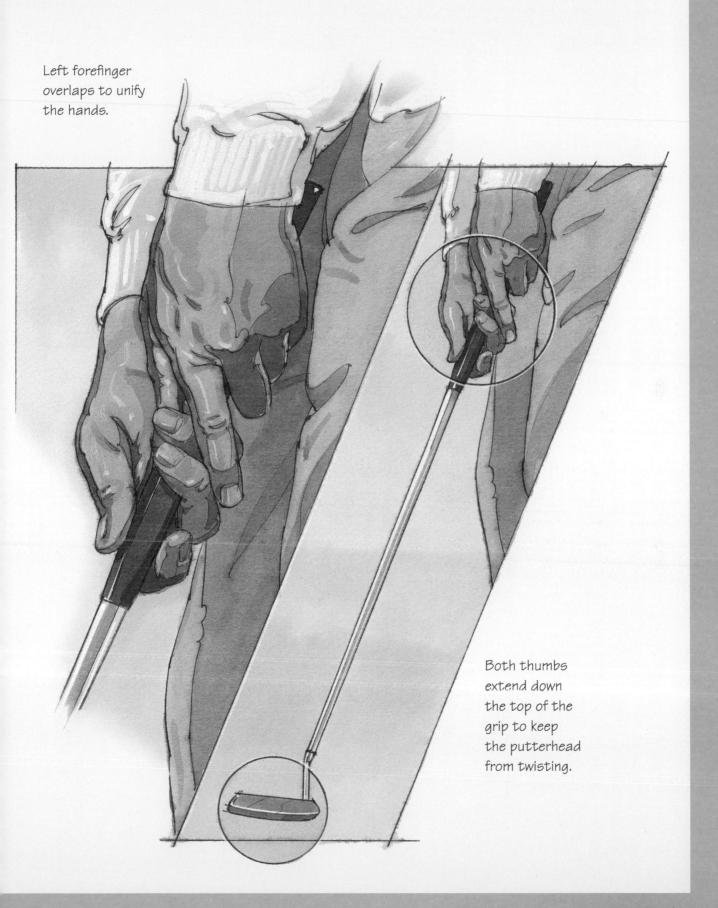

Left forefinger overlaps to unify the hands.

Both thumbs extend down the top of the grip to keep the putterhead from twisting.

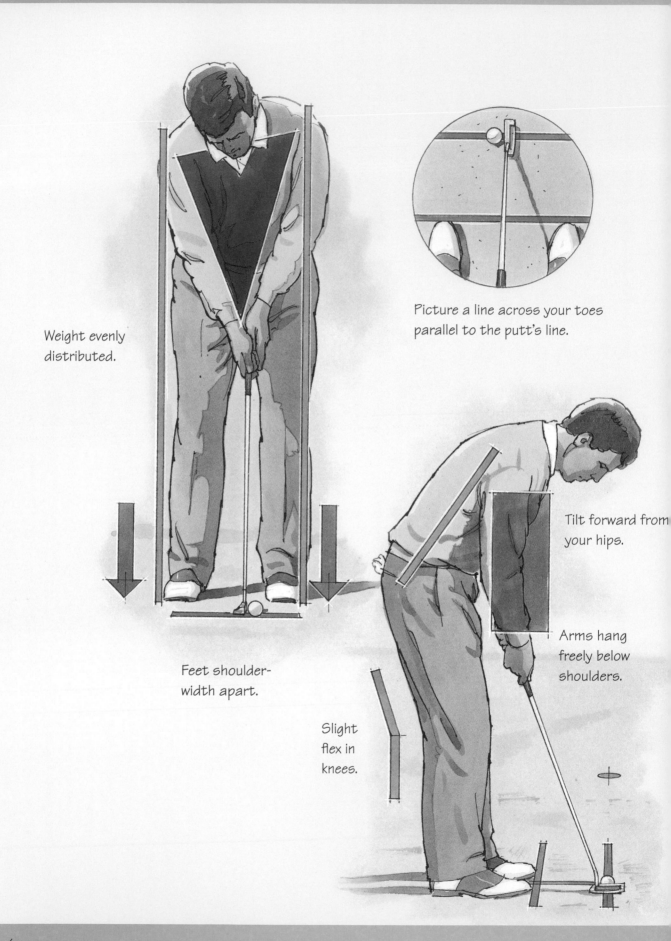

Weight evenly
distributed.

Picture a line across your toes
parallel to the putt's line.

Tilt forward from
your hips.

Feet shoulder-
width apart.

Arms hang
freely below
shoulders.

Slight
flex in
knees.

GET SQUARE AND STABLE

In the best putting strokes, your shoulders, arms and hands move as one unit while the rest of your body stays still. Even though your arms are initiating the motion, the positioning of your body plays a key role. A sturdy stance and good posture allow the stroke to make consistent center-face contact.

GET SQUARE, STAY STABLE

There's no rule that says your stance must be square, but it's the simplest way to line up. If your feet point 30 degrees left of the hole, for example, your shoulders tend to open, making it hard to square the putterface at impact. To square up your stance, picture a line drawn across your toes. That line should run parallel to the line the putt should start along.

Stability starts with your feet, so keep them shoulder-width apart, with your weight evenly distributed. Add a little flex in your knees and ankles to anchor your body.

Without letting your weight move to your toes, tilt forward from your hips until your arms hang freely from your shoulders. With your hands on the grip, a triangle will be formed with your arms and shoulders. Now you're in position to let the putter swing smoothly.

TRY THIS TEST

You can't see a putt's line clearly unless your eyes are over the ball. Here's how to check: Set up for a putt and then, staying in posture, bring the grip end of your putter to the bridge of your nose. The shaft should hang down and point at the ball. If it doesn't, you're looking at the line from a poor angle. Step out and try again.

Have a teacher
check your
mechanics.

Compete against a
partner in putting
games to create a
pressure environment.

SHORT PUTT SUCCESS

To consistently make short putts, you need solid mechanics and strong nerves. Do you work on either? Don't resign yourself to a career as a poor putter. Instead, make a commitment to practicing sound mechanics.

CHECK FOR FLAWS

Even with nerves of steel, you won't be successful if your setup or stroke is flawed. Have a PGA professional check your mechanics; once you know you're making a straight-back, straight-through stroke with a square putterface, you can work on making sure it holds up out on the course.

PRESSURE YOURSELF

With the exception of quick pre-round warm-ups, every session on the practice green should create a pressurized environment. Competing in putting games raises the stakes and puts your stroke to the test. If you're alone, use practice drills—like the four-point drill in the box to the right—that reward successes and penalize misses. Rehearsing under pressure is the best way to get ready for the real thing.

DRILL: FOUR-POINTS Picture a large clock around a hole on a sloped area of the practice green. Stick four tees in the ground, each three feet from the hole, at the 3, 6, 9 and 12 o'clock positions. Hit three putts from 3 o'clock. When you've made three in a row, move to 6 o'clock and hit three more, and so on. Because you're on a slope, each spot will present a different break. The goal is to make 12 putts in a row, three at each spot. If you miss, start the cycle over from that position.

On short putts, a square putterface is your top priority.

So, first place the putterhead behind the ball and align it to your starting line...

...then take your grip and stance without moving the face.

DROP THE SHORTIES

Missing short putts puts pressure on the rest of your game. Use these keys to improve your results.

SET IT STRAIGHT

On short putts, the putterface must be square to your target line at impact. Since the stroke is short, the face is likely to remain square at impact. Place the putterhead behind the ball and align the face to the line on which you want the putt to start. Then take your grip and stance without moving the face from its original position.

STEADY START

For many golfers, short putts add tension, which shows up in a quick or jerky backstroke. To be smooth, stay in motion at address: Tap the putter lightly on the ground or gently milk the grip with your fingers. Then, without opening or closing the putterface, begin the stroke with a slight forward press. Start smoothly, and you'll maintain good rhythm throughout the stroke.

STAY STILL

To maximize your chances of making a square, solid putt, keep your body still from start to finish. Be especially careful not to let your head move. If you become overanxious and look up even a fraction too quickly, soon the stroke will be affected. Rather than watching the roll, keep your eyes down and listen for the sound of the ball falling into the cup.

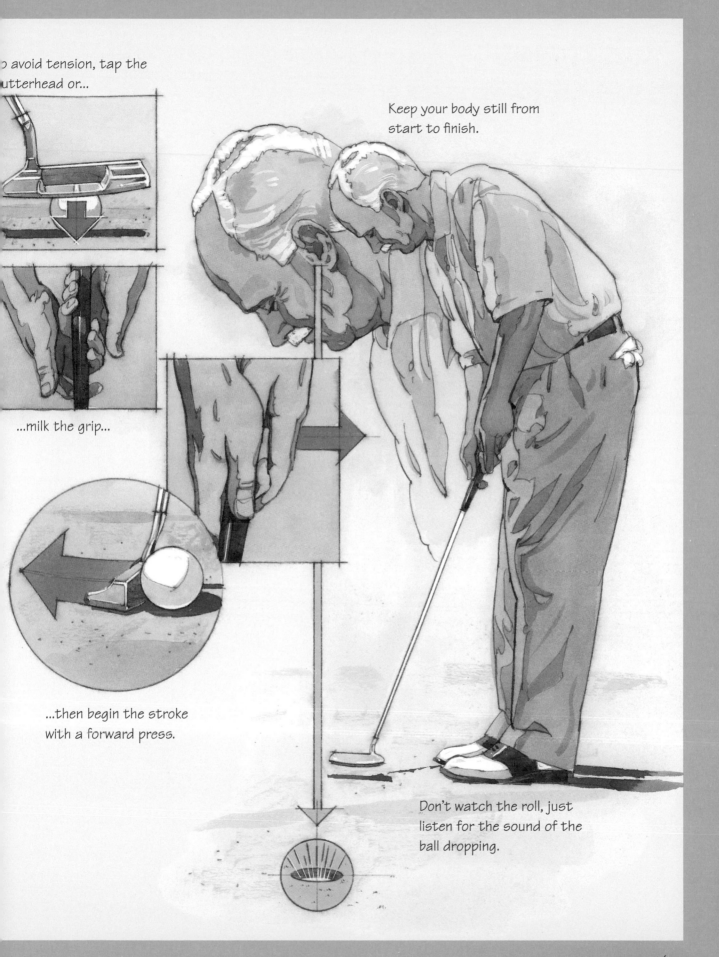

o avoid tension, tap the
utterhead or...

Keep your body still from
start to finish.

...milk the grip...

...then begin the stroke
with a forward press.

Don't watch the roll, just
listen for the sound of the
ball dropping.

MASTERING FAST GREENS

Every golfer knows how important it is to have a smooth putting stroke and an even tempo; however, fast greens can make this idea hurt your game more than it helps you, especially on downhill putts. Even with the shortest of strokes, a fast green can send a ball flying past the hole on a severely downhill putt, potentially costing you several strokes and even more frustration.

The next time you face a severely downhill putt, try making virtually no stroke at all on your backswing. Take the putter back no more than an inch, then tap it. With this method, there is no time for the putter to gain momentum on the backswing, and the shortness of the tap reduces the chance of twisting the putterface off line. While this method may sound like a piece of cake, you may find that you have to practice it a few times to control the putter properly. It's also helpful to grip the club a little more tightly than you're used to.

...tighten your grip slightly.

When facing a severely downhill putt on a superfast green...

Take the putter back no more than an inch, and then tap it.

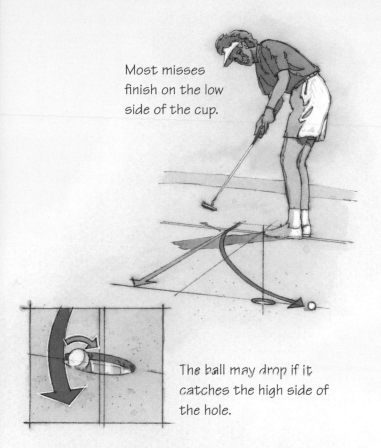

Most misses finish on the low side of the cup.

The ball may drop if it catches the high side of the hole.

PLAY MORE BREAK

Most golfers, even the pros, don't play enough break when putting. It's not that they don't see it; they just can't bring themselves to start the ball as far outside the hole as necessary. Afraid the ball won't track all the way back down, it seems easier for many players to take a lower, more conservative line, which is the reason about 90 percent of all misses finish on the low side of the cup.

Another reason higher is better: A ball has no chance of dropping in from the low side, but it may fall if it catches the high side of the hole.

To find the real line, start by tripling whatever break you feel comfortable playing (i.e., if you want to aim six inches outside the hole, actually aim 18 inches high) and see how that works. Then experiment down to doubling the break. Soon you should be starting the ball on the true line and watching more putts drop.

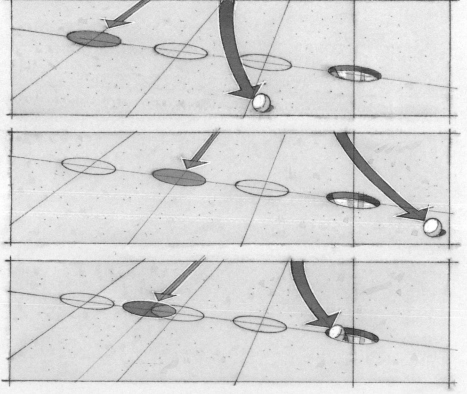

If you sense a six-inch break, experiment with higher breaking points until you find the true line.

HOW TO BECOME A CONFIDENT LAG PUTTER

Getting on the green in regulation—let alone getting the ball in the hole in only two putts—is a major challenge for most amateur golfers. Becoming a better lag putter, however, can give you a significant advantage over your fellow golfers, especially when you consider how large many greens are these days.

The first step in learning how to lag the ball with confidence is to develop a reliable feel for distance. Only then should you worry about getting the line of your putts perfect. Follow these steps to get your lag touch down:

Looking at the hole as you make your stroke forces you to putt by feel.

DISTANCE CONTROL

Take five balls and find a relatively flat 30-foot putt on the practice green. Place a tee in the green roughly halfway to the cup. With your first ball, don't even think about getting it close to the hole—just make sure that you roll it to a spot that's somewhere between the tee in the ground and the hole. On your second putt, try to get the ball to stop somewhere between your first ball and the hole, and then continue using this method with the last three balls until you're confidently rolling the ball to within a foot or two of the hole. Once you're done with the first five balls, choose a new hole and distance. This drill is also great as a pre-tournament warm-up, especially if you're playing a course with unfamiliar greens.

LOOK AT THE HOLE INSTEAD OF THE BALL

Move to various spots on the putting green and hit putts of 20 feet or longer. As you make each stroke, however, look at the hole instead of the ball. This will force you to make your stroke by feel rather than visually or mechanically.

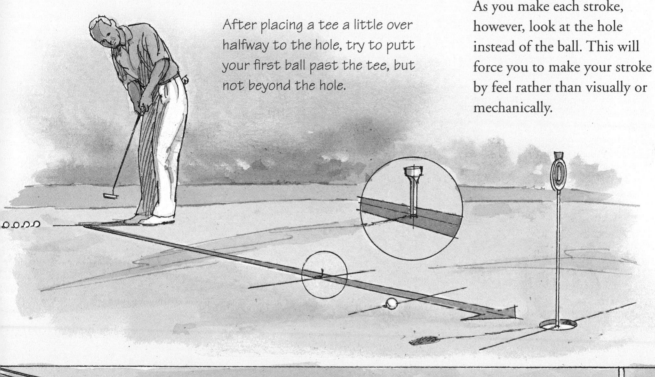

After placing a tee a little over halfway to the hole, try to putt your first ball past the tee, but not beyond the hole.

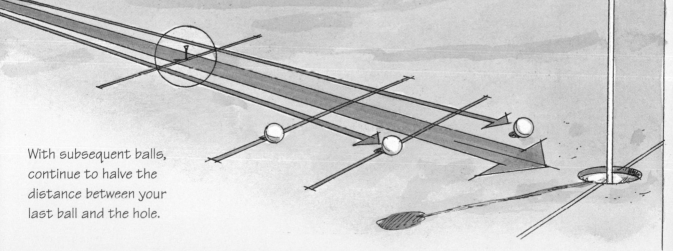

With subsequent balls, continue to halve the distance between your last ball and the hole.

THREE KEYS TO PUTTING

Even players who are long off the tee need to putt well to post low scores. Here are three ways to improve your performance on the greens.

LADDER DRILL SHARPENS LAG PUTTING

Most three-putts result from poor distance control on the first putt, so use the ladder drill to improve this critical skill.

Take six balls to the practice green and find a fairly flat area. Without aiming at a hole, putt the first ball about 10 feet, the next ball about 13 feet, then 16 feet. Keep stroking each ball three feet farther than the previous one, lining up the balls like rungs on a ladder. It shouldn't take long before you can roll the ball within three feet of the hole just about every time.

The Ladder Drill will improve your distance control.

10'
13'
16'
19'
22'
25'

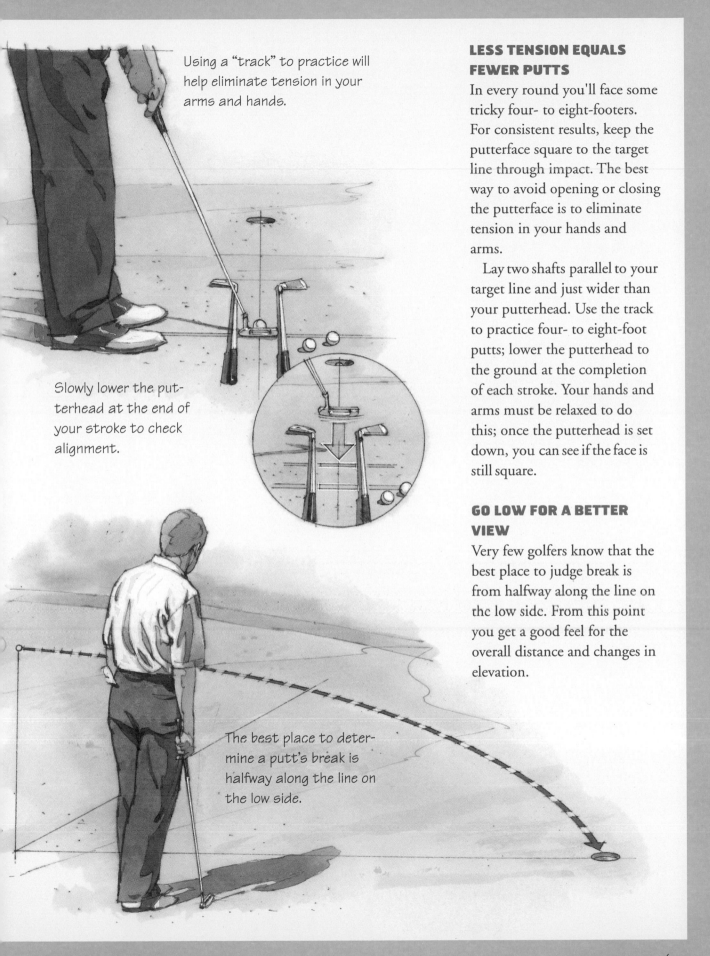

Using a "track" to practice will help eliminate tension in your arms and hands.

Slowly lower the putterhead at the end of your stroke to check alignment.

The best place to determine a putt's break is halfway along the line on the low side.

LESS TENSION EQUALS FEWER PUTTS

In every round you'll face some tricky four- to eight-footers. For consistent results, keep the putterface square to the target line through impact. The best way to avoid opening or closing the putterface is to eliminate tension in your hands and arms.

Lay two shafts parallel to your target line and just wider than your putterhead. Use the track to practice four- to eight-foot putts; lower the putterhead to the ground at the completion of each stroke. Your hands and arms must be relaxed to do this; once the putterhead is set down, you can see if the face is still square.

GO LOW FOR A BETTER VIEW

Very few golfers know that the best place to judge break is from halfway along the line on the low side. From this point you get a good feel for the overall distance and changes in elevation.

EVERY PUTT IS STRAIGHT

It takes the right combination of line and speed to sink a breaking putt. But the challenge is as much mental as physical: When your mind is forced to think of two things at once, you tend to alter your stroke at the last moment. To simplify the process, tell yourself, "I'm hitting a straight putt."

Picture the line the ball should roll on...

...and identify the apex of the break.

Then imagine a straight line running through that point to a target even with the hole.

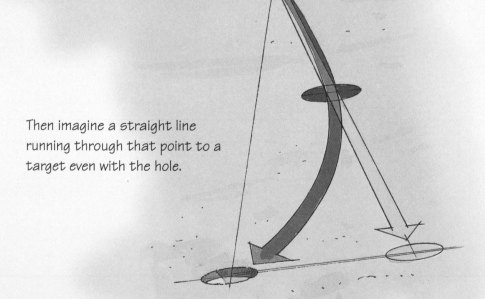

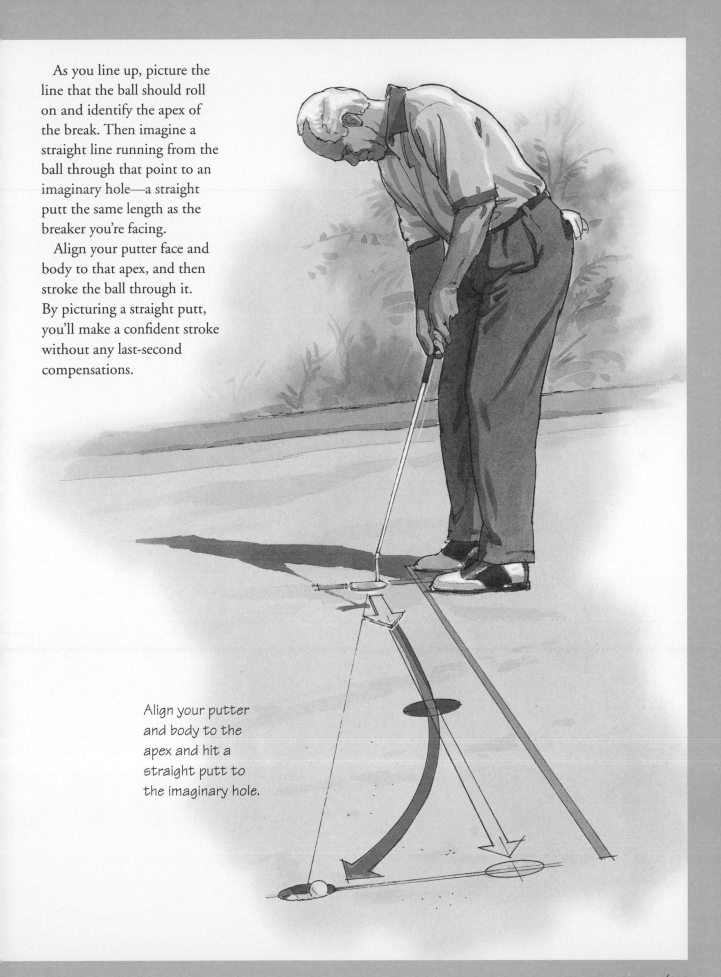

As you line up, picture the line that the ball should roll on and identify the apex of the break. Then imagine a straight line running from the ball through that point to an imaginary hole—a straight putt the same length as the breaker you're facing.

Align your putter face and body to that apex, and then stroke the ball through it. By picturing a straight putt, you'll make a confident stroke without any last-second compensations.

Align your putter and body to the apex and hit a straight putt to the imaginary hole.

WRIST COCK FOR LENGTHY PUTTS

While you might feel inclined to approach every putt with a methodical, pendulum-like rocking of your shoulders, you may be surprised to find that on putts over 40 feet, it doesn't matter how hard you try to hit the ball—with the pendulum method, the ball may never reach the hole. To avoid a costly three-putt, it's important to ensure that your first putt gets close enough to the hole to allow you to have a makeable second putt.

To make sure you get all the distance you can out of your first putt, try to incorporate a slight wrist cock into your backswing. The extra whip of your wrist will allow you to glean more yards from your stroke without running the risk of twisting or bringing the clubface off line (which often occurs with a long pendulum stroke).

A word of caution, however: Make sure to keep your wrist cock stroke short, or you may find yourself even farther from the hole on your second putt than where you started! It will take a bit of practice to

To get more distance control on your long putts, incorporate a slight wrist cock into your backswing.

get a feel for your wrist cock distance control, but once you have it down, you will find that it's very helpful, especially on putts from one side of the green to the other.

PUTT TO A SPOT

One of the hardest things about putting is one of the simplest: feeling confident that the clubface is perpendicular to your target line at address. It's tough, because you stand to the side of your target line, not on it. With a target (the hole) that's only about four inches wide, how can you be sure you have the face aimed correctly from 20 feet away?

It's much easier to aim at a target that's directly in front of your ball and on the target line. Think of it as putting to a spot. As you crouch behind your ball to read the break, find a spot about two feet or so in front of your ball and directly on the line that you want the ball to take. At address, aim your putterface at that spot, then set your body parallel to the line. You'll feel much more confident over putts if you aim at a target that is closer to you.

Once you're aligned, your goal is to roll your ball over the intermediate spot. If the line you've chosen is correct and you've gauged the speed properly, a putt that rolls over the spot will go in the hole.

Find a spot about two feet in front of the ball, on the target line . . .

. . . then align your putterface and body to that spot at address.

DO YOU MEASURE UP?

Putting well? Just wait—all good things come to an end, especially in golf. How will you regain your great putting touch when your stroke goes awry? When you're on a hot streak, record three key basics in your setup—your distance from the ball, head position and posture—and refer to them whenever the putts stop dropping.

DISTANCE FROM BALL

If you stand too close to the ball, your hands tend to swing the putterhead back outside the target line, leading to pulled putts. Standing too far from the ball results in pushes. When you're putting well, determine your perfect distance from the ball.

Address a putt, then take a piece of string and extend it across your toes, using tees to fasten it to the ground. It should be parallel to your intended target line. Measure the distance from this line to the ball and you'll know exactly how far to extend from the ball.

HEAD POSITION

Poor head position and unnecessary body movement during your stroke can cause direction problems. At address, hold a second ball against the bridge of your nose, then let it drop. When you're putting well, the ball will likely hit the inside-back part of the ball on the ground. If the ball lands on the outside portion of the ball, or misses it to the inside, adjust your head accordingly.

Determine your perfect distance from the ball.

To check your head position, drop a ball from the bridge of your nose...

...it should hit the inside-back part of the ball on the ground.

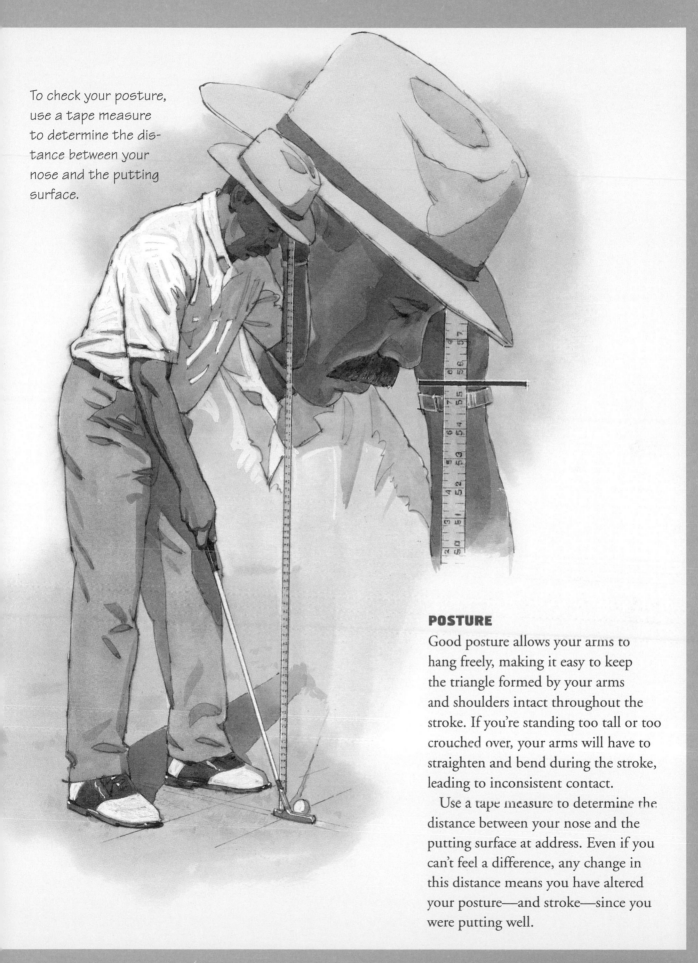

To check your posture, use a tape measure to determine the distance between your nose and the putting surface.

POSTURE

Good posture allows your arms to hang freely, making it easy to keep the triangle formed by your arms and shoulders intact throughout the stroke. If you're standing too tall or too crouched over, your arms will have to straighten and bend during the stroke, leading to inconsistent contact.

Use a tape measure to determine the distance between your nose and the putting surface at address. Even if you can't feel a difference, any change in this distance means you have altered your posture—and stroke—since you were putting well.

NO THREE-PUTT PARS

On those rare occasions when you string together two big shots on a par 5 and reach the green in two, you will likely face a lengthy putt for your eagle. From 50 feet, an eagle would be great and a birdie more in line with your level of play, but a three-putt par would be like giving up a shot. Keep the following keys in mind.

SPEED IS (ALMOST) EVERYTHING

As you look over the eagle putt, don't spend too much time trying to determine the perfect line; remember, a two-putt is your goal. Spend most of your preparation gauging the necessary speed, reading how the green will affect the putt and trying to get a feel for the required stroke. With the right speed, you can badly misread the break and still have a two-footer for birdie. At the same time, a perfect read does you no good if your putt rolls 10 feet past the hole.

Rather than determining the exact line, focus on how the green will affect the putt's speed.

SETUP YOUR BIRDIE

Taps-in are nice, but even a decent lag putt will sometimes leave you a three- or four-footer. Ideally, it will be a slightly uphill putt with little or no break. Draw an imaginary circle around the hole, but narrow your focus to a section of the circle—usually the lower half—that won't leave you with a downhill or severely sidehill putt. You won't completely eliminate the pressure of that second putt, but a little planning goes a long way toward preventing three-putts.

Your lag should leave you an uphill putt with little or no break.

DRILL: THREE IN ONE To learn how to make short putts at different speeds, work on this drill.

Find a sidehill four-footer on the practice green and drop three balls. Stroke the first so it takes the full break and barely topples in on the high side. Then ram the second one into the back of the cup, eliminating the break. Finally, split the difference on the third. Practice this drill often to develop an ability to handle short putts of all kinds.

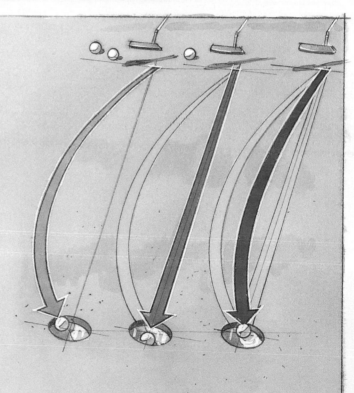

Short: Closest short of cup wins.

Long: Closest past the cup wins.

In: Sink the putt to win.

COMPETE IN PRACTICE

Whether it's playing in the club championship or in your regular weekend match, competition always sharpens your game. You know how important putting is to scoring, so why not work on your stroke while satisfying your competitive drive? Here are three advanced putting games to try.

SHORT, LONG, IN

You and an opponent each roll three putts with the goal of the first one finishing short of the hole, the second one long and the third one in the cup.

- **Short** Standing 30 feet away from the hole, each player has one ball to putt as near to the hole as possible without putting it in or past. The player whose putt rolls closest, but short of the hole, wins one point.
- **Long** Aim at a different hole from 30 feet away, and this time see who can putt the ball as close to the hole as possible, but past it. The player whose ball is beyond the hole and closest wins one point.

- **In** Now putt to a third hole—again, about 30 feet away—and try to knock the ball in. If you do, it's worth one point. If neither player knocks it in, the point carries over to when the goal again is to hole out.

Repeat this short-long-in rotation until one player wins the game by scoring 21 points.

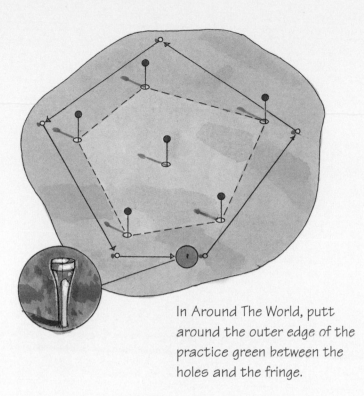

In Around The World, putt around the outer edge of the practice green between the holes and the fringe.

AROUND THE WORLD

The objective is to putt around the outer edge of the practice green in the fewest strokes possible.

- **Step 1** Place a tee between any hole and the fringe. That's your starting point. It's also where you'll finish.
- **Step 2** Each using one ball, you and another player putt around an imaginary boundary that runs from hole to hole. If you cross the boundary, putt back into play; if you putt off the green, place the ball where you last crossed the fringe. Each mistake incurs a one-stroke penalty.
- **Step 3** Complete the journey by returning to the tee where you started. Low score—total putts plus penalty strokes—wins.

DRILL: PLAY FOR QUARTERS Here's a game where you can win some spare change and make the hole look huge in the process. First, place a quarter on the putting green. You and your opponent each get 10 balls to putt to the quarter from five feet away. Each time you hit the quarter with the putt, add 25 cents to your total. Whoever has earned the most money after putting all 10 balls wins the game—and the change. Putting to such a small target will help you focus on your line and stroke, so when you go back to putting to a hole, it will look so large you'll feel like you can't miss.

BACK TO BASICS: KEEP YOUR HEAD STILL!

"Keep your head down!" It's one of the most popular tips any golfer hears. Just about every player has struggled with keeping his or her head down at some point—and this applies equally when you're on the green. A large percentage of off-line putts can be traced to a violation of the "head rule."

Head movement is usually caused by a desire to look at the ball's path before your putter makes contact with the ball, which causes the putter head to turn and send the ball left or right. To make sure you never violate the head rule, concentrate on maintaining your spine position throughout your stroke.

Another way to think about this is to imagine your shoulders swiveling around your spine. Here is the key: If your spine stays still, your body will, too. On short putts, listen for the ball to drop into the hole instead of watching it go in, and keep your head in place until the putterhead has passed your left ear.

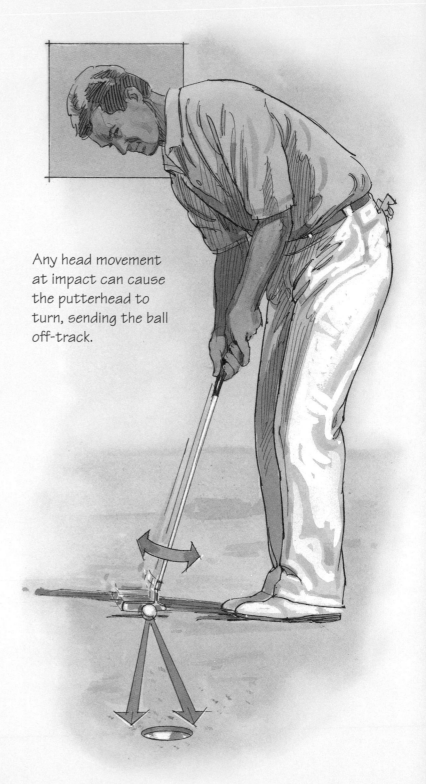

Any head movement at impact can cause the putterhead to turn, sending the ball off-track.

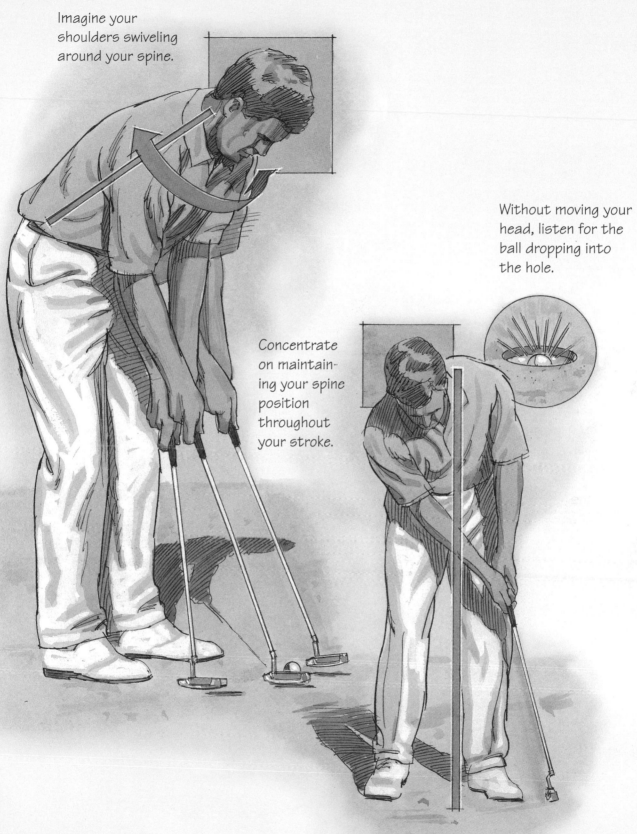

Imagine your shoulders swiveling around your spine.

Concentrate on maintaining your spine position throughout your stroke.

Without moving your head, listen for the ball dropping into the hole.

Keep your head in place until the putterhead passes your left ear.

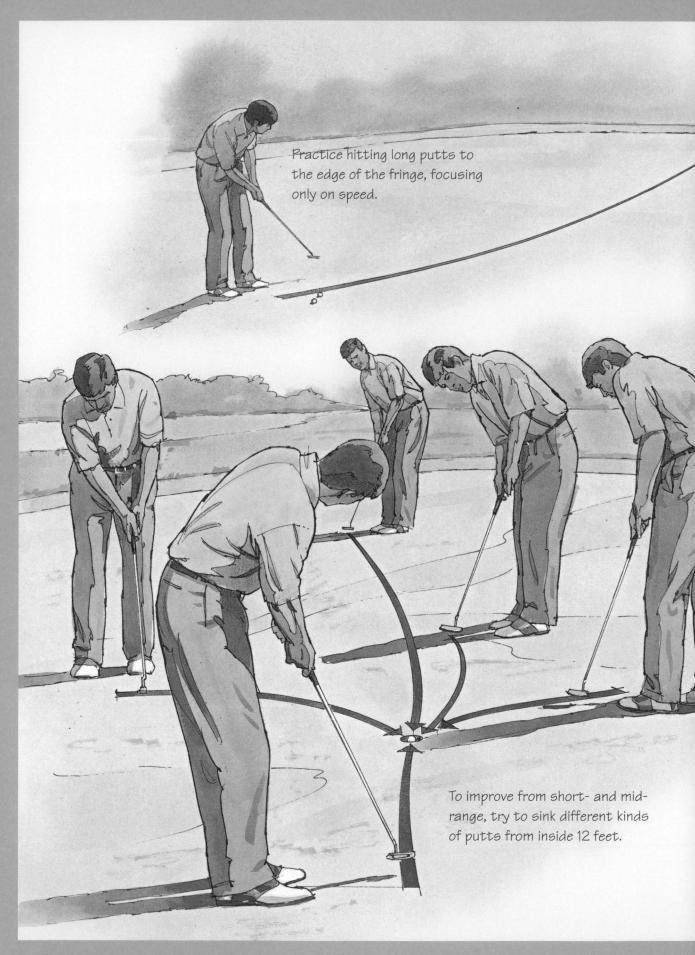

Practice hitting long putts to the edge of the fringe, focusing only on speed.

To improve from short- and mid-range, try to sink different kinds of putts from inside 12 feet.

FINE-TUNE YOUR FEEL

Your best rounds invariably come when you putt well. That's why you should concentrate on developing feel in your putting practice sessions and pre-round warm-ups. Here's how.

CONTROL LAGS

Success with the flat stick depends on how well you judge speed. Start every warm-up working on pace.

Begin by hitting 30- to 50-footers. Ignore the hole: Roll putts across the green, uphill and downhill, to a tee or to the edge of the fringe so you'll focus completely on speed and not on the hole. Learning to control distance will do wonders for your tempo.

VARY SHORT PUTTS

No two putts during a round are identical, so don't spend too much time in one spot when practicing short putts. Use one ball and vary the length and break of each putt as you move around the hole from three to 12 feet out. By hitting a different putt every time, you'll force yourself to adjust your stroke, just as you will on the course.

DRILL: 30 IN A ROW Surround a hole with six balls, each a foot from the cup. Sink all six, then place them at two feet from the hole and repeat. Move the balls out in one-foot increments until you sink six five-foot putts.

The catch: Any time you miss, you have to start over with the one-footers. You may never sink 30 consecutive putts, but the pressure of trying will ready your nerves for the course.

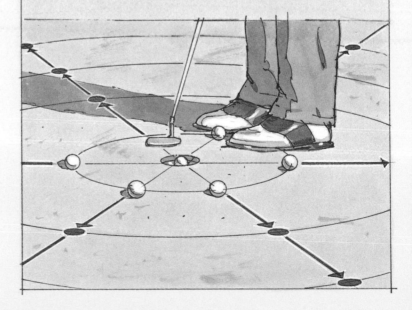

For shorter putts, use one ball and vary the length and break.

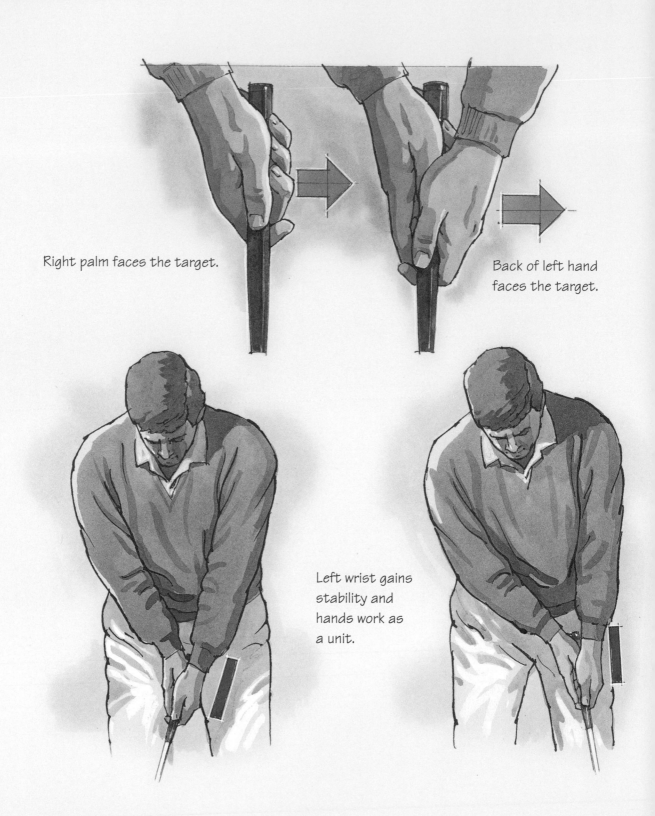

Right palm faces the target.

Back of left hand faces the target.

Left wrist gains stability and hands work as a unit.

CURE YOUR PULL

What's the most common putting fault? Left wrist breakdown. No matter how often you tell yourself to keep your wrist firm, it collapses and shuts the clubface, causing a pull. This will help: Try the cross-handed grip.

HOW IT WORKS

For right-handers, the cross-handed style puts your left hand below your right. Start with your right hand at the top of the handle, with your palm facing the target. Add your left hand with the back of it facing the target. This grip will stabilize your left wrist and help your hands work as a unit.

DRILL: GET IN THE ZONE With a cross-handed grip, long putts can be tough to judge at first. To develop a feel for distance, imagine a three-foot circular "safe zone" around the holes on the practice green. Hit putts of 20 or more feet to each hole. If your first putt finishes in the safe zone, putt out. If it's outside the zone, you have to repeat that putt. Add a little pressure by competing with a partner, seeing who gets "in the zone" first.

COURSE MANAGEMENT

There are only two ways to get better at golf—you can either hit the ball better or start playing the game itself better. Course management, which involves decision making and creativity, is the skill that bridges the act of hitting the ball with knowing which shots to attempt and which strategies to employ to get the best results.

On the following pages you will see how to make the ball curve in the direction you want, and how to use your clubs as tools instead of one-dimensional pieces of equipment. You will also learn how to develop a knack for spotting the best way to play a shot.

Improve your course management and your scores will assuredly go down, even if your swing does not get better.

Breaking up your round into six "matches" will help you focus on the hole at hand and stay in the moment.

BREAK UP YOUR ROUND FOR IMPROVEMENT

What are your goals? Are you yearning for the day when you'll break 100, 90, 80? Concentrating on shooting a specific score can put a lot of pressure on your game. Sometimes, all it takes to crack your goal score is a change in the way you think about your round. If your goal is to break 90, try separating your next round of 18 holes into six "matches" of three holes each, where the par for the course is 90. In order to be under par, you have to average between 14 and 15 strokes per three-hole match. For example, on a stretch of holes including a par 3, 4, and 5, you'd be allowed an average of two or three over par to maintain your goal of 14 or 15 strokes for each three-hole match. The same game can be played to break 80, 100, and so on. Breaking up your round in this way can help you concentrate solely on the holes at hand rather than what you have already faced or have yet to play. The best part is, you can get so caught up in the progress of each match that you just might be surprised to find that you are "under par" for the first time in your playing career.

HANDLING CROSSWINDS

Even the best players in the world are often bedeviled by wind. The wind is the most difficult variable to figure out for golfers at every level, and while shots into the wind or downwind can be overcome with experience and club selection, crosswinds are more troubling. Any wind of 10 mph or more will have a significant effect on your shots, especially those you'd like to land softly, such as an approach to the green. Here's our advice for hitting the right shot at the right time when faced with a crosswind:

Less than 10 mph: A slight draw will cancel a left-to-right breeze, so aim directly at the target.

LESS THAN 10 MPH

A crosswind of this speed is more of a solid breeze, and can be used to your advantage. Hitting a slight draw can easily cancel a left-to-right breeze blowing at this speed, while a fade works well when the wind is from right to left. When using this strategy, it's best to aim straight at your target, because if the breeze and ball flight cancel each other exactly, you'll be in great shape, but if you overwork the ball slightly, you won't be far off line.

More than 10 mph: For a strong right-to-left wind, aim to the right of your target line and let the ball ride the wind back to the target.

A punch shot can fly under the wind.

MORE THAN 10 MPH

The way to be successful is to ride the wind to your target. Even if you hit a natural draw or fade off the tee, you'll need to set up outside your natural target lines to end up where you want to be. Practice and experience will really help you here, as it's important to know the margin of error for your own shots as well as how much the wind you're dealing with will affect them. If all else fails, a knockdown shot can be the most effective way to take the bite out of strong, gusting crosswinds.

TIPS FOR ACCURATELY GAUGING YARDAGE

We've all experienced a round of golf where the on-course yardage markers just seemed a little bit off. However, most yardage markers are accurate, and it is up to us to calculate how much more or less distance than the marker's number is required to get the ball to the hole. Here's some advice for gauging distance when factors other than the simple length of the shot are involved:

THE TOPOGRAPHY

While understanding how many yards you should add and subtract for uphill and downhill shots is an acquired skill, many players forget that minor undulations in a course's topography can affect their shots as well. Dips and troughs in front of the green can make shots appear shorter than they really are. The same holds true for steep lips in greenside bunkers. The pin may appear to be directly behind the bunker, but in reality it is many yards beyond. Make sure to take into account the ground yardage, visual indicators, and pin placement on every approach shot.

Dips and troughs in front of the green can make the hole appear closer.

Always check the pin position, because the pin may appear to be directly behind a steep greenside bunker.

Throw a few bits of grass into the air to check the speed and direction of the wind.

Also study the treetops, especially around the green.

Taking the wind into account will help you judge distance more accurately.

THE WIND

The speed and direction of the wind is most easily tested by throwing a few bits of grass into the air before you approach the ball. While this method is a reliable one, it's also important to study the treetops, especially if they surround the green, because they can deaden the influence of a sturdy breeze. If you can keep the ball lower than the tree level, your shot will be more protected from the effect of the wind. For higher-trajectory players, however, surrounding trees may create a wind tunnel that can greatly affect the flight of the ball. Paying attention to these factors will not only help you to judge your distance more accurately, but also to develop better feel over time.

During your practice rounds, alternate conservative and aggressive play on each nine.

On your conservative nine, hit your driver only if the hole is wide open.

Play for the fat part of every green.

Lay up on par 5s unless you have a mid-iron or less to the green.

FIND THE RIGHT STRATEGY FOR YOUR GAME

Possessing power off the tee can occasionally become a liability when you lose strokes with wild mistakes. So when opportunity knocks, should you go for the big shot or play it safe and keep the ball in play? If you have any doubt about which strategy will yield the lowest scores, try the following test during your next few friendly practice rounds.

In the first round, play the front nine very conservatively. Hit your driver only if the hole is wide open, play for the fat part of every green, and lay up on par 5s unless you have a mid-iron or less to the green. Your distance advantage will only come into play on approach shots.

Then play an aggressive back nine. Hit your driver on every par 4 and par 5, fire at every pin regardless of its location, and go for every par 5 on your second shot. In your next round, play an aggressive front nine followed by a conservative back nine. Compare

On your aggressive nine, hit your driver on every par 4 and par 5.

Shoot for the pin regardless of its location.

Go for every reachable par 5 on your second shot.

the four nines to see if being aggressive or conservative significantly improves your score, but don't take the results as an indication that you should play either extremely conservatively or aggressively all the time. Rather, let the results help you decide what your strategic tendencies should be when you're not sure how to play a specific hole or course.

PAR 3 PLANNING

When it comes to tee shots, the stakes are high on par 3s. Hit the ball well and you've got a great chance at birdie or an easy par; hit it poorly and you're staring at bogey or worse. Here are four tips for playing par 3s.

1. USE A TEE

Start by teeing the ball up, no matter what club you're using. Even if the tee is no higher than the turf, it improves clubface-to-ball contact. With a tee, there's less chance that grass will get caught between your club and the ball.

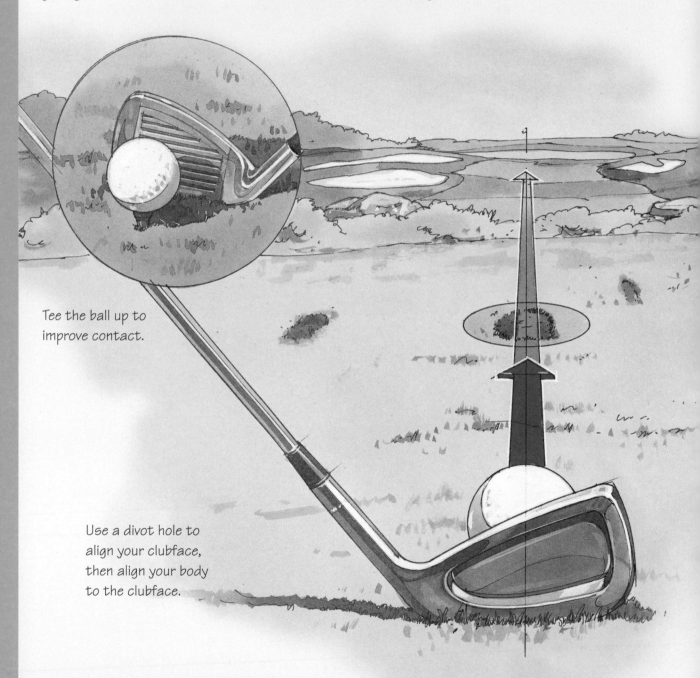

Tee the ball up to improve contact.

Use a divot hole to align your clubface, then align your body to the clubface.

2. USE A DIVOT HOLE

Divot holes can aid your aim. Tee the ball a few feet behind one, directly along your target line. Aim your clubface at the divot hole, then align your body parallel to your line. This is simpler and more accurate than trying to aim at the flag on the green.

3. USE ONE MORE CLUB

You'll find that most hazards on par 3s are between the tee and the green. So take one more club than your instinct tells you. With an extra club, you can make a smooth, relaxed swing and still get enough distance to clear any trouble.

4. AIM FOR THE FAT PART

Short holes often feature small, heavily guarded greens. Getting greedy can lead to disaster, so aim for the part of the green that gives you the largest margin for error. Even with a less-than-perfect swing you'll probably wind up on the dance floor.

Take one more club to ensure that you'll carry any trouble.

When the green is heavily guarded, play to the safest spot.

Playing the ball forward leads to easy outs.

Take a shallow cut of sand

BUNKER PLAY: THE SIMPLE ESCAPE

Bunker shots may seem intimidating, but mastering the basic technique allows you to play more aggressively from the fairways. If you have a long history of leaving shots in the sand, stop using the traditional technique—playing the ball inside your left heel and hitting an inch or two behind it—and try moving the ball forward a couple of inches; this widens your margin for error. The forward ball position promotes a shallower, more level cut through the sand. You can swing into the sand as much as five inches behind the ball and still apply enough force to pop it out. Just open your stance and the clubface and make a three-quarter swing. You'll be amazed at how easy a bunker shot can be.

HITTING DRIVER OFF THE DECK

Hitting a driver from the fairway can be a powerful weapon, but don't try it unless the conditions are right. The ball should be sitting up in the fairway or, even better, on a slight upslope. Your intended landing area should be dry and hard, letting you take full advantage of the low trajectory the ball will take.

The easiest way to get the ball airborne is to set up to hit a slight fade, which increases the clubface's effective loft by a few degrees. Aim your body a bit left of the target with the clubface square to the target line. Now make a smooth swing with a slightly out-to-in path through the hitting area. The ball should start left, then slide a few yards to the right before running hard to the green.

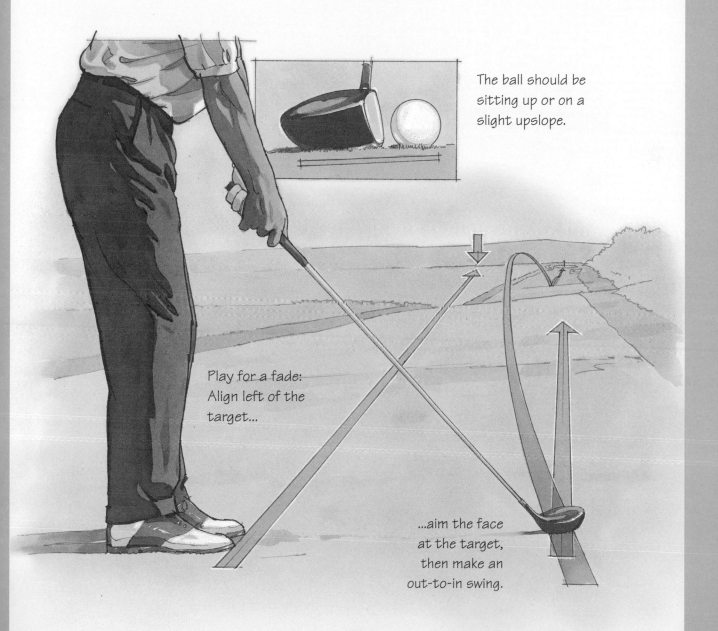

The ball should be sitting up or on a slight upslope.

Play for a fade: Align left of the target...

...aim the face at the target, then make an out-to-in swing.

PUTT FOR EAGLE MORE OFTEN

On par 5s, most long hitters have one overpowering inclination on the tee: to hit the ball as far as possible in order to have the shortest possible iron into the green. This isn't always the most productive strategy, however, because par 5s are designed to be hit in three shots. Often, it's smarter to think not only about what distance you'd like to hit your approach from, but also what kind of lie you'd expect to have from that distance. Smashing it off the tee can sometimes put you on a downslope for your approach shot. Even with a shorter iron, this scenario is not ideal if you want to have a makeable putt for eagle or birdie. Make sure to determine your ideal landing area from the tee. It may be smarter to resist the urge to smash your driver—instead, leave yourself with a 4-iron approach from a level lie instead of an 8-iron from a sidehill lie or heavy rough. Your extra distance off the tee doesn't mean much if you're in an undesirable spot for your approach.

Once you've conquered the drive, it's time to study your approach. Try to enlarge your

Determine your ideal landing area from the tee.

Try not to land your ball on a downslope.

It's better to leave yourself with a long iron approach from a level lie instead of...

target area by picking one side of the green that will be safe for a miss. That way, the worst third shot you'll face is a chip or a pitch, which can keep your hopes for birdie or better alive.

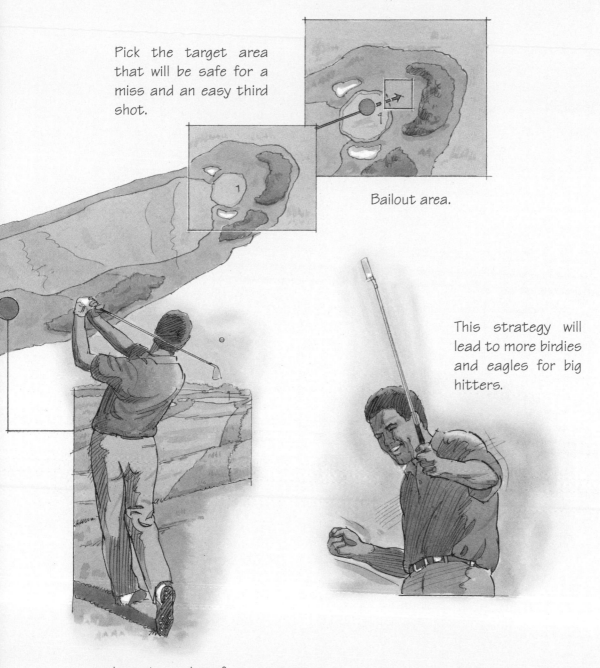

Pick the target area that will be safe for a miss and an easy third shot.

Bailout area.

This strategy will lead to more birdies and eagles for big hitters.

...a short iron shot from the rough or a sidehill lie.

SMART SHOTS FROM DEEP ROUGH

When you're in the thick rough, do you go for the green or pitch back to the fairway?

Your tee shot finds the long rough. What next? Go for the green, or pitch back to the fairway?

It depends on the lie, but most golfers want to shoot for the green no matter how bad it is. That kind of thinking usually sends the next shot into deeper trouble. Here's how to make the smart choice next time.

THE NEED FOR SPEED

How fast is your swing? The average golfer doesn't generate enough clubhead speed to reach the hole from the rough. (Tiger Woods can stick a 165-yard wedge on the green from the deep stuff—you can't.) Before taking a rip, be honest with yourself, because the less clubhead speed you generate, the more loft you need (e.g., a 9-iron or pitching wedge). Don't swing harder than normal; let the loft of the club advance the ball forward and leave a short approach for your third shot.

WHEN TO GO

If the lie in the rough is reasonable, use a lofted utility wood, such as a 7- or 9-wood, which will glide through the grass.

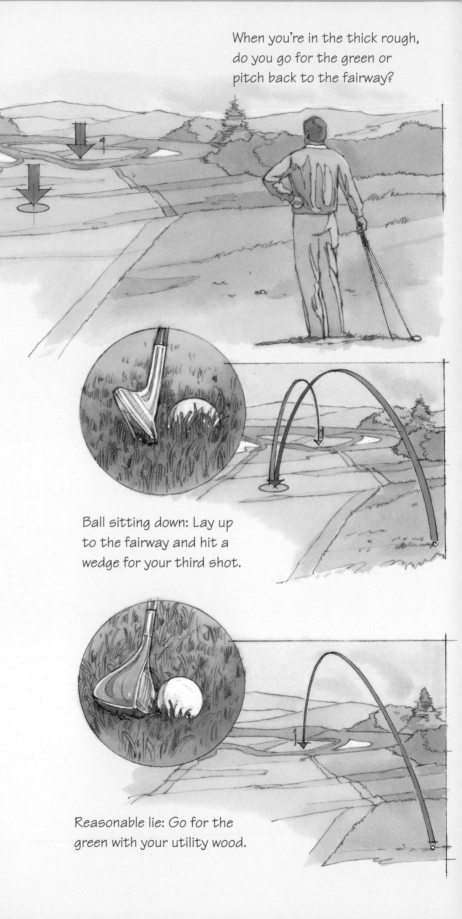

Ball sitting down: Lay up to the fairway and hit a wedge for your third shot.

Reasonable lie: Go for the green with your utility wood.

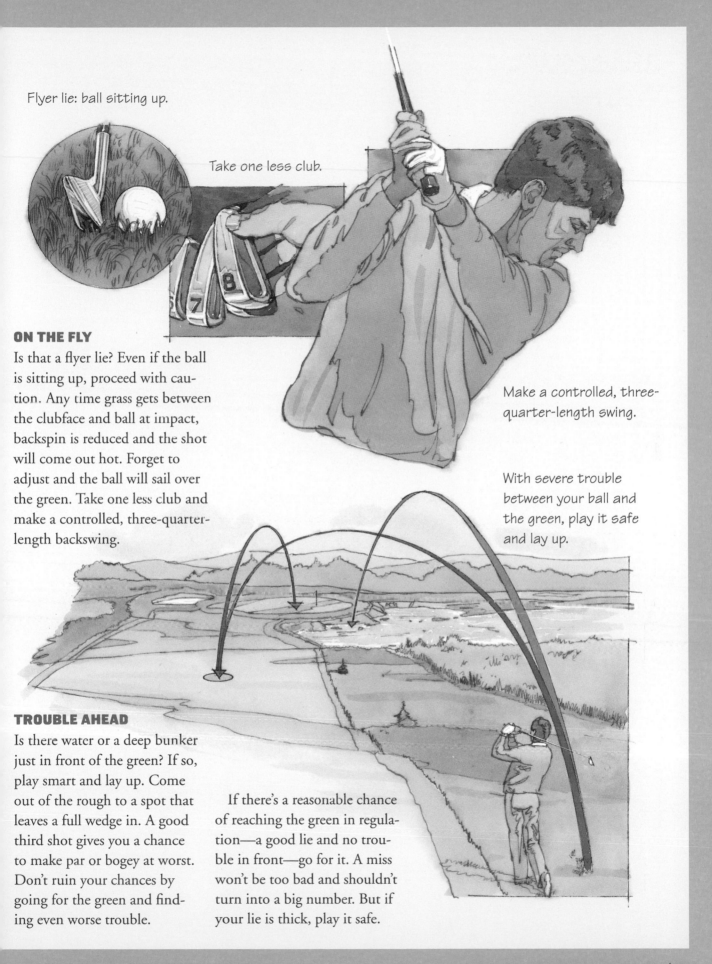

Flyer lie: ball sitting up.

Take one less club.

Make a controlled, three-quarter-length swing.

With severe trouble between your ball and the green, play it safe and lay up.

ON THE FLY

Is that a flyer lie? Even if the ball is sitting up, proceed with caution. Any time grass gets between the clubface and ball at impact, backspin is reduced and the shot will come out hot. Forget to adjust and the ball will sail over the green. Take one less club and make a controlled, three-quarter-length backswing.

TROUBLE AHEAD

Is there water or a deep bunker just in front of the green? If so, play smart and lay up. Come out of the rough to a spot that leaves a full wedge in. A good third shot gives you a chance to make par or bogey at worst. Don't ruin your chances by going for the green and finding even worse trouble.

If there's a reasonable chance of reaching the green in regulation—a good lie and no trouble in front—go for it. A miss won't be too bad and shouldn't turn into a big number. But if your lie is thick, play it safe.

DIVERSIFY YOUR SHORT GAME

When most players are around the green, they automatically reach for a high-lofted wedge. But there are a lot of ways to skin a cat, and the best short-game players are not afraid to use a variety of clubs and shots from tricky spots.

FAIRWAY-METAL CHIP

The ball is near the green in light rough. The wider, rounded sole of a 5- or 7-wood slides through the grass more easily than the upright head of an iron. So choke down to the bottom of the grip and take a fairly erect stance, so the shaft of the club is almost straight up and down. Then make your normal putting stroke. The ball will pop off the face and roll smoothly onto the green.

Stand tall.

Grip down almost to the metal.

Make a normal putting stroke.

PUTTING FROM SAND

If the sand is firm and there's no lip on the bunker, try putting out—especially if there's trouble behind the hole. Make your normal stroke with a little more oomph, taking care not to hit the ball with a descending blow, which would drive it into the sand. Even your worst putt from a bunker will be better than a bladed wedge over the green or a fluffed explosion.

Make a firm putting stroke.

Set hands ahead of the ball.

Use a narrow stance with the ball opposite the back foot.

CHIPPING FROM TIGHT LIES

Instead of trying a delicate sand-wedge shot from a tight lie or hardpan, try chipping with anything from a 6-iron to a pitching wedge. You can bounce the ball through the fringe or even light rough.

Take a narrow stance with the ball opposite your right heel, and set your hands slightly ahead of the ball. Now make a short, slightly descending swing for crisp contact.

Lean the shaft toward the target.

Open stance.

Make a low, wide swing using your arms and shoulders.

Keep the club-head low at the finish.

RUN IT TO THE FLAG

You're inside 50 yards and the flag is in the back of the green. Resist the temptation to fly the ball to the hole. Instead, use the entire green by playing a low pitch.

Using your pitching wedge, open your stance slightly, play the ball opposite your back foot and lean the shaft toward the target. Make a low, wide swing with your arms and shoulders, clipping the ball off the grass rather than taking a divot. Keep the clubhead low in your follow-through. Try to land the ball on the front of the green and get it to roll like a putt.

Align your body left and aim the clubface at the target.

THE LOW FADE

Under normal conditions it's tough to keep a fade from climbing quickly. But a low fade can be a great weapon when you need to carve a shot into a headwind and attack a far-right flag or escape low-hanging limbs.

Align your body left, where you want the ball to start, and aim the clubface at your target. The trick to keeping the ball down is to play it an inch or two farther back than normal, with your weight favoring your front foot. This will effectively de-loft the club slightly, so the shot should stay lower than normal. Make a three-quarter backswing and focus on keeping the clubhead's toe from passing the heel until well after impact. The shot will start left, then work to the right without ballooning.

Weight on back foot.

Ball back in stance.

Hold face open through impact.

When hitting to an elevated green, take at least 10 yards more club than what the yardage would normally require.

MASTERING ELEVATED GREENS AND TEES

Holes with elevated tees or greens can be tricky. Elevated greens are visually challenging because they make you feel as though you need to hit a higher-than-normal shot to a pin that you can sometimes barely see. Elevated tees allow you to see everything in front of you; however, it can be hard to judge how much the change in elevation will affect your shot. Here's our advice for tackling both situations:

For a shot to an elevated green, resist the impulse to try to hit a shot higher than normal. Instead, take up to 10 yards of extra club (more if you're also facing some wind)

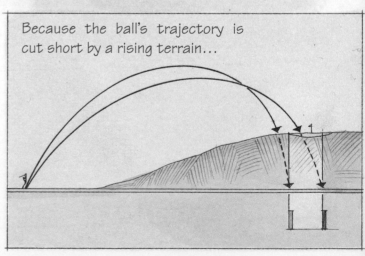

Because the ball's trajectory is cut short by a rising terrain...

...taking an extra club or two will get the ball all the way back to your target.

to compensate for the change in the green's elevation. The higher the green's elevation, the more club you'll need—sometimes as many as two or three more clubs than the yardage indicates.

Distance control is the most difficult aspect of hitting shots from an elevated tee. The higher you are above the tee, the more time the ball will spend in the air and the less club you'll need. The pin is an important factor to consider when judging distance. If the pin looks unusually long compared to the green, it means the green is relatively small. If the pin looks proportional, then the green is far below you. You should rarely have to drop more than two clubs, though—remember, there's a limit to how far forward a ball will fly before it drops straight down!

The higher the tee, the more time the ball will spend in the air and the less club you'll need.

Because a drop lengthens the ball's trajectory...

...less club is needed to reach the target.

MIND YOUR MAKEUP

If you are a beginner or a high-handicap golfer, carrying the wrong combination of clubs will cost you strokes, so optimize your 14 selections. Here are a few suggestions.

LONG CLUBS: HIGHER TRAJECTORY

There is a common misconception that a low, boring tee shot will maximize distance because the ball will roll forward after it lands. But test after test shows that to really go deep, you need to maximize your carry distance on your tee shots and long approaches. The long clubs in your bag should reflect this philosophy.

Start with your driving club. Even if you rarely have trouble getting your driver into the air, take it out of the bag. Yes, the 3-wood is designed to hit the ball shorter, but the higher trajectory it produces from your relatively low clubhead speed will provide more carry and, therefore, more distance.

In the same spirit, trade your 3-, 4-, and 5-irons for the 5-, 7-, and 9-woods for long approaches. High-lofted fairway woods get the ball up with less effort and are easier to hit from less-than-perfect lies.

The 3-wood's higher trajectory will provide more carry.

Lofted fairway woods will help you hit your long approaches higher.

SHORT CLUBS: CLOSE THE GAPS

Shots from 100 yards and in are easier when you don't have to make a delicate partial swing. Stock your bag with a variety of wedges. In addition to a pitching wedge (47–50 degrees depending on the model) and a sand wedge (54–57 degrees), consider adding a 51- to 53-degree gap wedge and a 58- to 62-degree lob wedge. Try to get four to five degrees of loft separation between each club. With four evenly spaced wedges, you'll almost always be able to make a full swing on short shots—and that will take the guesswork out of your wedge play.

Use a variety of wedges to cut down your number of partial shots.

47°–50°: Pitching Wedge

51°–53°: Gap Wedge

54°–57°: Sand Wedge

58°–62°: Lob Wedge

DON'T LET THE RAIN THROW YOU

Few players actively plan for a rainy round of golf, but whether you're grinding in a tournament or participating in a quick match with your buddies, knowing how to battle through the rain can give you a significant mental advantage over your opponents. Here are a few tips that can help make you as competitive as possible during a round in the rain:

Umbrella.

Extra towel.

Rain gloves.

Rain suit.

Golf bag cover.

For better traction, remove excess grass from your spikes with a tee.

Wipe your grip before every shot.

KEEP YOUR BALANCE

If your soft spikes are worn to the nub, replace them before a round in the rain. Since most courses don't allow steel spikes anymore, run a tee through your soft spikes as often as you can to get rid of excess grass. This will greatly increase your traction. If it's really slippery, cut your swing to three-quarter length to maintain solid footing.

BE AGGRESSIVE

Wet grass means less roll in addition to a reduced amount of spin on the ball. You can forget about bump-and-runs on a really wet day; instead, focus on trying to pitch the ball all the way to the hole. Putts will run more slowly and break less as well, so make sure to get the ball all the way to the hole.

Be aggressive with your pitch and chip shots.

ARRIVE PREPARED

Rain gear is a given, but it's important to protect your equipment, too. Keep your hands and grips dry to keep the club from slipping while you swing. If you don't have rain gloves, keep extra regular gloves in the original packaging in a pocket of your bag. (A pair of plain cotton gloves can also provide plenty of grip in wet weather.) Most bags come with a club cover— use it! Have an umbrella with you even if you're using a cart—that way you can shield yourself while you're waiting to putt or to hit from the fairway. The bottom line is, do your best to minimize your unprotected time in the rain.

HOT TIPS FOR COLD DAYS

Low temperatures won't keep a hardy soul off the golf course. Why should they? Take the following steps to make sure you enjoy yourself—and play to your potential—in the chill.

Dress in thin layers for warmth and mobility.

THE LAYERED LOOK

Warmth is a priority, but an unrestricted swing is key to playing well. Thin layers instead of bulky clothing let you swing freely. A combination of long underwear, a turtleneck, a thin sweater and an outer shell will keep you warm without sacrificing mobility.

Long underwear

Turtleneck

Thin sweater

HEAD AND HANDS

The most important body parts to keep warm are your hands and head. Wearing mittens or gloves (cover your non-gloved hand, too) between shots will keep your fingers from stiffening. And since body heat escapes through your head—*Mom was right about that*—wear a wool hat. It'll help keep your whole body warmer.

WARM UP LONGER

In cold weather, you're more prone to injury. Give yourself plenty of time to warm up before your round. When you arrive at the course, get your blood pumping by walking briskly and making fast circles with your arms extended from your sides. Then do some light stretching before starting your warm-up.

MIND YOUR DIMPLES

Temperatures near freezing reduce the distance a golf ball will fly, but it takes about 10 hours of exposure for a ball's performance to be affected significantly. The night before you tee it up, keep your golf balls indoors, not in your car or the garage. They'll retain their usual zip throughout the next day's round.

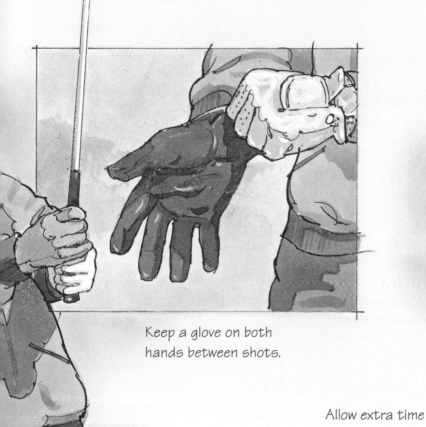

Keep a glove on both hands between shots.

dbreaker

Allow extra time to warm up before your round.

STROKE SAVERS

A unique aspect of golf is that when you practice, you usually are on a flat piece of ground, hitting from a perfect lie into a wide-open field. Nothing is in your way or restricts your swing. But golf course designers are devilish when it comes to incorporating slopes, trees, ponds and other natural obstructions. It is rare to find your ball resting in a good lie on a perfectly flat area with no hazards in sight.

So what do you do when your ball comes to rest in a less than perfect spot, such as a divot hole or under a tree? This chapter will explain how to adjust for those situations, plus other awkward shots that can either keep a good round going or lead to a big number.

Swing your right arm to chop down on the ball.

Shaft vertical.

Clubface square.

THE ONE-HANDED CHOP

Your ball has come to rest against a tree—so close, in fact, that your normal right-handed stance and swing are impossible. It may look like a trick shot, but in this position the one-handed chop is the most reliable, and possibly your only, escape option.

Hold a 9-iron or wedge in your right hand and grip down a few inches for more clubhead control. Stand with your back to the target so the ball is about six inches to the side of your right foot. Adjust the club so the shaft is perpendicular to the ground and the clubface is square to the target.

Now simply swing your right arm and chop down onto the ball. You'll find it's surprisingly easy to make solid contact, sending the ball scurrying toward the target. For longer shots, cock your wrist and lengthen the swing.

LOOK AHEAD ON HALF-WEDGE SHOTS

Plenty of golfers fail to reach long par 4s in two, and that means they face plenty of half-swing wedge shots into greens.

These can be some of the trickiest shots around.

The common mistake is trying to help the ball into the air with a scooping motion at impact. Instead, your setup and swing should encourage hitting down on the ball to produce solid contact and a high trajectory. Position the ball midway between your heels and angle the shaft toward the target so your hands are slightly ahead. Focusing your eyes on the front (target side) of the ball will help the club contact the ball before the ground.

Don't rush the swing. Good wedge players swing down at a smooth pace. At impact, the club's handle should be ahead of the ball, as it was at address.

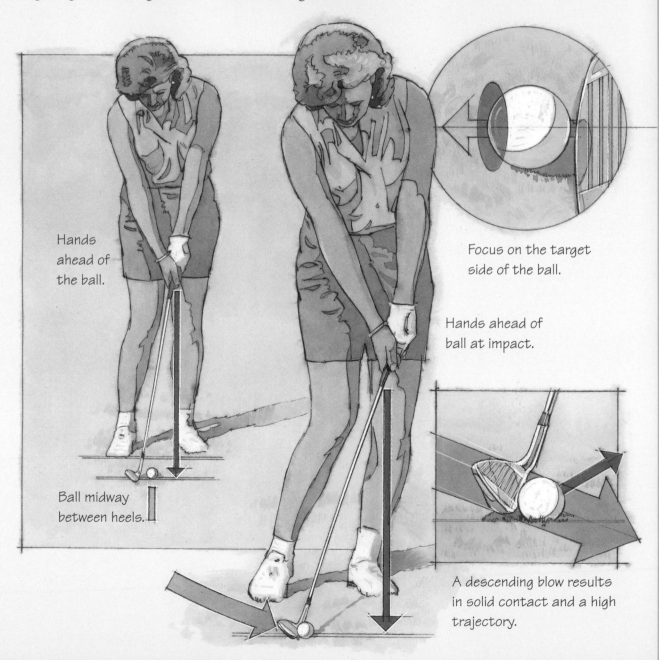

Hands ahead of the ball.

Ball midway between heels.

Focus on the target side of the ball.

Hands ahead of ball at impact.

A descending blow results in solid contact and a high trajectory.

MASTER THE PERCHED LIE

You may feel lucky to see your ball sitting up in the rough, but don't relax just yet. It's easy to make solid contact, but it's just as easy to slide the clubface under the ball and fluff the shot.

A ball perched in thick rough may be two or three inches above the ground, so plan accordingly. The key is to avoid a descending blow by swinging into impact on a shallow path, just as you would with a driver. Start by gripping down and hovering the clubhead at address, keeping the sole of the club even with the bottom of the ball. With your left shoulder slightly raised, start back with a wide, slow takeaway. As you swing through, keep your left shoulder high. You'll stay on a shallow path and make solid contact.

Hover the clubhead at address and swing through impact on a shallow path.

Left shoulder is lightly raised.

Start the swing with a wide, slow takeaway.

WHEN TO PLAY FOR BOGEY

Into a stiff headwind, your goal is to maintain control and reach the green in three.

Using your head can definitely help you score more pars and birdies, but there are times when you also have to be wise enough to avoid the big number. To that end, here are three situations that dictate you might need to forget about par, play for bogey and go quietly to the next hole.

1. LONG HOLE INTO THE WIND

Add a stiff headwind to a lengthy hole and the urge to overswing can be very strong. It's a great recipe for errant shots. Your first priority should be to hit the fairway. Instead of fighting the wind with a driver, go with a 3- or 5-wood and put an easy swing on it. The ball will pick up less sidespin from the more

With a hazard between you and a tight pin, hit safely onto the green.

lofted club, and therefore fly straighter. Next, hit a mid-iron that you can control and leave yourself a relatively easy wedge for your third.

2. RECOVERY OVER HAZARD

You've missed the green with your approach, and there's a hazard between your ball and the hole. You could try to hit a perfect lob shot, but the odds aren't with you. Rather than forcing yourself to be perfect, hit a simple pitch that steers clear of the hazard. As long as your next shot is a putt, you've significantly reduced your chances of making a big number.

3. SAFE IS NEVER SORRY

After blowing a drive into the woods, you usually have a couple of options: the dangerous route—a small window through the branches—and the smarter route, which means pitching out sideways. It's almost always best to take your medicine. By taking the safe route, you give yourself a good chance at bogey, maybe even par. More important, you minimize the likelihood of a big number.

By taking the safe route to the fairway, you give yourself a good chance at bogey.

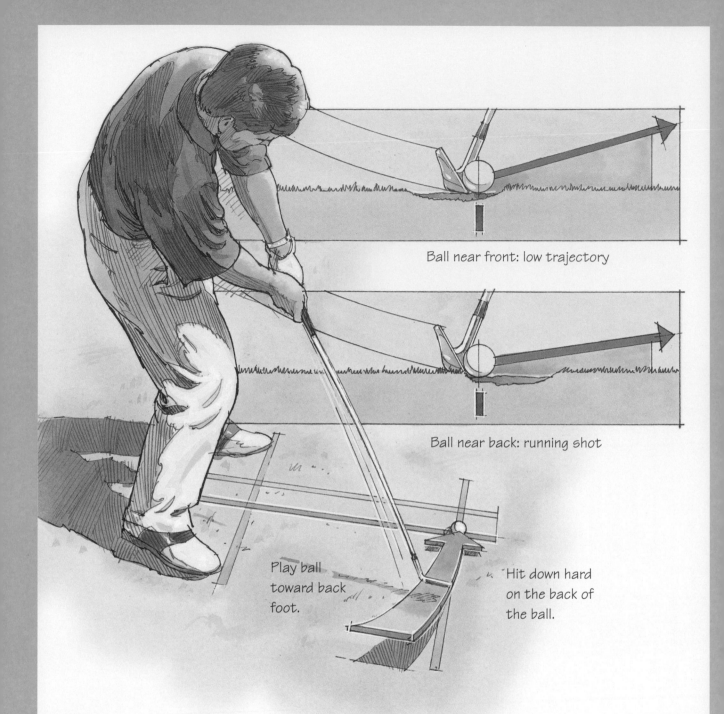

Ball near front: low trajectory

Ball near back: running shot

Play ball toward back foot.

Hit down hard on the back of the ball.

BEAT A BAD BREAK

Anyone who thinks golf is fair hasn't smacked a drive down the middle of a fairway only to find his ball in a divot hole. The good news: Recovery can be easy.

If your ball is at the front end of the divot hole, play it an inch farther back than normal, make a full backswing, then hit down hard on the ball. You'll probably make contact toward the bottom of the clubface and hit the shot lower than usual, but you should still reach your target.

If your ball is near the back of the divot hole, thin contact is a near certainty. Play for a very low trajectory and lots of roll. Take an extra club to compensate for imperfect contact and go for the green only if it will accept a running shot.

AGAINST THE COLLAR

With the ball against the second cut of rough...

...the toe of a mid- or long iron will snag and fan the clubface open.

Here's a dicey situation: Your drive has rolled into the first cut of rough, but it's nestled up against the longer second cut. As you set the clubhead behind the ball, the toe of the club is in the deep rough, but the heel is not. How do you compensate for this half-and-half lie?

In truth, it depends on the club. There's less effect on a short iron, because the angle of attack is steep. But if the shot calls for a mid- or long iron, be prepared for the toe to get snagged, which will fan the clubface open. How much is hard to predict, so you're better off making a three-quarter swing with a lofted fairway wood. Its rounded head will be far less affected by the long grass.

A wiser choice is a three-quarter swing with a fairway wood.

The wood's rounded head will be less affected by the long grass.

CLOVER, SANDY ROUGH AND PINE NEEDLES

Your ball might not find an unusual lie very often, but when it does, you should know what to do. We're not talking about uphill, downhill or sidehill lies, but the really odd ones that can give even good players fits.

CLOVER

Clover is easier to swing through than most rough, but because of its relatively weak stems, the ball will sink below the surface. This makes contact unpredictable. Resist the temptation to chop down as you would from thick rough and, instead, play the ball like a flyer, taking one less club than normal (e.g., a 7-iron instead of a 6-). Make your normal swing, keeping your wrists firm; the clubhead should glide through the clover easily.

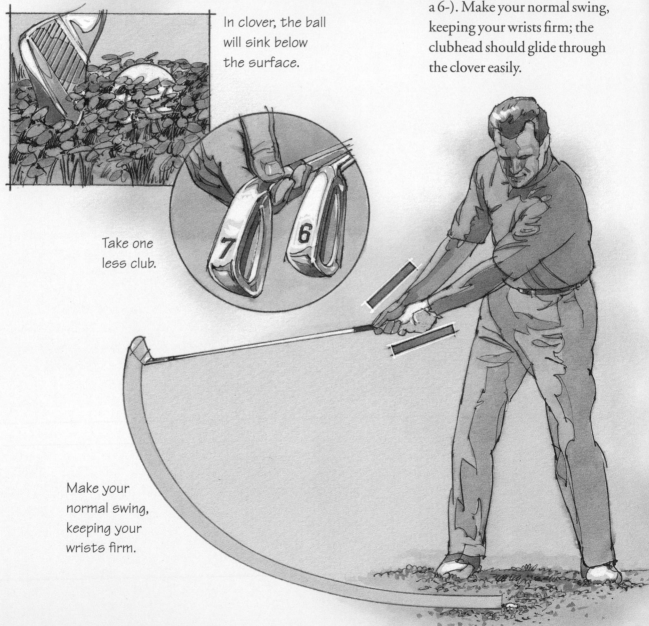

In clover, the ball will sink below the surface.

Take one less club.

Make your normal swing, keeping your wrists firm.

SANDY ROUGH

Especially common in coastal regions, sand-based rough creates indecision due to variations in texture. Feel the ground around your ball: If the sand is soft, sweep the ball as you would from a fairway bunker; if firm and dry, take a wider-than-normal stance, increase your grip pressure and hit the ball with a downward blow. In either case, the shot will have plenty of backspin, so take one more club than normal.

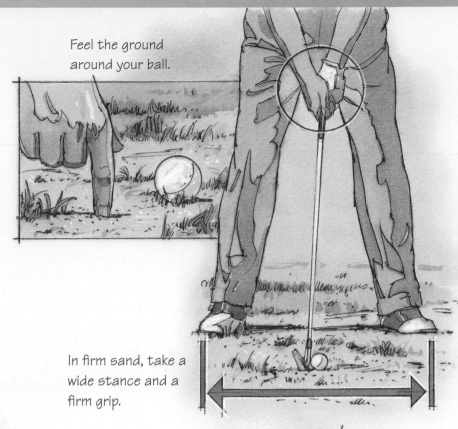

Feel the ground around your ball.

In firm sand, take a wide stance and a firm grip.

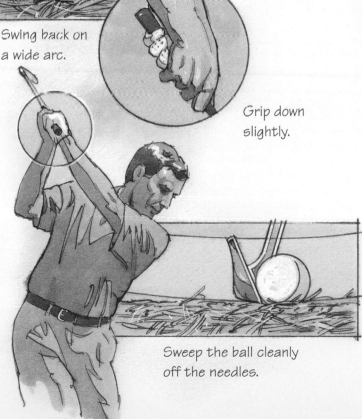

Swing back on a wide arc.

Grip down slightly.

Sweep the ball cleanly off the needles.

Make a descending blow.

PINE NEEDLES

Pine needles create an unstable surface, so merely grounding your club can set off a chain reaction that accidentally moves the ball—costing you a penalty stroke. Pretend you're in a hazard and don't ground your club. Gripping down slightly will help you do this. Then, swing the club back on a wide arc and sweep the ball cleanly off the needles.

Choose a club with enough loft to clear the bunker lip.

Sink your feet just enough to stabilize your stance.

Grip down.

Weight favors front foot.

FAIRWAY SAND MADE SIMPLE

Rule No. 1 from fairway bunkers is to get the ball out of the sand and back in play. Club selection is vital; you must choose a club with enough loft to clear the lip of the bunker. Here's a good guideline: If you are unsure whether your club has enough loft to clear the lip, take more loft than you think you need. Think twice before ever using anything stronger than a 7-iron.

Make a three-quarter swing.

The result will be a low screamer that clears the lip.

To quiet your lower body, imagine your legs are thick concrete pillars.

Keep weight favoring front foot.

Instead of digging your feet deeply into the sand, sink them only enough to stabilize your stance; you should stay as tall as possible. Choke down on the grip about an inch, which will give you more control and also discourage hitting behind the ball. Finally, set more weight on your front leg and play the ball in the middle of your stance to promote ball-first contact.

STRONG, SILENT LEGS

Now that you have the right club and the right setup, you must find a way to maintain your balance despite the instability of the sand. The key is a quiet lower body. Keeping the majority of your weight on your front foot, make a three-quarter swing. Don't worry about shifting your weight. Instead, as you swing the club back and through, imagine your legs are thick concrete pillars. The more stable your legs, the easier it will be to make solid contact.

SETUP FOR THIN CONTACT

Perfect contact would be nice, but a more realistic goal is to hit the ball a little thin, with the leading edge of the clubface making contact just below the ball's equator. If you've chosen the right club, this will produce a low screamer with enough height to clear the lip.

TRICKY BUNKER SHOTS

If you want to shoot consistently low scores, you must be able to handle the curveballs a course throws you. And one prime spot for those is the sand. Here are some hints for tackling three out-of-the-ordinary bunker shots.

1. DOWNHILL TO A TIGHT PIN: FOLLOW THE HILL

The key to this awkward shot is to do everything you would on a regular sand shot, while accommodating for the hill. Your stance remains slightly open, but play the ball a couple of inches back and angle your shoulders parallel to the slope. Lay the clubface wide open and start your backswing with a sharp wrist hinge. As long as the angle of attack is steeper than the hill and the clubface stays open through impact, the ball will float out. The trajectory will be low, but it should have a little backspin.

Sharp wrist hinge.

Ball back in stance.

Steep descent into sand.

2. PLUGGED IN THE FACE: DON'T FOLLOW THE HILL

Your ball is buried in the bunker face. In this case, an upward swing following the hill's slope is a mistake. Instead, lean into the hill, square the clubface and play the ball in the middle of your stance. From there, swing hard: Smash the wedge into the bunker face just below the ball and try to follow through—even though you won't be able to. The club will cut into the sand and pop the ball up and onto the green.

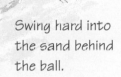

Lean into the hill.

Swing hard into the sand behind the ball.

Blast the ball out with an 8- or 9-iron.

3. THE "TWEENER": USE A SHORT IRON

A bunker shot of 30 to 50 yards is a classic "tweener": It's too long for a standard explosion but too short to nip the ball clean. The simplest method is to blast the ball out with an 8- or 9-iron. Open your stance and the clubface slightly, and play the ball just in front of center. Then make a full swing along your stance line. Your setup is designed to make the club enter the sand behind the ball; the sand you displace will push the ball out.

FLIP THE CLUB FOR SWITCH PITCHING

Everyone misses fairways during a round, and bad luck can strike even the friendliest people. So if you find your ball sitting next to a tree, take heart in knowing that even the best shotmaker gets jittery when his next shot calls for a left-handed swing.

Don't panic—the lefty shot is not as tough as it looks. You have two options: Take an 8- or 9-iron and turn it so the toe of the club is soled behind the ball; or, turn a long iron around and hit the ball with the back of the clubhead. The former method often works better for short shots, the latter for long ones.

After reversing your grip to left-hand low, try a few practice swings using no more than a half-swing. Keep your right arm extended, swing slowly and stay in your posture.

Keep your right arm extended, swing slowly and stay in your posture.

Reverse your grip.

Turn a short iron upside down.

A SURE OUT FROM THICK LIES

Use a short iron and open the clubface slightly.

Leave hitting through deep rough with a 4-iron for the pros. Take your medicine and use a more reliable method for getting the ball safely back into play.

Pick a club with plenty of loft, nothing longer than an 8-iron. Open the clubface slightly to keep the long grass from wrapping around the hosel and shutting the face. Play the ball back, opposite your rear instep, and open your stance slightly to encourage a steep, out-to-in downswing. Then swing the club up sharply, keeping your weight forward, and pull it down and through the ball. Keep your grip firm to stabilize the clubface. It may not be glamorous, but it works every time.

Open your stance and play the ball back.

Swing the club up sharply.

Pull down and hold on through impact.

Weight favors the front foot.

THE MENTAL GAME

As challenging as golf is physically, perhaps no other sport is as demanding mentally. There are a lot of reasons for this. First, you have plenty of time between shots to think about the swing you just made. Secondly, while the ability to hit the ball a long way is important, often the shortest shots are the most perplexing and stressful. How you handle those easily overlooked shots can mean the difference between a great round and another day of frustration.

The best players in the world are mentally the strongest, and that's no accident. On the following pages you will learn how to improve your thought process in order to perform better on the course. From building a better pre-shot routine, to breaking through scoring plateaus, to putting the brakes on a poor stretch of play—it's all here.

KEEP YOUR STATS

One of the best ways to pinpoint the weakest areas of your game is to keep a running list of your statistics during every round you play. Create a tally of each fairway and green you hit in regulation, what club you use on each approach, the number of putts you make on each green and every up-and-down and sand save. If you miss a fairway or a green, be sure to jot down whether you missed to the left or to the right. When you analyze your data after the round, keep in mind that on most courses a perfect regulation round consists of 14 fairways, 18 greens, and 36 putts. If the number of greens you hit is less than 18 and your putts total more than 36, you'll know that it's time to spend some serious time on your short game! Even if you feel satisfied with the state of your game and your handicap, keeping continuous statistics can alert you to fix minor problems or unconscious alterations in your swing before they create a full-blown slump.

To pinpoint the weakest areas of your game, keep a list of statistics for every round you play.

HOLE	1	2	3	4	5	6	7	8	9
PAR	4	4	5	3	5	4	4	3	4
FAIRWAYS	D	3W	P/SW		D/4W	D	3W		
MISS L/R	L		3W/R			R			
GREENS	5	6	8	4	9	8	5W	7	6
MISS L/R		R	R			R		L	
PITCH CHIP		W	7						
SAND						SW		SW	
PUTTS	2	1	2	2	2	2	3	2	3

BALANCED PRACTICE LEADS TO BETTER SCORES

Beginners tend to see improvement in proportion to the amount of time they spend on the range, because better ballstriking tends to yield lower scores. But as you improve and gain experience, an interesting thing occurs: The effects of your practice diminish, because you've reached a ballstriking plateau—that is, you're hitting it as consistently as you can.

Once you start striking the ball consistently solid, you need to change your practice routine to improve your score. If you analyze your average round, you'll see that 40 percent of your score is on the green, while 25 percent of your score is from 50 yards and in. With these statistics in mind, here's a practice routine that will allow you to see continued improvement: Spend about a third of your time practicing putting, a third of your time practicing short shots (25 yards and in) and a third of your time practicing half-swing wedges and your full swing. Taking it a step further, make the first third

Spend a third of your time practicing putting...

...a third of your time practicing greenside shots...

of your practice on putting, the second third on greenside shots and the final third on the full swing. The faults or patterns in your full swing tend to show up in your short game. By improving your technique on and around the green, you'll also improve your full swing.

...and the final third practicing half-swing wedges and your full swing.

PERFECT YOUR PRE-SHOT ROUTINE

Start with a physical gesture to focus your concentration.

Experienced players know that a good pre-shot routine can help you stay calm, gather your focus and lead to more consistency. You may think you have a pre-shot routine that works. But does it really? If not, it might be time for some routine refinements. Don't simply mimic what the pros do; an effective pre-shot routine should fit your temperament, game and pace of play. The key is knowing what to include and what to avoid.

Select an intermediate target.

WHAT TO INCLUDE

According to *GOLF MAGAZINE* Mental Game Consultant Dr. Richard Coop, there are three elements to all good pre-shot routines: an obvious physical signal, an intermediate target and a deep, cleansing breath.

1. Start with a physical gesture, something to draw your concentration inward and tell you it's time to get started. It can be as simple as tugging at your shirt sleeve, tapping the clubhead on the ground or reattaching the Velcro on your glove.

2. Select an intermediate target, such as an old divot lying between your ball and the target, and aim the clubface at it. Besides improving alignment, this step signals the first psychological commitment to the shot.

Take a deep breath to reduce tension in your arms and torso.

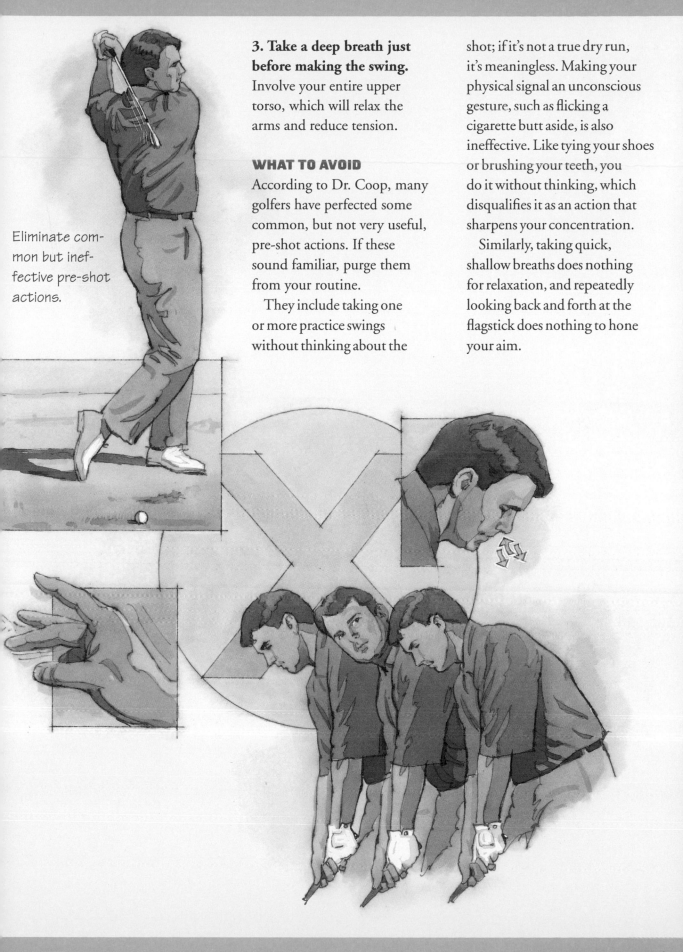

Eliminate common but ineffective pre-shot actions.

3. Take a deep breath just before making the swing. Involve your entire upper torso, which will relax the arms and reduce tension.

WHAT TO AVOID

According to Dr. Coop, many golfers have perfected some common, but not very useful, pre-shot actions. If these sound familiar, purge them from your routine.

They include taking one or more practice swings without thinking about the shot; if it's not a true dry run, it's meaningless. Making your physical signal an unconscious gesture, such as flicking a cigarette butt aside, is also ineffective. Like tying your shoes or brushing your teeth, you do it without thinking, which disqualifies it as an action that sharpens your concentration.

Similarly, taking quick, shallow breaths does nothing for relaxation, and repeatedly looking back and forth at the flagstick does nothing to hone your aim.

LOSE THOSE FIRST-TEE JITTERS

No shot produces more anxiety than the first one. Stripe it down the middle and you're thinking this will be a career round. Top it 30 yards left and you're already asking yourself, "Why did I get up this morning?" With so much mental baggage riding on a single shot, it's no wonder many golfers are nervous wrecks on the first tee. Here are four ways to overcome those first-tee jitters.

1. DRIVER REHEARSAL

On the practice range before the round, pretend you're on the first tee. Imagine the shot shape you want, then hit that shot as if hitting to the first fairway. If you don't have time to warm up, play the first tee shot in your mind while driving to the course. Picture the last time you played the shot to perfection and replay it over and over in your head.

Simulate the first tee shot while on the practice range...

...or play it in your mind while driving to the course.

2. THE "SURE" CLUB

No confidence in your driver? Then leave it in the bag. Take out a 3- or 5-wood—the longest club that gives you the best chance of hitting the fairway. Keeping the ball in play is more important than an extra 20 yards.

3. ONE THOUGHT, NO MORE

Keep it simple: One swing thought or none at all. Running through a long list of swing keys is a sure way to freeze over the ball and create tension. If your thought is to complete the backswing, key on one thing, such as turning your left shoulder under your chin. Or, choose a target— such as a tree at the end of the fairway—and focus on the image of it as you swing.

4. WAGGLE RELIEF

Hover the clubhead in the air and waggle it back and forth, feeling the weight of the clubhead in your fingers. This relieves tension in your hands and arms while promoting a full shoulder turn and a powerful coil. Golfers who rest the clubhead on the ground tend to pick it up with their hands to start the backswing, which leads to tense muscles and an abbreviated backswing.

Hit the club you trust most.

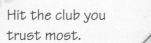
Key on one swing thought.

Focus on a very precise target.

Less tension means a better shoulder turn.

Waggle the club-head to relieve tension.

Hitting practice balls from a divot will help groove a descending blow at impact.

A descending blow reduces effective loft, resulting in more distance.

PRACTICE FROM DIVOTS

Want more distance from your iron shots without having to increase your clubhead speed?

Then change your angle of attack. A slightly descending blow on the ball with a mid- or short-iron decreases the club's effective loft, producing a more penetrating trajectory and five to 10 extra yards. You can groove this by hitting practice balls out of shallow divots.

Place the ball in the middle of the divot and address it with your normal setup. The only way to make solid contact will be to drive the clubface down into the back of the ball. After practicing this drill, you should find it easy to hit from a normal lie and create this improved angle of attack.

Focus on a specific target.

COOL UNDER PRESSURE

Clutch players get just as nervous as other golfers when the pressure mounts. But what saves clutch players is their ability to focus on the target instead of on the trouble around it.

To do this, choose a specific target. Don't just aim for the fairway or green. Pick a small area—a patch of grass, a single tree—and fix that image in your mind. Keep it there and you'll come through when it really counts.

To recover from a bad shot, take a break, clear your mind and refocus.

STOP SNOW-BALLING

Every golfer has been there: After a string of good shots, a bad one shatters your confidence. Your mind races, your tempo quickens; suddenly, that one bad shot has snowballed into a series of bad holes.

Learning to recover quickly from mistakes might lower your scores more than improving your swing or putting stroke. The key is managing frustration: Instead of rushing your next shot, clear your mind for 30 seconds. Take a short walk, do some deep breathing—whatever it takes to refocus.

Work on clearing your mind over the ball as well. Don't get overwhelmed by mechanics. Instead, key on one basic swing thought, like "smooth back and through." Keeping it simple will calm you, allow your body to perform to its highest potential and let you have more fun out there on the golf course.

PLAY FOR A FULL APPROACH SHOT ON PAR 5s

On par 5s, golfers generally hit their second shot as far as they can to allow for the shortest possible approach shot. This strategy isn't always the best idea, however, because you may frequently find yourself in between clubs when you hit to the green.

A better way to approach a par 5 is to let the club you'd like to hit on your third shot dictate your strategy for your second shot. For example, if you hit your drive 225 yards on a 475 yard par 5 and then try to blister a 3-wood 210 yards to get as close as possible to the green, you leave yourself with a 40-yard approach shot. That can be a difficult shot to execute if you haven't practiced from that distance. A full shot is always easier to execute than a half- or three-quarter "feel" shot. If you know you hit your sand wedge 80 yards and your pitching wedge 100 yards, hit a second shot that will leave you with one of those distances to the green.

Strategizing your yardages this way will not only make you a smarter player, but will take the guesswork out of how to tweak and finesse your swing to make the ball travel the appropriate yardage—leading to shorter putts and more birdie opportunities.

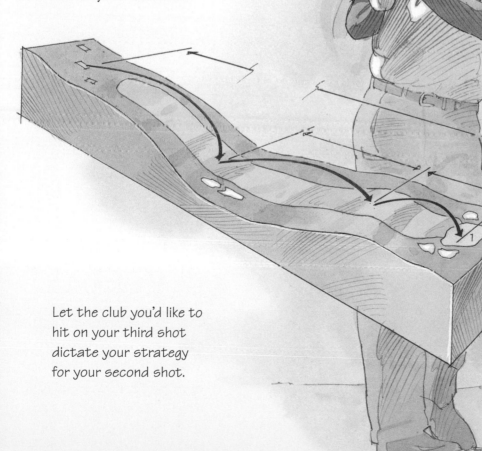

Let the club you'd like to hit on your third shot dictate your strategy for your second shot.

MATCH PLAY MECHANICS

Grasping the subtleties of head-to-head play can mean the difference between victory and defeat. Here are three simple keys to exploiting an opponent's weaknesses.

1. WATCH AND LEARN

Watch everything your opponent does. For example, if you're torn between hitting a driver or a long iron on a tight driving hole and he blasts his tee shot out of bounds, he's made the decision for you: Grab the iron.

Look for subtle signs of indecision or excessive emotion. If your opponent's routine changes—he gets fidgety or takes extra practice swings—he may be feeling the heat. Sharpen your focus: One or two good shots from you could make him self-destruct.

If your opponent gets into trouble, play it safe.

2. STAY IN PLAY

Don't strive for spectacular shots in head-to-head competition. You can put pressure on an opponent by keeping every shot in play. When you stay out of trouble, he'll start to press to hit better shots.

Even when he does hit a better shot than you do, try to make it your advantage. For instance, if he out-drives you, you still can hit the green first and put the heat right back on him. Maintain this pressure and you'll wear him down.

You can regain momentum with one stellar shot.

Step up the pressure on your opponent by keeping the ball in play.

3. NEVER SAY DIE

Match play is all about momentum, which will shift several times during a match. So never give up. If your opponent hits the green on a par 3 and you're in a bunker, the momentum is clearly his. But if you stick your sand shot close, the pressure shifts to him. If he three-putts and you win the hole, the momentum is all yours.

Don't give up even if you're four down with four to go. Win the next two and the momentum is yours. There's a good chance he'll react defensively and blow the match.

HOW TO PLAY FOUR-SOMES

Every other year, courses throughout the United States host Ryder Cup–style team competitions in the weeks preceding the real event. But few American golfers ever play the alternate-shot format called *foursomes*. If you're looking for something new for your weekend group, try foursomes.

HOW IT WORKS

Two teams of two golfers play one ball per team. Player A drives and then his partner, Player B, hits the second shot. Player A hits the third, and they continue alternating until the ball is holed. On the next tee, they trade places: Player B drives, Player A hits second and so on.

HELP YOUR PARTNER

Your foursomes partner can only play as well as you let him, and vice versa. If you're driving the ball into the rough all day, he will probably struggle hitting into the greens. A conservative approach to shot selection often works best: Try to hit fairways rather than swinging for huge drives, and play to the fat parts of the greens, steering clear of tucked pins.

A conservative approach often works best.

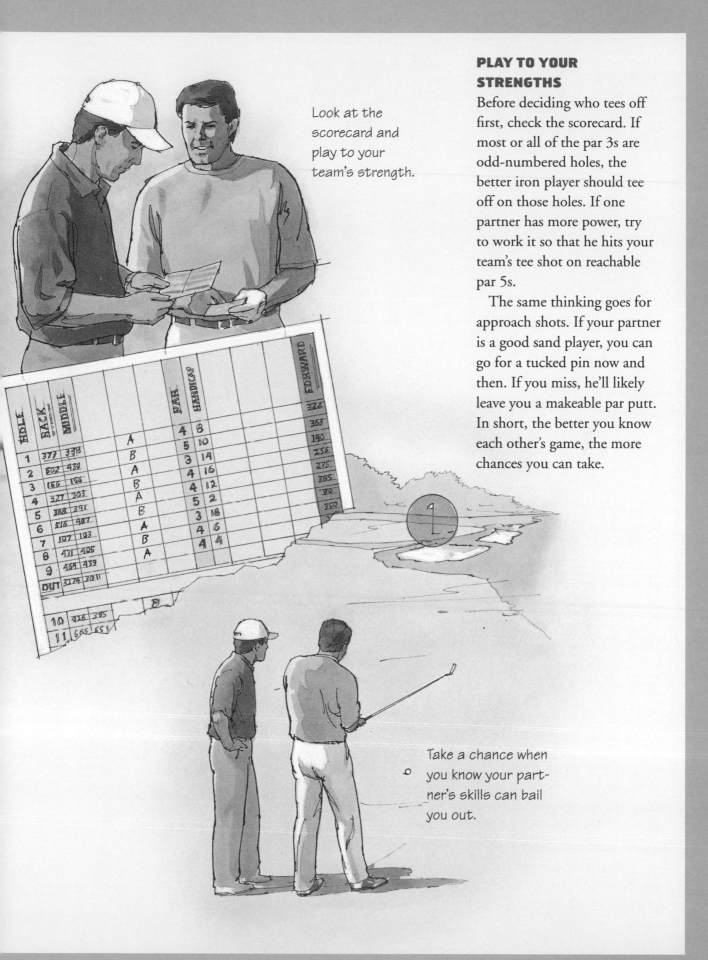

Look at the scorecard and play to your team's strength.

HOLE	BACK	MIDDLE			PAR	HANDICAP				FORWARD
			A		4	8				322
			B		5	10				363
1	373	338	A		3	14				140
2	502	439	B		4	16				256
3	166	156	B		4	12				275
4	327	303	A		5	2				385
5	368	341	B		3	18				90
6	516	487	A		4	6				350
7	107	103	B		4	4				
8	431	405	A							
9	464	439								
DUT	3274	3011								
			B							
10	416	395								
11	565	553								

PLAY TO YOUR STRENGTHS

Before deciding who tees off first, check the scorecard. If most or all of the par 3s are odd-numbered holes, the better iron player should tee off on those holes. If one partner has more power, try to work it so that he hits your team's tee shot on reachable par 5s.

The same thinking goes for approach shots. If your partner is a good sand player, you can go for a tucked pin now and then. If you miss, he'll likely leave you a makeable par putt. In short, the better you know each other's game, the more chances you can take.

Take a chance when you know your partner's skills can bail you out.

HOW TO SALVAGE A BAD ROUND

Bad days on the course are a part of life for every golfer. Every player in the world is prone to struggle off the tee, from the fairway, and on the green on any given day. If you feel yourself sinking into a slump, here's our advice to reverse your momentum and reclaim your game.

DRIVER DIFFICULTIES: PLAY A HARD FADE

A hard fade is a great go-to shot because it allows you to swing aggressively and still keep the ball in play. To execute a hard fade, aim down the left side of the fairway, make a full turn, and hit the ball hard with your right side. Be sure to hold on past impact with the last three fingers of your left hand, as this will keep the clubface slightly open, thereby producing the fade.

INCONSISTENT IRONS: TAKE MORE CLUB WITH LESS SWING

When your irons let you down, your first priority should be to regain the feeling

Hold on past impact with the left hand to keep the club face slightly open.

To execute a hard fade...

...aim down the left side of the fairway.

of solid contact. The best way to do this is to take an extra club and make a three-quarter swing. By swinging more easily, you'll allow your muscles to relax a little and help relieve the tenseness that comes with hitting a series of bad shots. Three-quarter swings also allow you more control over the clubhead and the ball, which should bring the smooth, powerful strikes of your good days back in no time.

Take an extra club and make an easy three-quarter swing.

PATHETIC PUTTS: BOUNCE IT OFF THE BACK

While bad putting and its solutions take many forms, an off day on the greens is usually most apparent from 10 feet and in. If you can't seem to get it in the hole, change your approach. Instead of trying to finesse the ball into the cup, sometimes it helps to simply ram the ball into the back of the hole. This technique will not only take your mind off the mechanics of your stroke, but will also eliminate the break in many putts and help you regain the most important thing of all: your confidence.

Ram the ball into the back of the hole.

FAULTS AND FIXES

All players have a nemesis shot that they desperately want to improve. Maybe longs putts are your Achilles' heel, or you just can't seem to make crisp contact on your iron shots. With so many facets to the game, it seems like there is always something that could use a little polishing.

To that end, here are the fixes for several of golf's most common faults.

SPEED DETERMINES BREAK

How much a putt breaks is not only determined by undulations in the green, but also by how hard you hit the ball. The faster the ball rolls, the less it's affected by the slope. Slower rolling putts, on the other hand, break more. This is an important reason to be diligent about gauging speed, especially on longer putts.

Another reason to make speed your primary concern is more obvious: If you misread a putt's line but get the speed right, you'll still finish close to the hole. On the other hand, a combination of good line and bad speed will almost always leave you with a testy second putt—and a higher risk of three-putting.

To better gauge speed, trace the putt's expected path with your eyes as you take your practice strokes. The strong visual impression created while looking down the line will provide a sensory guide for how hard to stroke the putt.

Take a few practice strokes with your eyes looking down the line, imagining the path the ball should take.

When you practice, go through your complete pre-shot routine.

When playing alone, drop a few extra balls and experiment with a variety of shots.

START MAKING PRACTICE MORE MEANINGFUL

Good shots are easier to hit on the range than on the course. Hitting at the same target time after time helps you develop a good rhythm, there is less tension in your body and the lie is always perfect. But to make your work on the practice tee translate into lower scores on the course, follow this advice.

ON THE RANGE

Mix elements of actual play into your practice sessions. Every few swings, go through your complete pre-shot routine: Stand behind the ball, identify your target, visualize the shot and align the clubface and your body. When your routine becomes second nature, it will help you focus and relax on the course.

Next, vary your club selection. Hitting dozens of 7-irons in a row is not as useful as hitting a few balls each with the driver, 3-wood, 5-iron, 7-iron, pitching wedge and then alternating through the bag.

ON THE COURSE

If possible, play a few nine-hole rounds by yourself. Don't worry about your score; in fact, don't even putt out or keep score.

Playing alone takes the pressure off and helps increase your percentage of good shots. If the course isn't crowded, drop extra balls and experiment with shots you would not ordinarily hit. This variety will breed confidence the next time you tee it up.

DRILL: THE ONE-MAN SCRAMBLE Hit three drives off the tee, then pick the best. Hit three approach shots from the best possible lie, pick the best result then hit three shots from that spot, and so on until all the balls are in the hole. Move on to the next hole and repeat.

Having three chances at each shot and hitting from ideal lies helps develop good rhythm. In this exercise, keeping score is important: Try to go low as you play these best-case scenarios. You'll feel more comfortable the next time you're on the verge of breaking a scoring barrier.

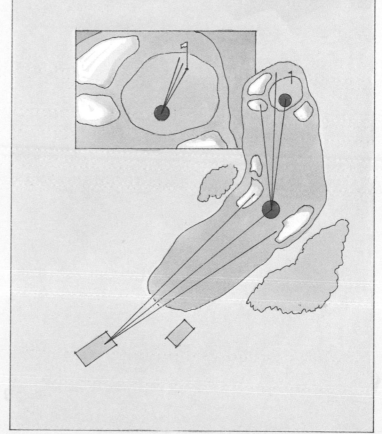

Estimate how fast the ball should roll over an intermediate target.

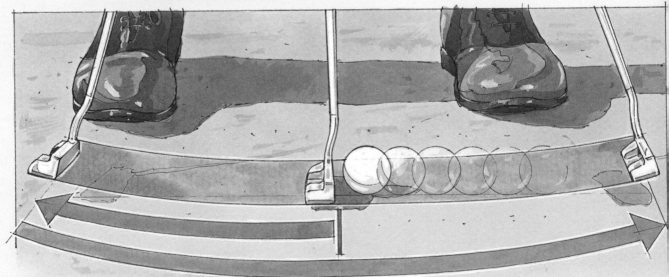

Keep a consistent rhythm throughout your stroke.

SHAKE THOSE THREE-PUTTS

"Don't three-putt." That's what you may tell yourself when faced with a putt from 30 feet or more. Problem is, that's the last thought you want running through your head. Worrying about three-putting can add tension and bring on a tentative stroke. To roll long putts close to the hole, you need to have freedom—in your mind, body and stroke.

READ THE SPEED

Distance is more important than direction on long putts, so don't worry about the precise break. Read the putt, then pick an intermediate target—a spot about 10 feet in front of the ball—and decide how fast the ball should roll over that spot in order to die at the hole. Make practice strokes while imagining the ball moving too quickly, then too slowly. Choose a speed in between, then roll the ball over your spot at that pace.

STAY IN RHYTHM

Don't get too mechanical. Good long putting calls for consistent rhythm. Once you have settled on an appropriate speed, take a deep breath and focus on making a relaxed stroke. Feel the putterhead's weight as you move it away from the ball, then swing it forward and through the ball at the same pace as the backstroke. Smooth rhythm can make up for some minor shortcomings in technique.

DRILL: GET SOME SHUTEYE On the practice green, sharpen your feel for pace by closing your eyes just before starting your stroke. With no visual distractions, you'll have a stronger sense of the stroke's rhythm. Practice with your eyes shut until you are stroking the ball with the same pace back and through.

DRAIN MORE THREE-FOOT PUTTS

Three-foot putts should be easy—that's what can make them so maddeningly hard.

Knowing you should make a putt creates an extra layer of pressure.

The best way to conquer those "must-make" nerves is by focusing on a physical key instead of the consequences of missing. Here are four good ones.

1. STAY STILL

If your head doesn't move, neither will your body. With your body steady and your arms in control of the stroke, you have fewer moving parts to synchronize. That makes it easier to keep the putterface square through impact.

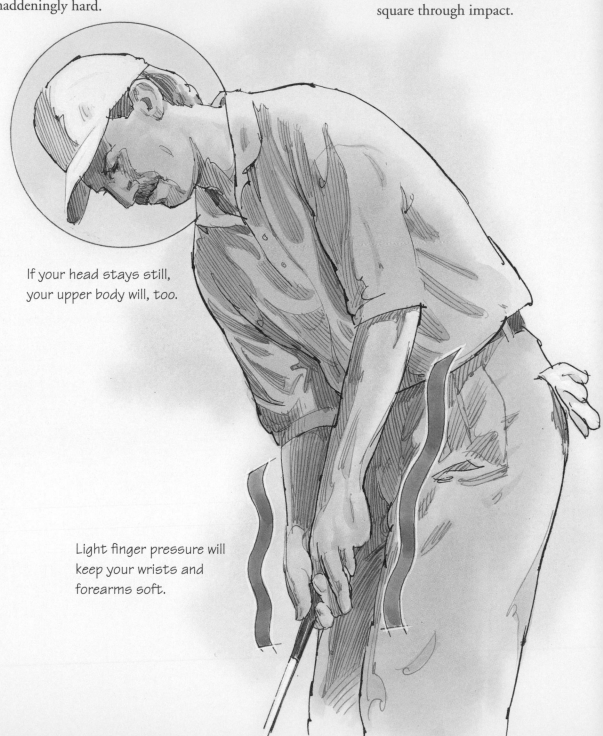

If your head stays still, your upper body will, too.

Light finger pressure will keep your wrists and forearms soft.

2. GRIP LIGHTLY

A tight squeeze creates tension, which can inhibit rhythm. Light finger pressure and soft wrists and forearms throughout your motion will increase your chances of hitting your putts where you aim them.

3. STROKE THROUGH

Focusing on making a straight-back, straight-through stroke can make you less result-oriented. Take the putter straight back, then reverse direction and retrace that path. If the face is square, the putt will drop.

4. GET IT THERE

A tentative stroke is no way to approach knee knockers. So send the ball firmly to the back rim of the cup on these short putts. You'll see that an aggressive stroke is easier to make and helps you keep the ball on line.

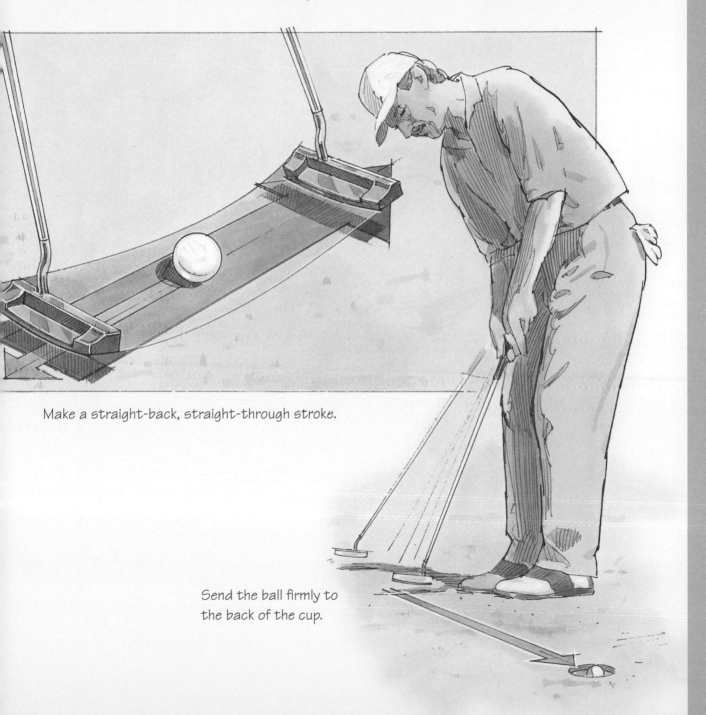

Make a straight-back, straight-through stroke.

Send the ball firmly to the back of the cup.

For pitches, consider at least two ways
to play the shot, accounting for the wind,
obstacles, and ease of execution.

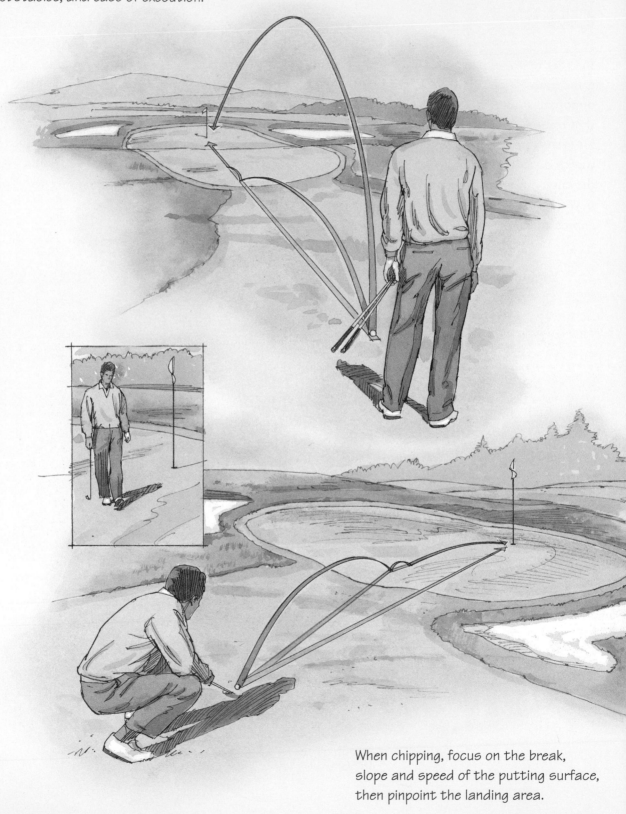

When chipping, focus on the break,
slope and speed of the putting surface,
then pinpoint the landing area.

STRENGTHEN YOUR SHORT GAME

In order to fine-tune your game from 50 yards and in, it's important to establish a pre-shot routine that you can follow for every chip or pitch. One way to do this is to go through the same motions for a pitch as you would for a drive or an approach, and for a chip as you would for a putt.

For pitches, try to consider at least two ways to play the shot. In most cases, you can play a high, soft shot or a low, running ball. Factors to consider include the wind, obstacles in front of the green and which of the two shots will be the least difficult for you to perform.

Chip shots should be treated like putts. Focus on the break, slope and speed of the putting surface. You have to pinpoint where you'd like the ball to land and how much it will run out, depending on what kind of chip you elect to hit.

The most important thing to focus on during your pre-shot routine for both shots is getting the ball started on the target line. Sticking to your routine until it becomes second nature will allow you to do this, and you'll soon notice a big difference in the quality of your shots.

Use the same pre-shot routine on both pitches and chips, and focus on getting the ball started on the target line.

FAT-FREE CHIPS

Set up with the ball back and your weight over your front foot.

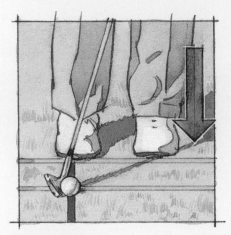

Sometimes a thinly struck chip works out okay because it can roll all the way to the hole. But hit it a little fat and the ball will dribble only a few feet.

To trim the fat, think about hitting the ball before the ground. The setup is the key: Place the ball back in your stance, opposite the rear foot, with most of your weight over your front foot. This promotes a steep, downward blow, reducing the likelihood of the clubhead bottoming out early. Swing back and through with your shoulders, keeping your weight forward and your hands ahead of the clubhead.

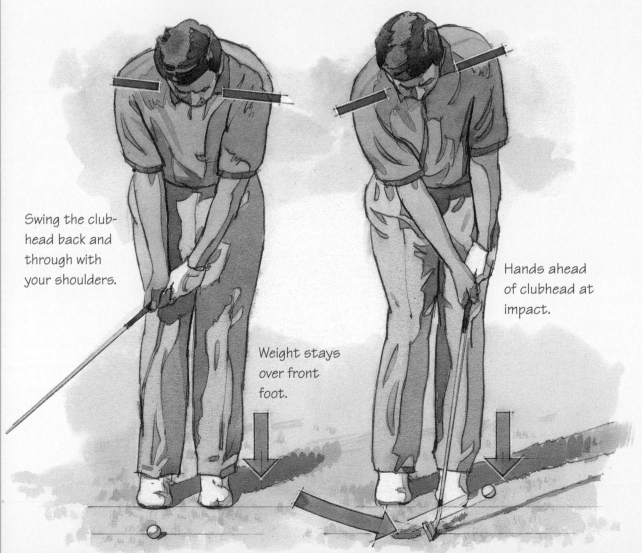

Swing the clubhead back and through with your shoulders.

Weight stays over front foot.

Hands ahead of clubhead at impact.

Feet shoulder-width apart.

Drive your knees forward and finish the swing.

Square your stance and clubface to the target.

1

THE LONG BUNKER SHOT

Do you get a sinking feeling in your stomach when you're facing a long bunker shot? Fear not: With a few adjustments, the 30- to 50-yard shot from the sand can be easy to hit.

Instead of opening your stance and clubface and making a steep swing, use a flatter motion. Align your feet and the clubface square to your target and stand as you would for a full iron shot—with your heels shoulder-width apart and the ball just ahead of center. Make a long, slow backswing, then drive your knees toward the target, taking a shallow sliver of sand and swinging to a full finish. By taking less sand and hitting with a square face, you will get the ball to the hole.

SHATTER SHORT-GAME MYTHS

Many golfers struggle around the greens because they believe two popular, but incorrect, myths: "Keep your body still" and "chip like you putt." Here's how to erase them from your game.

PITCHING: LET YOURSELF GO

Holding your body stock-still while pitching will turn your swing into a stiff, robotic motion, destroying feel and making it hard to achieve solid contact. Any shot longer than a putt needs some body movement to support the club's motion. Don't purposely move your body, but let it react to the momentum of your swing. You'll have better rhythm and make more consistent contact.

When pitching, let your body react to your swing's momentum.

Putting stance

Chipping stance

CHIPPING: DESIGN DICTATES TECHNIQUE

Putters are designed for a stance that sets the eyes directly over the ball and promotes a pendulum-like swing arc. Your chipping clubs are not. So trying to "chip like you putt" demands using an unnatural motion that fights the design of your equipment.

When chipping, stand tall with an open stance. The butt end of the club will be about a hand's width from your body, and your eyes will be well inside the ball. Swing the clubhead on a semi-circle arc from the inside, out to the ball and back to the inside. You'll swing with less tension and develop better touch.

Club swings on a semicircle arc: inside-to-square-to-inside.

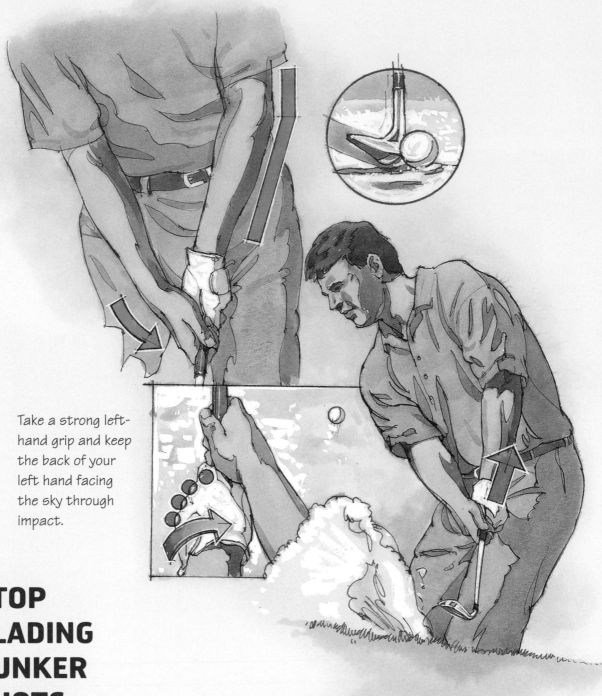

Take a strong left-hand grip and keep the back of your left hand facing the sky through impact.

STOP BLADING BUNKER SHOTS

The bladed bunker shot is often the result of trying to lift the ball out, which causes your right hand to flip and your left arm to bend. When this happens, there isn't enough arm extension to slide the clubface under the ball, so you catch it thin.

Try this: Set up normally—clubface and stance open, ball forward—then dig your feet in just below the level of the ball. Rotate your left hand clockwise on the grip so you can see four knuckles. This strong grip makes your left arm less likely to break down. Finally, focus on keeping the back of your left hand facing the sky through impact.

TEMPO TOUCH-UP

If your ballstriking has suddenly soured but you feel that your fundamentals are sound, your tempo may be the problem. Swing tempo is personal—some people have success swinging quickly, while others prefer a smooth, deliberate motion. Regardless of your personal preference, if your natural tempo gets off-kilter, you're going to have problems in every area of your game. Here's our advice for restoring your natural rhythm:

Take a few practice swings. Practice swings generally feel effortless, controlled and well-balanced because you aren't worried about hitting the ball and where it might end up. The key is to maintain this feeling of confidence on every shot. One way to practice this is to hit plastic practice balls. Because they are so light, impact is barely discernible and you can focus on swinging the club instead of hitting the ball.

Another way to improve your tempo through the impact zone is to practice with half swings. Use a long iron or hybrid, and you'll find that to get any distance out of the shot, you have to swing all the way through the ball, not at it. After practicing this way for a while, try to hit full shots again, and you will have a much more powerful and well-balanced feeling through impact.

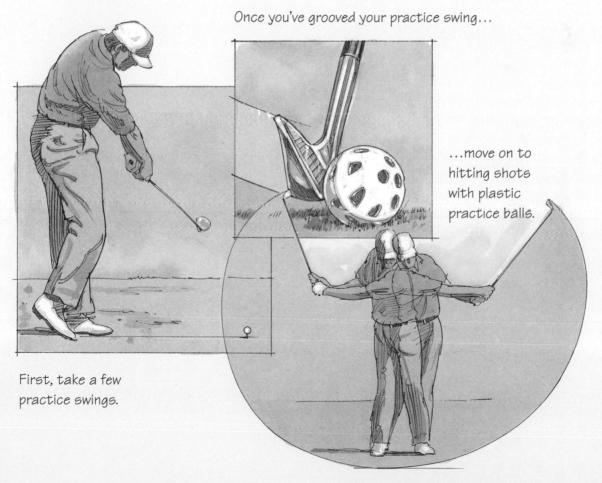

Once you've grooved your practice swing…

…move on to hitting shots with plastic practice balls.

First, take a few practice swings.

Finally, practice hitting real balls with a half-swing.

CALLUS ANALYSIS

The key to diagnosing your swing problems is often literally etched right into your hands. Calluses are helpful indicators of the places where your palm and fingers absorb pressure during your swing. Because the left hand is the foundation of a standard grip, most right-handed players develop calluses there, whether they wear gloves or not. You know you are gripping the club correctly if you have calluses where the base of your pinky, ring and middle fingers meet your palm. If you have calluses on the base of your left forefinger or on the pad of your left thumb, you are probably suffering from a slice or reduced distance because you are exerting too much force on those fingers by gripping the club too tightly.

Your right hand should be

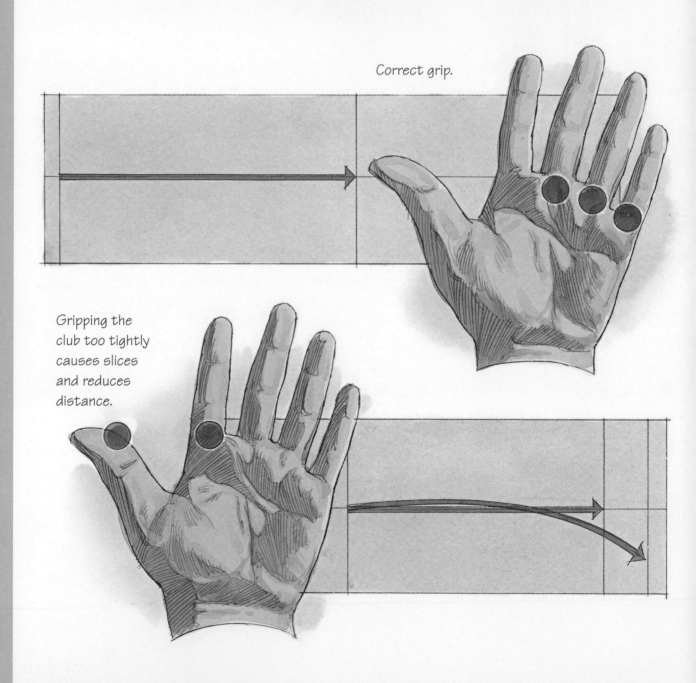

Correct grip.

Gripping the club too tightly causes slices and reduces distance.

less callused than your left, as only the insides of your ring and middle fingers touch both the club and each other. It's also possible to develop a callus on the outside of your right ring finger where it touches the forefinger of your left hand. If you notice calluses on your right forefinger or thumb, you are likely suffering from frequent slices or pulls, because putting pressure on these fingers causes the shoulders to stiffen, creating an undesirable inside-out path and ball flight.

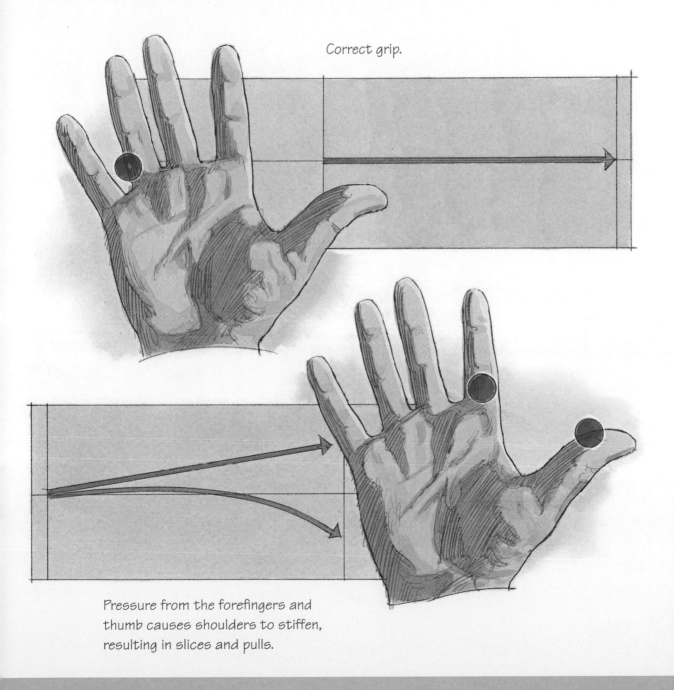

Correct grip.

Pressure from the forefingers and thumb causes shoulders to stiffen, resulting in slices and pulls.

PLAYING FAIRWAY WOODS FROM THE ROUGH

For many players, it can be difficult reaching long holes in regulation, especially when you hit a wayward drive into the rough. While some players are strong enough to pound long irons out of the rough up to 200 yards away, many need to get comfortable hitting a well-lofted fairway wood or hybrid from the rough. The goal for any shot out of the rough is to minimize the effect of the grass by making clean contact with the ball and swinging on a steep,

To make clean contact, you must swing on a steep, descending path.

Play the ball in the middle of your stance and open the club face slightly.

Aim your feet left of the target.

descending path. Play the ball in the middle of your stance (opposite your chin) and aim your feet a few yards left of the target. Open the clubface slightly and swing along a line parallel to your feet (on an outside-in path) across the ball. This swing will produce a steeper path and a cut shot, which has a higher trajectory and a little more spin, so the ball will not only get out of the rough but also stop more easily on the green.

This swing will produce a high-trajectory cut shot that will stop on the green.

Swing along a line parallel to your feet on an outside-in path across the ball.

TRANSFORM A SLICE INTO A DRAW

If you want to lose that slice and groove a draw, set yourself up at the far left end of the practice range, align your feet parallel to the netting or trees that define the perimeter and swing away. With no room to the left, you'll be forced to start the ball right of your target—the first step toward eliminating that out-to-in slice swing.

Old habits die hard, so expect to hit the first few shots into the net. This feedback will force you to change your swing path. Set a modest goal for yourself of getting each shot to land somewhere right of the range's left boundary. Don't worry if the ball finishes right of the target. As long as it starts right, you're swinging on an in-to-out path, which is the foundation of a draw.

Focus on an in-to-out swing path to start the ball right of your target. Then work on curving it back to the left with draw spin.

Feet parallel to the left border of the range

Once you have every shot starting to the right, it's time to curve it back to the left with draw spin. To create this right-to-left spin, the clubface must be slightly closed at impact relative to your swing path. If most of your shots fly straight right or they start right then curve right, the clubface is either square relative to the path or open.

Visualize getting your club's toe to pass the heel before the moment of impact. Using a stronger grip can make it easier to do this and rotate the clubface closed. If you're still unable to turn the ball back to the left, imagine hitting the ball with the toe of the club instead of the face. This will help you create more forearm rotation during the swing, helping you generate right-to-left spin.

Toe passes heel.

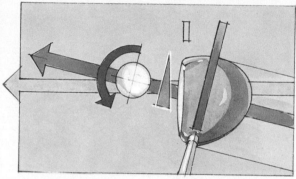

To create draw spin, the clubface must be slightly closed relative to your swing path at impact.

Seeing three knuckles on your left hand indicates a strong grip, which will make closing the clubface easier.

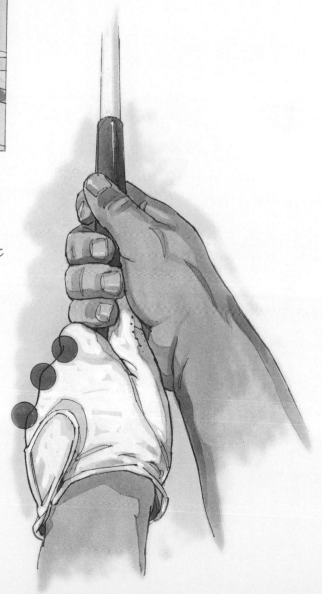

CURE YOUR PUSH

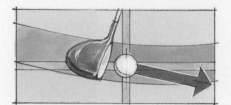

In a push, the club swings on an in-to-out path and is square to that path.

Missing wide right does not necessarily make you a slicer. If the ball starts right and stays right (for righties), you've hit a push. Believe it or not, this shot is closer to a hook than it is to a slice. A push happens when the clubhead swings on an in-to-out path and the clubface is square to that path. In moderation, an in-to-out path works: If you can

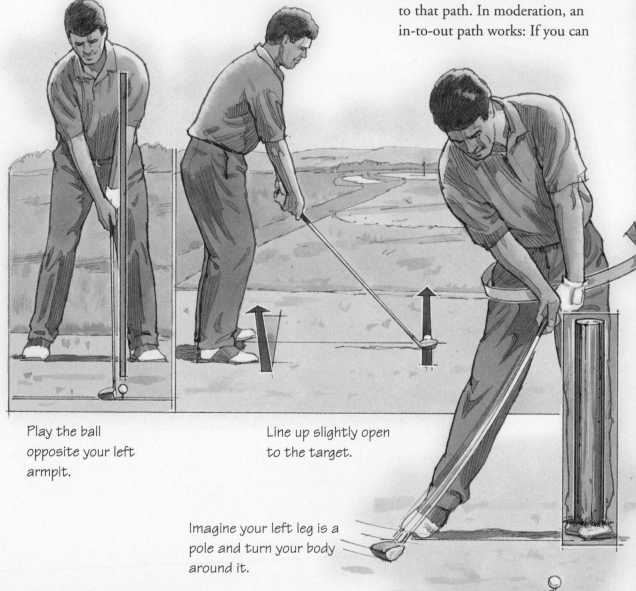

Play the ball opposite your left armpit.

Line up slightly open to the target.

Imagine your left leg is a pole and turn your body around it.

square the clubface to the target at impact, you'll hit a draw. So the key to turning pushes into good shots is squaring the face.

MOVE THE BALL UP

Playing the ball too far back in your stance makes it hard to square the clubface at impact. Setup with the ball opposite your front armpit when hitting your driver and no farther back than three inches inside your left heel, even with your shortest clubs.

DON'T BE WIDE RIGHT

Most golfers align their bodies right of the target; if a pusher does that, he'll have trouble squaring the face at impact. Check your alignment: Work toward setting up parallel to your target line, but try a slightly open stance for a while to help you break out of lining up closed.

TURN, DON'T SLIDE

Sliding your hips toward your target on your downswing can move your body ahead of the ball. Instead, imagine that your left leg is a pole in the ground and turn your body around it. This move will keep you from sliding forward, letting your arms release and square the clubface.

DRILL: SPLIT-HAND GRIP: Grip a 7-iron, leaving a three-inch gap between your hands. Swing your hands back to hip height and check that the club's toe points up, then swing through to hip height and do the same. The split grip trains your arms to rotate through the hitting area, which will get the ball to turn to the right. Feel the forearm rotation this drill promotes, then re-create it with your regular grip.

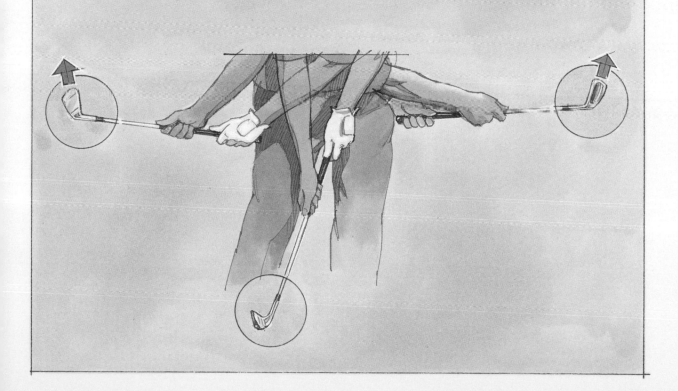

Align your body on the line you want the ball to start on; aim your clubface at the target.

Aiming away from your target to compensate for a hook or slice can make their effect worse.

Outside-in swing path.

Clubface aimed at target.

NEUTRALIZE A HOOK OR SLICE

Swing follows inside-out path.

If you compensate for your hook or slice by aiming even farther to the left or right, you're actually exacerbating your problem. While it's natural to "play" your tendencies by aiming slightly left or right, it's really only useful for a draw or fade of five to 10 yards, not a severe hook or slice. Aiming away from your target to compensate for severe curveballs will simply create a bigger curve.

The next time you find yourself aiming into the hazard on the left in an attempt to get your slice in the fairway,

align yourself in the opposite direction—toward the right— and close your stance slightly. This will encourage your swing to follow an inside-out path, as opposed to outside-in. The same idea applies to a severe hook. Aim your body slightly left of the target— instead of out to the right— by opening your stance. This

body position will allow you to make an outside-in swing and should help to straighten out your ball flight. But whether you're trying to neutralize a hook or a slice, make sure that your body alignment is the only thing you alter. Keep the clubface square to the target, not open or closed like your stance.

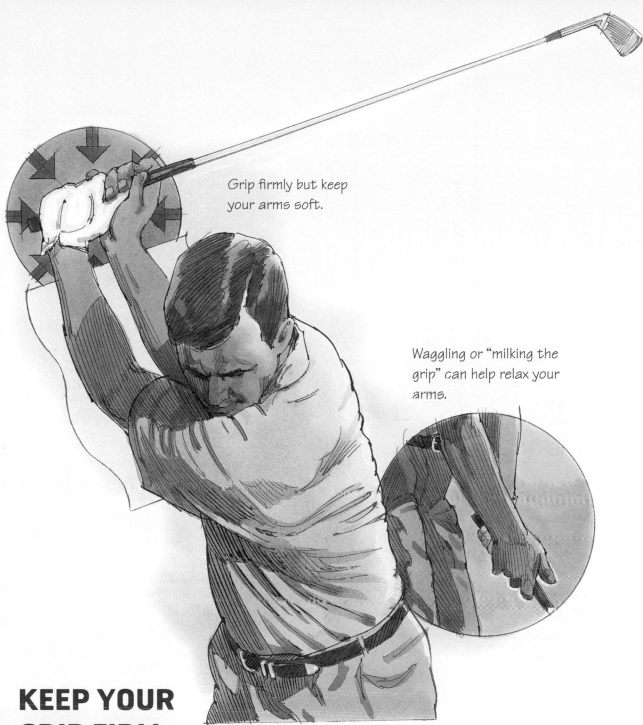

Grip firmly but keep your arms soft.

Waggling or "milking the grip" can help relax your arms.

KEEP YOUR GRIP FIRM AND ARMS SOFT

Arm tension can ruin any swing, but if you get too relaxed, your swing can break down. Moderate pressure in your fingers solidifies your connection to the club and keeps it from slipping at the top. The secret is gripping firmly while keeping your arms soft.

Take a secure grip at address, but relax your arms. For many golfers this is an acquired feel. Waggling the club can help; so too can gripping and re-gripping a club with your fingers, called "milking the grip."

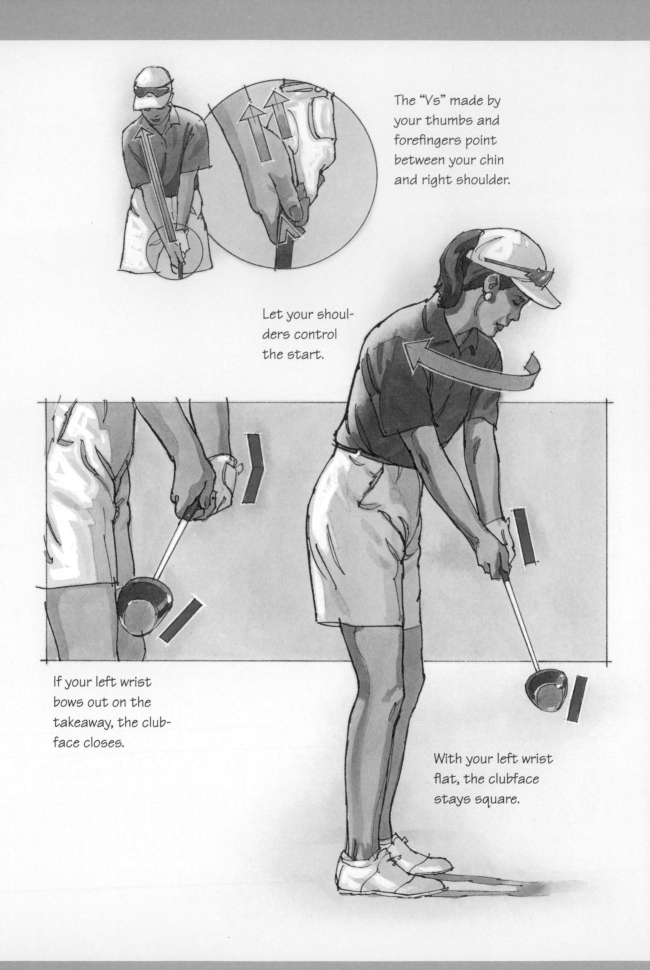

The "Vs" made by your thumbs and forefingers point between your chin and right shoulder.

Let your shoulders control the start.

If your left wrist bows out on the takeaway, the clubface closes.

With your left wrist flat, the clubface stays square.

STOP THE SMOTHER

The smothered shot is as frustrating as it is ugly. Though it behaves like a topped shot, the smother is caused by an extremely closed clubface at impact. Diagnosis: Your grip is too strong or your left wrist is bowed.

WEAKEN YOUR GRIP

Gripping the club with your hands too far to the right can lead to a closed face at impact. Make sure your grip is neutral. Set the clubface square and then grip the handle in your fingers. When you close your hands on the grip, the "Vs" formed by your thumbs and forefingers should point between your chin and right shoulder.

USE YOUR SHOULDERS

Even with a good grip, the clubface will close if your left wrist bows out during your swing. This is most common in the takeaway: Instead of staying flat while the club swings back, your left wrist bows out as your right hand snatches the club to the inside. Here's the fix: Let your shoulder turn control the start of your swing. With your hands quiet, the face will stay square going back, setting up square impact.

DRILL: THUMB IT Start with a neutral grip. Swing to the top and stop. Your left thumb should be directly under the grip, pointing toward the target. Hit a bucket of balls with "thumb down" as your swing thought and you'll square the face more often.

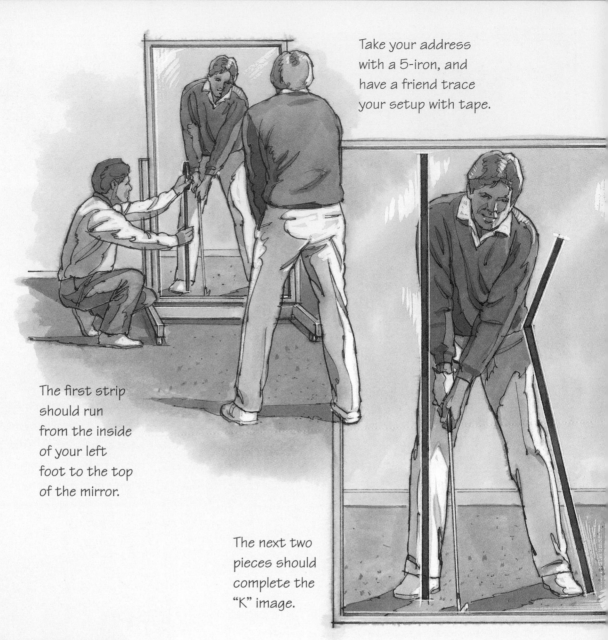

Take your address with a 5-iron, and have a friend trace your setup with tape.

The first strip should run from the inside of your left foot to the top of the mirror.

The next two pieces should complete the "K" image.

MAKE USE OF A MIRROR

Checking your fundamentals in a full-length mirror is a great way to breed good habits. The following drills work for three crucial areas.

SETUP: THE LETTER "K"

Because your right hand is lower than the left on the grip, your body should naturally appear in a "K" position in the mirror. To check this, face the mirror and take your address with a 5-iron. Have a friend stick a piece of tape on the mirror running vertically from the inside of your left foot to the top of the mirror. Your left hip, arm and shoulder should all run along this vertical line.

Add two more pieces of tape: one running from outside your right foot to your right hip, the other from your right hip to the outside of your right shoulder. These form an angle—the front of the "K". Step away from the mirror and take a good look, then step back in and use the tape to guide you into the proper setup.

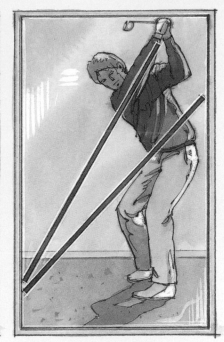

BACKSWING: ON PLANE

Take your stance with a driver so the mirror is to your right. Have your friend stick a long piece of tape on the mirror that runs up the shaft and through your body. Run a second piece from the clubhead over the tops of your shoulders. The lower piece is a guide for the takeaway; the clubhead should trace this line until about hip height. The higher piece represents the proper plane for the top of the swing. Ideal positioning would have your left arm running along it at the top.

DRILL: STEADY HEAD Set up with a 5-iron; your head should be behind an imaginary line running up from the ball. Have your friend face you, holding a driver and extending it so the grip is a fraction of an inch from your left ear. Make slow, easy swings: If your head hits the grip before impact, your body is shifting too soon.

NO SHANKS

If there's anything worse than hitting a shank (a ball hit off the club's hosel that darts off sideways), it's knowing that they tend to come in bunches. They're usually caused by an extreme in-to-out path that forces the clubhead outside the target line. But even if you know that, the shanks can be hard to stop.

Try this drill: Using an iron instead of your driver, put two balls side-by-side about four inches apart, and address the outside ball. Make a normal backswing, then hit the inside ball. To do it, you'll pull the club toward your body, which eliminates the in-to-out path and hosel contact. After 10 practice shots this way, go back to hitting drivers. Your shanks will be memories.

Put balls side-by-side and address the outside ball...

...then hit the inside ball to avoid the extreme in-to-out path—and the shank.

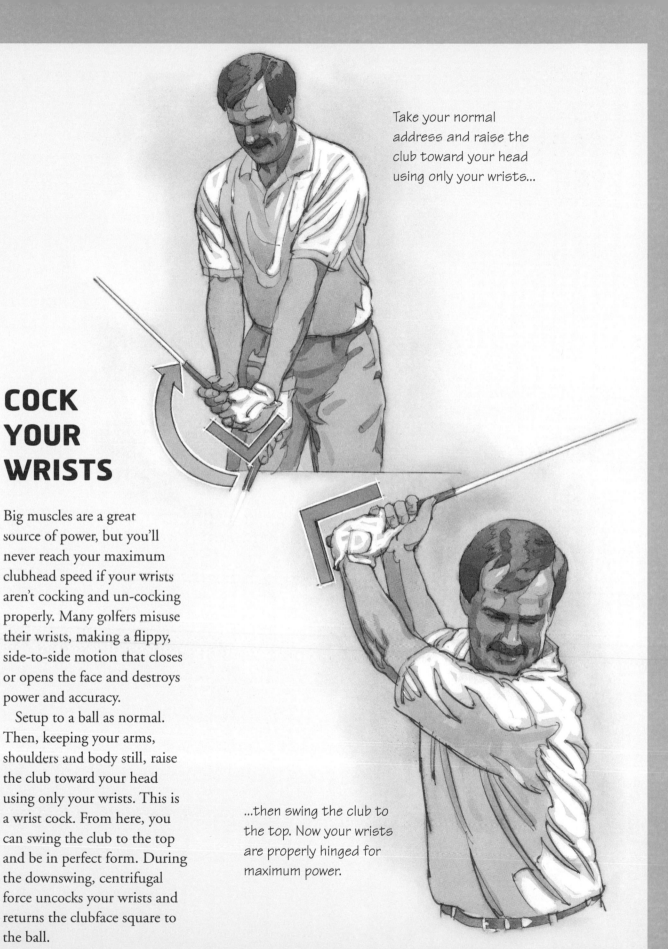

Take your normal address and raise the club toward your head using only your wrists...

COCK YOUR WRISTS

Big muscles are a great source of power, but you'll never reach your maximum clubhead speed if your wrists aren't cocking and un-cocking properly. Many golfers misuse their wrists, making a flippy, side-to-side motion that closes or opens the face and destroys power and accuracy.

Setup to a ball as normal. Then, keeping your arms, shoulders and body still, raise the club toward your head using only your wrists. This is a wrist cock. From here, you can swing the club to the top and be in perfect form. During the downswing, centrifugal force uncocks your wrists and returns the clubface square to the ball.

...then swing the club to the top. Now your wrists are properly hinged for maximum power.

TWO MORE WAYS TO TRIM THE FAT

Next to the shank, the fat shot is the most penal mis-hit. Here's how to avoid hitting the ball heavy.

1. STAY TALL

To make solid contact, you must maintain your forward tilt from address through impact. Dipping your upper body toward the ball as you swing down can cause fat shots. To make sure you stand tall, practice swinging from your address position through the hitting area without a club, keeping your forehead pressed against a wall or doorway. If your head stays in place, you'll learn to stay in your forward tilt.

Dipping your upper body on the down-swing can lead to fat contact.

To learn good posture, mimic swings with your forehead against a wall.

Stop a reverse pivot by starting your hands, arms and club together.

Reverse pivot.

2. KEEP IT TOGETHER

Another cause of the fats is the reverse weight shift. Instead of shifting toward the target coming down, you fall away from it, which moves your swing's low point behind the ball. Result: You hit the ground first.

Here's the cure: Start your backswing moving your hands, arms and clubhead together. This will transfer your weight to the inside of your back foot as you coil to the top. With your weight behind the ball, you'll shift toward the target on the downswing.

DRILL: MISS THE HEADCOVER Stick a tee in the ground and place a headcover about 12 inches behind it. Make practice swings with your 5-iron, trying to clip the tee without touching the headcover. You can only do it if you transfer your weight to your front foot.

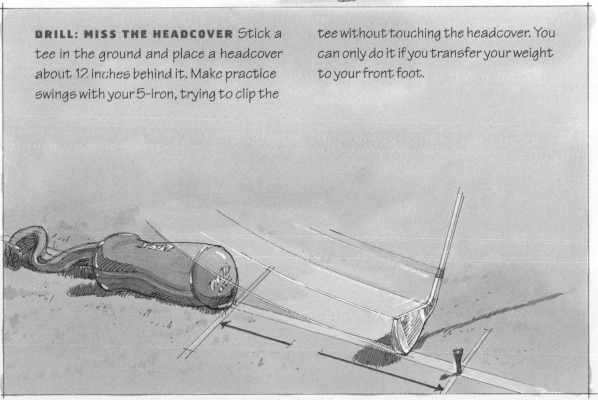

HIT ONE–HANDED TO STRIKE THE BALL BETTER

Forget about swing mechanics for a moment. Consistently flush contact comes when your hands find the ball by instinct, without any how-to clutter. That's why hitting shots one-handed improves your ball-striking; it trains each hand to feel its way back to the ball individually, so that when they come together, they're doubly effective.

WORK THE RIGHT

After a little warm-up, hitting with your right hand will prove fairly easy for right-handed golfers. Tee a ball about a half-inch above the ground, choke down a few inches on your 5-iron and be sure your palm is facing the target. This is where your hand should be in a regular grip. The key to solid contact is controlling your right elbow, which tends to fly away from your body on the backswing. Focus on keeping it tucked against your side as you make half-swings. As your contact improves, gradually lengthen your swing until you're hitting full shots.

Grip down.

For solid contact, focus on keeping your right elbow tucked against your side.

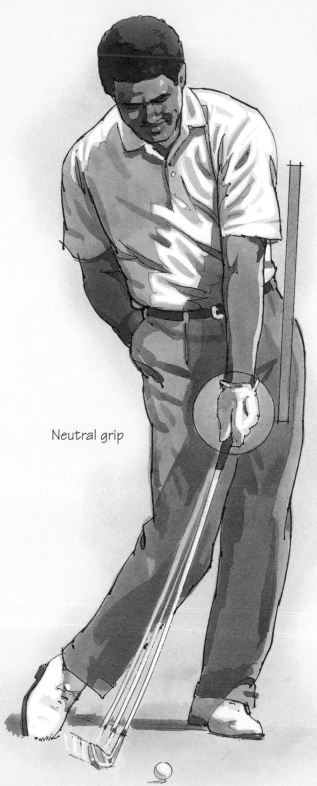

TRAIN THE LEFT

Isolating your left hand will be awkward for most golfers, but it's a great way to learn to hit with a solid left side. Your left wrist and arm should be straight, not bent, at impact. Plus, there's the added benefit of grip analysis: Because your left hand is not strong enough to manipulate the club during the swing, you'll be able to make contact with a square face only if your left hand is in the correct neutral position at address. Start with short pitch shots until you get a feel for the motion, then move on to longer swings.

Your left wrist and arm should be straight at impact.

Neutral grip

Failure of the right arm to rotate over the left through impact results in contact with an open clubface and a blocked shot.

Open clubface

BAN THE BLOCK

Many players try to steer the club down the target line. Often this leads to failing to let the clubhead release so contact is made with an open clubface. The results are blocked shots that travel high and to the right, significantly reducing distance.

There are a variety of causes that can contribute to the failure of your right arm to rotate over your left through impact, producing an open face. Check the following areas in your setup and swing to ban the block from your game.

A BLOCK-FREE SETUP

Make sure you're not standing too close to the ball. At address, there should be at least a full hand's width between the club's butt end and your left thigh. Standing too close causes your head to bury against your chest, hindering shoulder rotation. This promotes an open clubface at impact.

Also, check that your left-hand grip isn't rotated too far counter-clockwise (toward the target). The "V" formed by your left thumb and forefinger should point slightly right of the chin.

There should be at least a full hand's width between the club and the left thigh.

The "V" formed by your left thumb and forefinger points slightly right of your chin.

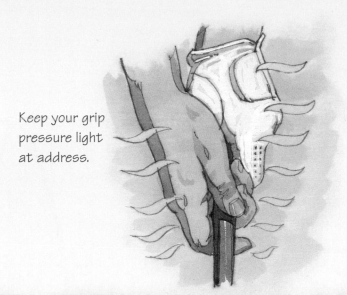

Keep your grip pressure light at address.

BLOCK OUT EXCESSIVE TENSION

If grip pressure increases significantly at the beginning of the downswing, it's difficult for your arms to remain relaxed. This tension keeps your arms from rotating the clubface through impact. If you sense that you are re-gripping or tightening your hold during the backswing or transition, lighten your grip pressure at address and monitor it as you warm up. Becoming conscious of grip pressure will help you keep it lighter.

DRILL: SPLIT YOUR GRIP If everything else checks out, focus on developing better clubhead rotation during your downswing. To learn the correct feeling, hold a 7-iron with your hands spaced six inches apart. Keeping your left hand soft, swing back until the club is parallel to the ground. The toe should point at the sky.

Make a smooth swing down and through until the club is parallel to the ground on the other side. If the toe is pointing skyward, your arm rotation is correct. Repeat until you have learned the feel of this rotation.

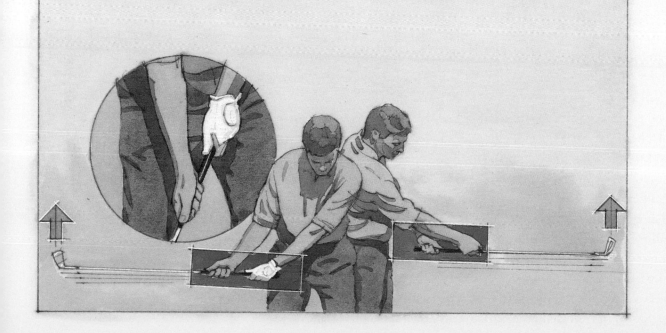

INDEX

Written by Susan Burke

ACKNOWLEDGMENTS

My name may be on the cover of this book, but the success of *Private Lessons*—both as a monthly series within *GOLF MAGAZINE* and this book—has been the result of a lot of work by a lot of very talented people.

This book reflects the efforts and passion of these *GOLF MAGAZINE* staff members, both past and present: Dave Allen, Lorin Anderson, John Andrisani, David Clarke, Michael Corcoran, James A. Frank, Julie Hansen, Greg Midland, Peter Morrice, George Peper and Hunki Yun.

At Abrams Publishing, designer Robert McKee, editor Margaret L. Kaplan and project coordinator Harriet Whelchel also deserve credit for bringing this book to life.

But perhaps no one deserves more credit for *Private Lessons* than Barry Ross. From his studio in Fairfield, Iowa, Barry's illustrations and art have come to define the style and feel of this series. Without his talent, *Private Lessons* as we know it might not exist.

Editor: Margaret Kaplan
Designer: Robert McKee
Production Manager: Ankur Ghosh

Library of Congress Cataloging-in-Publication Data

Golf magazine private lessons / by David Dusek, illustrations by Barry Ross. —Updated ed.
    p. cm.
ISBN 978-0-8109-8482-0 (pbk. flexibound w/ round corners)
1. Golf. I. Dusek, David. II. Golf magazine book.
GV965.G5458 2010
796.352'3—dc22

2009035063

Printed and bound in China
10 9 8 7 6 5 4 3 2 1

Abrams books are available at special discounts when purchased in quantity for premiums and promotions as well as fundraising or educational use. Special editions can also be created to specification. For details, contact specialmarkets@abramsbooks.com or the address below.

THE ART OF BOOKS SINCE 1949

115 West 18th Street
New York, NY 10011
www.abramsbooks.com